THE NEW POLITICS OF HUMAN RIGHTS

THE NEW POLITICS OF HUMAN RIGHTS

James Avery Joyce

ST. MARTIN'S PRESS NEW YORK

Library of Congress Cataloging in Publication Data

Joyce, James Avery.
The new politics of human rights.

Bibliography: p.
Includes index.
1. Civil rights. I. Title.
JC571.J66   1979   323.4   78-13333
ISBN 0-312-56880-0

For HELEN

in respect and admiration

Contents

Preface and Acknowledgements

This is not a book for lawyers, though it covers many legal issues. Nevertheless, a work of this kind depends on a considerable documentation and these sources have been brought into the main text, as far as possible, so as not to interfere with a flowing narrative. Where technical language is unavoidable, as in quoting from United Nations resolutions, the citations have been reduced to their essential passages.

On a more personal level, it would be impossible to designate the wealth of inspiration and information drawn from so many friends and colleagues over so long a period. Some of my previous works have been briefly cited under relevant topics, and in these I have already acknowledged my deep indebtedness to my mentors and masters, especially Lord Gardiner, Professor Quincy Wright, Sir Alfred Zimmern, Lord Philip Noel-Baker, and the late Dr C. Wilfred Jenks.

Since I have been directly associated with United Nations action in this field, I must place first and foremost my admiration for Dr Marc Schreiber, former Director of the Division of Human Rights, and for Mr Niall MacDermot, Director of the International Commission of Jurists, who have given such brilliant and untiring service to the movement over the years.

For advice and assistance on factual questions and also for their kindness in reading parts of the manuscript or proofs, I am particularly grateful to Colonel Patrick Montgomery, Secretary of the Anti-Slavery Society; Mr Frank Field, Director of the World Federation of UN Associations; Nigel S. Rodley, Legal Adviser of Amnesty International; Dr M. E. Tardu; Dr B. Ramcharan, barrister, and Dr George Brand of the Human Rights Division; Miss Mary Tom, editor of the *Year Book on Human Rights*, and Mrs Ciceil Gross, JD, attorney, of New York. For so much skill in typing my variegated and troublesome manuscript, I owe deep appreciation to Miss Janet Taylor, former United Nations official in Geneva.

Since this book does not aspire to be a legal treatise as such, but a broad survey aimed at the cultured reader, a legalistic style has been avoided as far as is compatible with accuracy and clarity, and notes have been kept to a minimum. References to legal documents and other sources have been confined to essential descriptions, rather than standard publication or pagination details. With a similar aim in view, lengthy titles to institutions or public documents have been given their short or popular forms where the context is clear; for instance, 'World Court' stands for both the Permanent Court of Justice and the International Court of Justice, while the Covenant on Economic, Social and Cultural Rights has sometimes been referred to as the economic Covenant.

In thus aiming for directness and simplicity, rather than scholarly exegesis, the main arguments must obviously leave many points to be further debated. A more substantial reason for this rejection of a primarily legalistic approach is that the serious study of human rights has become today an interdisciplinary exercise, involving history (origins), geography (frontiers), diplomacy (negotiations), sociology (group structure), psychology (motivation), ethics (standards), and many other formal disciplines, as well as constitutional and international law.

Moreover, the newness of many of the topics dealt with so briefly here, which have so recently come within the scope of human rights, means that some of the author's personal interpretations of matters still under sharp public dispute will have to be tested, and doubtless revised, by time and experience. Consequently, this work cannot pretend to be a definitive one; it is a pioneer survey aiming to present an all-round and often exciting picture of human rights as a key factor today in the evolution of a more worthy human condition.

A final caution: some readers will be surprised at how closely human rights questions are bound up with world politics today. For this reason this survey will have to probe into some of the most controversial aspects of national foreign policy. This author believes that to approach foreign policy primarily from the point of view of human rights, instead of in terms of alleged national security, leads to revolutionary or – at least – challenging conclusions. If, therefore, the author's own convictions obtrude with unusual candour and even, at times, with vehemence, it is because no one can confront

today the grossness and perfidy of so many assaults on human
dignity and not become, like this author, a committed crusader in
the cause of world peace and personal integrity.

Geneva   JAMES AVERY JOYCE
February 1978

Note: Many of the official documents cited or referred to in this book are
reproduced in their entirety in the author's compilation entitled: *Human Rights:
Basic Documents* (Leyden: Sijthoff, 1978) 3 vols.

The author's great indebtedness for so generous a use of citations from and
reproductions of United Nations public documents can best be acknowledged by
his sincere hope that the present volume will bring the principles and purposes of
the Organisation to the attention of a world-wide public.

Introduction: The Challenge

Man has the capacity to push aside from his mind unpleasant problems.
– Seán MacBride (1977)

Torture is on the increase in sixty-two countries. Dissidents are being clapped into psychiatric wards in the Soviet Union. A rule of terror dominates the military regimes of Uganda, Ethiopia and the Central African Empire. Arab trade-unionists are groaning in Israeli jails and two-score Chilean labour leaders have just 'disappeared' without trace. Some sixty MPs in seventeen countries have also 'disappeared' or are imprisoned for 'political reasons'. Britain was charged before the Strasbourg Court of Human Rights to punish soldiers if found guilty of torturing detainees. Twenty young men and women have been on hunger strike in West Germany, clamouring to be treated as prisoners-of-war under the Red Cross Convention. Black leaders of a potential multiracial South African Republic have been exiled for life to an Orwellian no-man's-land called Robben Island. While President Carter's call for vigorous action to promote human rights in other countries is being blunted in credibility by the United States's own repeated refusal to ratify some dozen human rights treaties, including two key Covenants (discussed in this book) which came into force in 1976 and led to the setting up in the summer of 1977 of the first United Nations Human Rights Committee to listen to and act on individual complaints, with the United States absent. The United States' withdrawal from the International Labour Organisation (ILO), too, has been described by the UN Secretary-General Kurt Waldheim as a 'retrogressive step from the principle of collective responsibility'.

Are all these new and impressive official documents just a paper façade for camouflaging reality? Or is the fiery and undaunted Brazilian Archbishop Dom Helder Camara on a good point in calling for a World Peace Conference in India in 1979, because, he says, 'Peace without justice is impossible, while injustice affects two-thirds of the people in the world today'?

Nobody knows for sure what 'human rights' are, or where they begin. But everybody knows what they are *not*, and where they stop.

The thirtieth anniversary of the Universal Declaration of Human Rights, which was proclaimed on 10 December 1948, has opened up a new Decade of Freedom for mankind in 1978. And the new decade has been ushered in by the conferment of the Nobel Peace Prize on Amnesty International, with its headquarters in London and branches in over fifty countries.

At last, governments are being pushed to act by a growing multitude of movements and pressure groups of all shapes and sizes. Amnesty International has mobilised its 100,000 members in professional, religious and local groups in fifty countries in the battle against torture. Prisoners locked up behind bars in the Philippines, Argentine and South Korea, without any charges being brought against them, have finally been released following outside investigation by some of the world's leading jurists, as detailed in these chapters. The UN Human Rights Commission, so frequently assailed for its lethargy by truculent mass media – in search of quick and easy remedies – is now involved in forward planning to clean up the earth's worst cesspools of misery and suffering, inflicted by mad dictators and a callous public.

Some sobering words of Kurt Waldheim are taking on more and more meaning as this Decade of Freedom opens:

> The issue of human rights is of fundamental importance. But we must not overlook the difficulties of applying this concept in a world of differing ideologies, political systems and concepts of society. The two International Covenants that came into force this past year and other earlier United Nations instruments are modest steps towards giving international legal content to a comprehensive range of human rights . . . Questions of human rights come almost daily to the Secretary-General, and I have used the possibilities of my office in a variety of specific cases with varying degrees of success. In doing this I have had to judge in each case which approach is likely to be productive – quiet diplomacy and direct contacts with the Governments concerned, or a public approach. Whatever approach is adopted, the main objective must be to alleviate the suffering of the people whose human rights are being violated.

Where can we best begin our exploration of so vast a terrain – some of it never traversed before – than by looking into how it all began; or, at least, how the *modern* concept and practice of human

rights sprang into social consciousness and international organisation? In Chapter 1, therefore, we survey what a previous century
has contributed to our study. The famous *Droits de l'homme* of the
French Revolution will, in fact, be celebrating its bicentennial in
1989, following close on the heels of the dogmatic phrases of the
1776 Declaration of Independence (even if they were true – as one
historian has said – at the time nobody really believed them). The
nineteenth century was illuminated by these two declarations and
(a newly coined word) the 'humanitarian' principles that they
enshrined. We shall seek to outline in our first chapter, then, how
some of them were slowly translated into international law, laying
the foundation stones of the League of Nations in our own century,
with its revolutionary provisions for minority rights and the well-
being of 'peoples not yet able to stand by themselves'.

The contemporary scene, described in Chapter 2, brings us to the
Universal Declaration itself, which is often quoted in parts, but
seldom read as a whole. It was put together with remarkable speed
and accepted by the UN General Assembly in 1948 without a
dissenting voice. This was followed in 1949 by the equally famous
Geneva Conventions, added to which were the 1977 changes in the
Laws of Armed Conflict, covering today's 'liberation movements'
and the status of guerrillas. From that point onwards, we can paint
later in this book the broad picture of the successive covenants,
protocols and other legal instruments that have marked the last
three decades with *conscious planning* of the Rights of Man through
global co-operation – a remarkable effort of the collective will.

But, in Chapter 3, we begin a violent descent from these lofty
aspirations and plunge into a dark abyss of tortures and cruelties
inflicted on all sorts and conditions of men and women because their
ideas or their skin pigment or national origin are different from
those of the governments under which they have to live. Not
everyone will agree, of course, on how best to remedy such
violations. Yet there is emerging today a closely knit tapestry of
individual rights woven by hundreds of committees and organisations (some enumerated in this chapter) which form a visible
pattern of civilised standards against which infringements can
nowadays be tested in exact legal terms.

The real trouble, however, does not lie in the clear language of
the international instruments – be they enforceable or merely
declaratory – but in a quaint notion which has recently gained the
editorial eye and disturbed the timid governmental mind: the

hybrid term 'politicization', the controversial topic of Chapter 4. Evasive though this notion is, it is not an invention of political philosophers. On the contrary, it is an escapist device of hard-headed diplomacy caught in a web of international law and common justice, frantically looking for a cop-out. This is the gimmick of the 'double standard' *in reverse*: 'Why pick on *me*, when the other man is worse?' It has brought forth some of the most disgraceful financial boycotts of the Human Rights system and, some of the most vituperative verbal attacks on it, as well as on the innocent UN Secretariat itself, as we shall examine in that chapter.

Chapter 5 also presents some difficult problems, with the emergence of the Third World at a time when the West's traditional prerogatives are under increasing challenge. The 'right of self-determination' is studied in some depth, because there exist certain Western doubts about it and also because some authorities are worried about dangerous trends which they perceive as 'African imperialism', perpetrated by the countries of the Third World themselves.

From politics in the raw we move on, in Chapter 6, to what at first blush might seem to be a depersonalised realm of modern technology: computers, kidney-machines, heart transplants and the nebulous 'right to privacy'. Unanswered questions such as 'Who pulls the plug?' when a human life hangs perilously on a brain-surgeon's decision, or on a criminal trial conducted by the mass media, put human rights both into legislative policy and under judicial scrutiny.

Unless it be thought that the thirty years since the Universal Declaration have produced little or nothing to set what Shelley called 'the tune of the future', we shall examine in Chapter 7 the procedures laid down by the 'new' Conventions of 1976, as well as noticing, in passing, how the European Convention, with its prestigious Strasbourg Court, has outstripped them in the provision of legal remedies. Hence, we also ask: Has the time arrived for a High Commissioner of Human Rights? And is it time, too, for Britain to enact a Bill of Rights?

In Chapter 8 we seek to gather together some of the trends revealed during the preceding enquiry, but also to open up some new vistas for the 1980s. Has the UN established a new right – the Right to Development? If so, how does this square with the present arms race? Or do we yet have to discover the Right to Peace? In final analysis, does it not all depend on how the individual performs his *duties* towards the world community as a world citizen?

*   *   *   *   *

Certain factual considerations will become clearer as our study develops along these lines. The first is that the global movement of human rights since the Second World War is founded on and inspired by the United Nations Charter. In a truer sense, the UN system as a whole is founded upon the 'fundamental human rights and freedoms', which have been enlarged in subsequent declarations and covenants. Without the constitutional existence of the international system of the UN Charter – which is taken for granted today – no international order of human rights could exist at all. Nationalistic politicians or conservative publicists frequently utter glib warnings that, unless the United Nations does this or that or refrains from doing this or that, it will somehow disintegrate. None of these detractors seems to have observed that the present global framework of a viable international order would also disappear. Any serious approach to the study of human rights has to accept the UN system, as it exists *now*, as the bed-rock on which all future progress in human rights must be erected.

A second general consideration that is bound to emerge, as the reader proceeds, is that the separate 'rights' surveyed here form a fabric all of one piece. Like love and marriage, as the song runs, the human rights enumerated in the various instruments 'go together'. There may be some nuances of definition between them, from time to time, and some definitions may not be immutable (for example, 'the right to found a family'); but it will be seen, as our study develops, that the protection of one right (e.g. freedom of the person) needs the support of another (e.g. prohibition of arbitrary detention). It will also be seen that there is a good deal of duplication between one declaration or instrument and another. This is due to the different historical origins or legal categories of the separate instruments; and also because the aim of the various drafters has naturally been to make each document complete in itself. Duplication thus brings a strengthening, rather than a weakening, of the total fabric of human rights law.

A third consideration is the factor of TIME. A 150-nation corporate effort, with all that it implies in rival emphases and sometimes hostile attitudes towards the same proposals – either of principle or method – cannot be produced quickly. It required twenty years to frame and reach enforcement action on the two major Covenants. The United States did not accept them till 1977, when President

Carter signed them – but still subject to Senate ratification.

Implementation particularly brings in the time element, because of inevitable delays – designed or tactical – in the national procedural processes. Impatience with the formulation and procedural timelags of human rights can be corrected by noting a wise warning of the late C. Wilfred Jenks in *The Common Law of Mankind*:

> To secure the recognition of these rights as binding on an international basis, to secure reasonable uniformity in their interpretation and application in a manner acceptable to the free world, and to devise adequate national and international procedures and guarantees for their effective implementation, may well represent a succession of tasks for several generations.

Some casual observers of Human Rights questions, whose knowledge has hitherto been derived mainly from the general press, and who have never before given their minds to a detailed study of some aspect or another of the subject, will be astonished, as they read these chapters, at the growing number and considerable range of both the legal and political, as well as the social and psychological, reverberations of Human Rights in the contemporary world. For lawyers, as for serious students, Human Rights can never be a 'soft option', either for study or practice.

Finally, the reader must be warned, too, that, since the primary emphasis in the present study is on the international protection of human rights, many important issues on the *national* level must be omitted altogether. The declarations and instruments which form the basis of our enquiry are essentially expressions of a global concern, because they envisage the individual in terms of his potential world citizenship as a human being in his own right, irrespective of his own nation or race or colour or creed.

1 Some Earlier Principles

The sacred rights of Mankind are not to be rummaged for among old parchments or musty records. They are written, as with a sunbeam, in the whole volume of human nature by the hand of Divinity itself, and can never be erased or obscured.

— Alexander Hamilton (1787)

The noted historian Professor W. E. Woodward raised a fundamental issue that rational men have never been able fully to answer, when he wrote:

The Declaration [of Independence] contained statements that none of them really believed . . . Even with the slaves left out, the assertion does not fit in with ordinary common sense . . . and everybody knows that men are not created equal . . . As to inalienable rights, man has none.[1]

How can we, then, at the beginning of our study, surmount this initial obstacle of irrationality, which challenges the validity of serious enquiry and will reappear many times, in one form or another, in the following chapters?

One provisional answer might be to accept the same historian's own evaluation of that horrendous 4 July 1775 event. The Declaration was never intended, he said, to be more than a philosophic document, a 'reverberation of the ideas of John Locke reworded in Jefferson's luminous style'. For, even if the signers may not have believed in the equality of man, *the common people did*.

This point was put more adroitly quite recently by a British MP, Raymond Fletcher, in *The Times* of 6 December 1976: 'Even though Jefferson's magnificent statement that "all men are created equal [and] endowed by their Creator with certain unalienable rights" is neither self-evident nor true, there can be no civilized society unless it is assumed to be both.'

The same pragmatic approach might equally be applied, but with less confidence, to the *Droits de l'homme*, drafted in September 1789, and proclaimed to all French citizens on 1 September 1791. For these two revolutions were really all of a piece, though Edmund

7

Burke did not think so. He said in his speech on the Army Estimates on 9 February 1790:

> They made and recorded a sort of institute and digest of anarchy, called the rights of man, in such a pedantic abuse of elementary principles as would have disgraced boys at school; but this declaration of rights, was worse than trifling and pedantic in them; as by their name and authority they systematically destroyed every hold of authority by opinion, religious or civil, on the minds of the people. By this mad declaration they subverted the state; and brought on such calamities as no country, without a long war, has ever been known to suffer; and which may in the end produce such a war, and perhaps, many such.

But the late British historian Christopher Dawson, in the last book he wrote, points out with a hindsight not available to Burke that:

> In the victory of the American Revolution, European liberals saw the justification of their ideals and the realisation of their hopes. It turned the current of the Enlightenment in a political direction and infused a revolutionary purpose into the democratic idealism of Rousseau.[2]

Lafayette, who helped the Americans in their freedom struggle, returned to his own land as the Hero of Two Worlds and with the prestige of an apostle. However, perhaps a more influential living link across the Atlantic, uniting the two revolutions spiritually, was none other than the agnostic Thomas Paine. His *Rights of Man* had inspired Lafayette, when he had written:

> Government founded on the moral theory of universal peace, on the indefeasible hereditary Rights of Man, is now revolving from west to east by a stronger impulse than the government of the sword revolved from east to west. It interests not particular individuals but nations in its progress and promises a new era to the human race.[3]

And Christopher Dawson sums up this mighty *fin de siècle* movement in its proper setting and in capsule form:

> Thus the French Revolution falls into place as part of a world revolution which would restore to mankind the original rights of which it had been robbed at the very dawn of history by the tyranny of kings and priests.

What do we then notice, looking back two centuries later, about this West-to-East reverse commitment?

For one thing, there is a feeling of incompleteness, of amateurishness, of improvisation, to which Professor Woodward has called attention. A modern French historian worries about this, too, and says:

> One might ask today whether the authors [of the *Droits de l'homme et du citoyen*] had not opened a credit account too big for the reasoning faculties of man, in so far as, by exalting only the rights of the individual, they suppressed in their consciences the imperative need for duties.[4]

This same misgiving will make itself evident as our study proceeds; but it is significant that some of the most recent United Nations resolutions (still not implemented) go so far as to bear such titles as 'The Economic Rights *and Duties* of States' (our italics).

Another reflection of hindsight – now obvious, but of overriding importance – is that both the 1776 and 1789 pronouncements were drafted by small, select groups and were conditioned by the local contemporary necessities of their respective nation-states, still in the throes of revolutionary upheaval, rejecting one form of government and erecting another in its place. No contrast could be greater than that with the Universal Declaration, proclaimed by the world community in 1948, after three years of strenuous open debate, following immediately on the cessation of global war. It was not compiled *in abstracto* from the surmises of philosophers, but pieced together, word by word, article by article, from a thousand disparate strands marking mankind's moral, social, and political progress since the beginning of time.

Nevertheless, the intrinsic novelty that must strike every thinking person, as we watch the slow evolution of some concepts of human rights in this chapter, is that the 1948 Declaration carries at its head the qualifying word 'universal'. It is true that the authors of both the American and the French documents assumed that what they had planned for their own countrymen applied to all men everywhere. Yet the fact that the Universal Declaration actually is, for the first time in civilised life on this planet, global in its inspiration and intention, renders it one of the most difficult and enormously challenging enterprises of Man during the twentieth century, and beyond. If its complications and apparent inconsistencies – as we shall find later in this book – are baffling and often tantalising, it is not because its framers and promoters were stupid or mistaken, but because the global civilisation it both serves and represents has itself become more complex and demanding. There is no worse enemy of human rights than the simplistic belief that the Universal Declaration is a sort of rule-of-thumb that can be applied to any human predicament.

Brief though these preliminary thoughts are, we cannot leave the Transatlantic parallel two hundred years behind us without noting also that, hardly does the ink run dry on the respective parchments, than they require revising and amending. The *Droits de l'homme et du citoyen* was published as the preface of the first revolutionary constitution on 14 September 1791, but a review of its chequered history over even the ensuing half-dozen years, as the Revolution frantically struggled, as revolutions do, to become a stable government, provides interesting food for thought, and is not without its lessons today. As Professor John A. Hawgood has said,

> The constitution of 1795, in its reaction against the lack of precision of 1791 and the lack of restraint of 1793 and 1794, did not go so far as Bonaparte in 1799 and *omit a declaration of rights altogether*; but it did label its declaration 'Rights and *Duties*' . . . Equality had not been mentioned in 1789 when the rights had been listed as 'Liberty, Property, Security, and Resistance to Oppression'; but had been inserted next after Liberty by the Girondists in 1793 (who completed their list with Property, Sovereignty of the People and Resistance to Oppression) and the Jacobins put Equality first of all . . . This Jacobin declaration elaborates its statement of the rights of man to the extent of asserting (Article 21) *the right to work or subsistence* from society. This article casts a longer shadow into the Nineteenth and Twentieth Centuries than perhaps any other clause from the constitutional documents of the first French Revolution [*our italics*].[5]

Across the Atlantic, the amending process began almost at once. The insertion of a Bill of Rights, by way of amendment, in the Philadelphia Constitution had, in fact, a history that had preceded the Declaration itself, for it had already appeared in one form or another in at least seven of the state constitutions of the rebelling colonies. Dr Valerie Fifer of London University has pointed out that

'the trend was eventually highlighted in the early 1770s by the new Provincial Congresses which marked the beginning of a political transformation and a westward shift of power. The Provincial Congresses, with their new Constitutions or Declarations of Rights, became strong centres of political innovation. They prepared the way for the Continental Congresses, proposed by Virginia in May 1774 and convened first in Philadelphia the following September.[6]

The Constitution was amended by Congress on 8 June 1789, when Madison moved the first ten amendments. This was, as Professor James T. Shotwell reminds us,

> the work of those who, while accepting the Constitution as a necessary structure for government, demanded that it include as well definite guarantees of the rights of citizens against any possible tyranny by government, guarantees of freedom of religion, speech, and the press, and the protection of life, liberty, and property by due process of law.[7]

Were we not dealing in this book with the modern movement for international human rights, it would be tempting to take the reader back some way into English constitutional history and discuss how – from the Magna Carta (1215) onwards, through the *Habeas Corpus* Act of 1679 and the Bill of Rights of 1689 – the British have sought to solve the same problem as faced the Americans by other means. (The present author has already sketched this history briefly in his *Justice at Work*, Chapter XIII, 'This Mysterious Freedom'.)[8]

A considerable degree of authoritative opinion in Britain today seems, however, to be swinging the other way. We shall return to this significant trend in later chapters; suffice to record here that a distinguished judge, Sir Leslie Scarman, speaking of what he terms 'the challenge from overseas', has tersely put the issue on record in the Hamlyn Lecture for 1974, as follows:

> The legal system must now ensure that the law of the land will itself meet the exacting standards of human rights declared by international instruments, to which the United Kingdom is a party, as inviolable. This calls for entrenched or fundamental laws protected by a Bill of Rights – a constitutional law which it is the duty of the Courts to protect even against the power of Parliament.

To the student of human rights in their global context, the

nineteenth century (which, for some observers, did not terminate until the First World War) is full of innovation. For the rest of this chapter, therefore, we shall attempt to elucidate the topics listed in a brief summary presented by Dr C. Wilfred Jenks of parallel trends that led up to the modern movement. He says:

> Historically, the preoccupation of international law with human rights has developed in four main contexts: (a) international action for the suppression of slavery and the slave trade, from the Congress of Vienna to the adoption in 1956 of the Supplementary Slavery Convention; (b) other international measures for the protection of backward peoples, notably the Berlin and Brussels Acts of 1885 and 1890, and the mandates and trusteeship agreements; (c) international arrangements for the protection of minorities . . . culminating in the minorities treaties and declarations administered by the League of Nations . . . and (d) the development in the law of State responsibility of the concept of an international standard for the treatment of aliens.[9]

SLAVERY

A year before the *Mayflower* landed at Plymouth Rock in New England, bringing its living cargo of religious freedom, another ship, the *Treasurer*, armed as a privateer and owned by the Earl of Warwick but commissioned by the Duke of Savoy, came to Jamestown with a fettered cargo of slaves, captured from a Dutch vessel and now under the orders of Captain Samuel Argall, Governor of Virginia. The chronicler of this incident was equally explicit in describing how the Dutch transported the first slaves to Manhattan's Island, 'as soon as they obtained foothold in America':

> They tried, at first, after the custom of the times, to enslave the aboriginal inhabitants, but the task was found so harassing and unprofitable that they soon sought supplies of blacks from Africa. In fact enslaving red men led to such trouble that a wall was built across the lower end of Manhattan Island where Wall Street is now found, to keep red lovers of liberty from driving the Dutch slave-catchers over the Battery beach into the bay.[10]

The mention of Wall Street so early in the history of the American slave trade is by no means fortuitous, for economics has never been divorced for long from human rights – a theme developed later in this book. Economics and conscience were compressed into this minimum formula by the same author:

In short, slaves were introduced into United States territory in answer to a demand for labor. They were purchased by men who were accustomed to the purchase and sale of laborers, and no one's conscience was in any way hurt by the transaction. It was a good business proposition for that day, and for two centuries, at least, thereafter.

Nor were the ventures of the *Mayflower* and the *Treasurer* quite so remote from each other in ethical terms. Professor R. H. Tawney, himself an economist, pointed out in his famous analysis that 'organised' Christianity had never failed to insist that all men were brethren:

But it did not occur to it [*sic*] to point out that, as a result of the new economic imperialism which was beginning to develop in the seventeenth century, the brethren of the English merchant were the Africans whom he kidnapped for slavery in America, or the American Indians whom he stripped of their lands, or the Indian craftsmen from whom he bought muslins and silks at starvation prices. Religion had not yet learned to console itself for the practical difficulty of applying its moral principles by clasping the comfortable formula that for the transaction of economic life no moral principles exist.[11]

During the eighteenth century the slave trade became the most flourishing branch of the fast-growing commerce of the new financial empires. The vast numbers of ships of all sizes and draughts crossing the Atlantic from West African ports and Arab slave-markets have never been counted; but the revenues of the insurance-brokers and investment bankers that serviced the slavers are written in the blood of a thousand thousand victims – many of them kidnapped – crammed for weeks or months on end under the rotten decks of infested hulks, shackled and allotted only two feet of 'living' space. Yet a Rhode Island diarist could record in 1787 that 'This trade in human species has been the first wheel of commerce in Newport, on which every other movement in business has depended. That town has been built up, and flourished in times past on the slave-trade, and by it the inhabitants have gotten most of their wealth and riches'.

But the classical turning-point in this 'odious traffic', as Lord Mansfield was to call it, was reached on 22 June 1772, when that famous judge held that slavery had no standing in the law of England, so a writ of *Habeas Corpus* was good to release the slave Somersett from a ship then lying in the Thames. For a hundred years the abolition battle was waged, first on a national and soon on an international front – now an almost forgotten freedom struggle but by no means terminated yet. This was a time when Englishmen were talking of their constitutional rights as 'fundamental law', and judges like Mansfield were rediscovering 'natural justice' in contesting the royal prerogative. General rules of the Common Law were being built up case by case in the English Courts.[12]

Although the Somersett decision was made in 1772, it was not until 1787 that a recognised 'Society for the Abolition of the African Slavetrade', was set up in London. A committee had been formed on 7 July 1783, however, 'to consider what steps they should take for the relief and liberation of the Negro slaves in the West Indies, and for the discouragement of the Slave-trade on the coast of Africa'; and it prepared the ground for the formation of the Society for the Abolition of the African Slave-trade, of which Granville Sharp became chairman, and Thomas Clarkson an active member. In Parliament, William Wilberforce, MP, became the champion of the society, aided by the work of Clarkson. The motive of Wilberforce and the Claphamites was a religious one, according to a recent historian: 'In their view, the principal reason to think West Indian slavery deplorable was not so much that it whipped and bullied Negroes – though that was a crying shame, too – as that it denied their souls opportunity for salvation and tempted masters to cruelty and fornication.'[13]

Yet the American abolitionists who followed later lacked the same respect for facts and the humanitarian approach of the Claphamites. Meantime, David Hartley, MP for Hull, moved in the House in 1776: 'That the slave-trade is contrary to the laws of God and the rights of man'. He laid on the table of the House some of the irons used in securing slaves on the slave-ships. (The motion failed even of a respectful hearing.) Similarly, a bill of 1783 failed, but an Order in Council, dated 11 February 1788, directed that a committee of the Privy Council should sit to take into consideration 'the present state of the African trade'.

Progress was infinitesimal. On 17 June 1788 a Bill passed the House of Commons by a vote of fifty-six to five, by which slavers were allowed to carry 'five men to every three tons in every ship under one hundred and fifty tons and which had the space of five feet between the decks'. Parliamentary investigation of the trade followed.

Internationally, the initiative came from Britain. In 1806 Britain proposed to the United States a treaty 'of amity, commerce, and navigation' under which the two nations were to 'agree to use their best endeavours to procure the co-operation of other Powers for the final and complete abolition of a trade so repugnant to the principles of justice and humanity', but the United States refused to sign it. In 1811 Parliament declared participation in the trade by any British subject a felony punishable by fourteen years' transportation. Across the Channel, Napoleon, on his return from Elba, decreed the abolition of the slave trade, and this Decree was re-enacted in 1818 by the Bourbon dynasty.

In 1814 Great Britain and the United States at last agreed to 'use their best endeavours' for the abolition of the trade. And in 1815 five of the principal Powers (Britain, Russia, Prussia, Austria and France) made a solemn engagement 'in the face of mankind, that this traffic should be made to cease, in pursuance of which these Powers have enacted municipal laws to suppress the trade'. In 1817, Britain and Portugal made a treaty whereby 'ships of war of each nation might visit merchant vessels of both, if suspected of having slaves on board acquired by illicit traffic'.

But the slavers were still sailing the high seas! So, in 1818, Britain and the Netherlands contracted for a mutual right of search, and in 1824 Britain enacted that any British subject found guilty of engaging in the slave-trade should 'be deemed and adjudged guilty of Piracy, Felony and Robbery', and should 'suffer Death without Benefit of Clergy'. The same year, Sweden and Britain agreed to a mutual right of search on the slave coast. The US again declined. In 1831 and 1833 Britain and France agreed to a mutual right of search, and then together invited the United States to join them. Other treaties followed thick and fast.

It should not be overlooked that the majority of slaves shipped across the Atlantic were already slaves in Africa when the Europeans appropriated them. The strongest protesters against the abolition of the slave trade were the 'kings' of the Guinea Coast, deprived of their most profitable export market. Private profits had become the worst enemy of private rights.

Though a pirate had long been, by the law of nations, a man

without a country, and was the lawful prize of all honest ships, the USA informed the British government that in *their* law the slave-trade was only 'statutory piracy', and so was different from high-seas robbery under international law. Hence, the US government could not admit that an American slaver should be treated as a high-seas robber, except by an American court. Nevertheless, a treaty for the suppression of the slave trade was finally signed by Daniel Webster and Lord Ashburton of Britain on 9 August 1842.

We have lingered somewhat over these early decades of the nineteenth century, since they are a forewarning of the interminable delays which not merely 'human nature', but hard money and national 'interests' constantly put in the path of social reformers. But if this brief sketch seems to underestimate the tremendous impact of abolishing slavery on American economic and political life in the South – above all, the long-term ravages of the Civil War of 1861–4 it is because these essential issues are too complex and too controversial for cursory treatment in the present context.[14]

Until the League of Nations was founded at the end of the First World War, no sustained campaign of world-wide investigation and action had been feasible, for protection of human rights on so vast a scale required international political machinery to ensure it. According to evidence presented in one of the League's typical reports:

> During a period of 250 years 'the trade' had established machinery and vested interests in every European and American State. The highest personages in more than one country were involved. Crowned heads and royal princes drew large revenues from the traffic. Planters, merchants, even clergy and missionaries, had together invested millions of capital in it . . . Different shipping lines had built hundreds of craft only fit for the purpose of carrying slaves; thus the shippers were resolute opponents of Emancipation.

Hence, the problem of slavery and the slave trade was recognised, even at the beginning of the nineteenth century, to be essentially of an international character. Though it was not until 1890 that the General Act for the Repression of African Slave Trade was concluded in Brussels. The Brussels Convention was mainly concerned with the African continent; but the wider question of slavery throughout the whole world fortunately became the concern of the League of Nations in 1920.

Under the leadership of Britain, a Slavery Convention was framed in 1926 and signed by over forty nations, including the United States, who committed themselves to the active tasks of abolition and emancipation. That was something; but it revealed that more was needed. Conventions do not execute themselves, and lagging signatories need to be kept up to their professions. The League of Nations Council accordingly appointed seven persons with expert knowledge to watch the working of the Convention and advise the League on all matters connected with it. That again was not enough. Yet it was the awakening of an international conscience.

The Slavery Convention of 1926 expressed in twelve Articles the maximum agreement obtainable at that time which would recommend itself to the States. But it lacked clarity on many points and it neglected to provide machinery for supervising the application of the Convention. Six years elapsed before steps were taken to meet that deficiency by setting up the Advisory Committee of Experts on Slavery. Until 1926 definitions of slavery reposed upon national enactments or legal and philosophic opinions. This Slavery Convention, to which forty-four states later adhered, defines slavery in the following simple terms: 'Slavery is a status or condition of a person over whom any or all of the powers attaching to the rights of ownership are exercised'.

The last League pronouncement on the legal status of slavery was in the Report of the Advisory Committee on Slavery for 1938, which stated: 'There is no evidence to suggest that outside Africa and Arabia there are still any *born* slaves'. But it pointed out that in some countries

> extreme poverty has driven some parents to transfer their children, either by gift or sale, to others who desire to adopt them as their own children or to exploit their labour. This is generally done in the mistaken belief that the lot of the child will be improved by entry into a more affluent family. In other countries girls are sold by their parents to be wives. The girl is sold without her consent and sometimes before she is born. On the death of her husband she is inherited, with her children, if any, by her husband's heir-at-law.

All of these forms of enslavement, except perhaps enslavement of prisoners-of-war, are still operating in the world today.

The Charter of the United Nations (1945) does not make any

specific reference to slavery. However, its Article 1, paragraph 3, defines one of the objectives of the United Nations as 'promoting and encouraging respect for human rights and for fundamental freedoms for all without distinction as to race, sex, language, or religion'. Three years later the General Assembly adopted the Universal Declaration, which, in its Article 4, declares specifically: 'No one shall be held in slavery or servitude; slavery and the slave trade shall be prohibited in all their forms'. A Protocol, moreover, was concluded in 1953, by which the 1926 Convention was placed in the care of the United Nations. In September 1956 a new instrument was debated and approved under the title 'Supplementary Convention on the Abolition of Slavery, the Slave Trade and Institutions and Practices Similar to Slavery'.[15] It went further than the 1926 Convention and covered abuses analogous to slavery, such as debt bondage, serfdom, the sale of women into marriage without their consent and the sham adoption of children to exploit their labour. Thus the United Nations is now in possession of two important instruments dealing with the problem of slavery. Ratification, however, has been rather slow, although there has been some progress towards that end in recent years.

Eighty-five states are parties to the 1956 Supplementary Convention on the Abolition of Slavery, the Slave Trade and Institutions and Practices Similar to Slavery. It binds those governments to do their best to eradicate chattel slavery, serfdom, debt bondage and certain institutions affecting women and children. But until 1975 no machinery existed to implement that Convention. In 1975, yielding to eighteen years of persuasion, the UN established a Working Group of Experts to study evidence and make recommendations. Their unanimous report found that slavery persists, particularly in new disguises, and that it has not diminished in the past decade.

The Anti-Slavery Society was founded in 1839 by friends of William Wilberforce (then deceased). In 1909 it merged with the Aborigines Protection Society, founded in 1837. It has consultative status at the Economic and Social Council (ECOSOC), is supported entirely by private subscription and has members in twenty-eight countries, representing all continents. Its Secretary, Colonel Patrick Montgomery, states:

What does slavery mean in the seventies? In 1973, twenty Ghanaian girls aged fourteen were sold into unpaid 'domestic service' in Lebanon. Detection was followed by prompt punishment and preventive action. But to remove the incentive is more difficult . . . Amerindian children caught with their parents in Government-sponsored expeditions in Paraguay to 'clean' the forests were being sold as household drudges for two dollars each in 1975. Nigerians who escaped from Equatorial Guinea described in January 1976 the conditions of slavery in which 30,000 of them had been working in cocoa plantations without pay. Slavery in the seventies also means enforced prostitution.[16]

The Times on 4 December 1976 had a good word for Colonel Montgomery's splendid organisation:

Do not imagine that slavery has vanished from the face of the earth. Chattel slavery, serfdom, debt bondage, pseudo-adoption and servile forms of marriage persist in many parts of the world. The Anti-Slavery Society exists to detect, investigate and challenge these and other abuses and violations of human freedom, as it did so successfully in earlier generations.

But over and beyond these voluntary and privately financed pressure groups, whose work is still indispensable, our own generation has seen the creation of intergovernmental bodies whose goals and operations in the field of human rights reach beyond the wildest dreams of the early reformers. One of these intergovernmental bodies, the International Labour Organisation (ILO), will round off the historical survey we are attempting in this chapter. But the cynics who scoff at these long-overdue innovations in the world community and who hide their ignorance under a cloud of outmoded nationalism, are occasionally brought up with a sharp shock at what is happening in the next street or village or workplace:

'The story of Michele Di Benedetto, sold by his parents as a farm labourer at 11 and a suicide at 14, has left Italy a slightly more sober place,' writes Patricia Clough from Rome. The son of a poor family at Altamura, in Apulia, he was first sold to a farmer at the age of 11 in the annual labour market in the town's market place. The price – 40,000 lire (about £26) a month and a few kilograms of cheese, to be paid to his parents, for a year's work. Each year his price went up until in 1974 he fetched his parents 125,000 lire a month, 10 kilos of cheese, about 7 cwt of wood, 12 litres of olive oil and 12 kilos of salt.

The end of the tragedy came out in the Court, when his parents were indicted: 'Michele worked 15 hours a day, seven days a week, rising at a quarter past three to milk 200 ewes and take them to graze. His food was a piece of bread at lunchtime and a plate of pasta for supper. At night he was locked up in the cowshed to sleep in the straw and filth. At the age of 14 he shot himself with his latest boss's gun.'[17]

HUMANITARIAN INTERVENTION

Although not specifically listed in Jenk's summary (p. 12 above) of the precursors of the modern movement – possibly because of its doubtful respectability under international law – what has been loosely called 'humanitarian intervention' can be linked at this point with some more recent views on 'state responsibility', which Jenks placed last on his list. But the reader must be warned that this topic plunges us immediately into politics of the most blatant kind. Critics who have been complaining that human rights today are becoming 'politicized' might look again at what some of their forebears thought and did. Happily the right of 'humanitarian intervention' – if it were ever a 'right' at all – has been pronounced by most international lawyers as either extinct or moribund. For one thing, the recent General Assembly Definition of Aggression includes no provision to permit it. It is all too obvious, alas, that *in*humanitarian intervention is still very much with us!

The former Director of the UN Division of Human Rights, Professor John P. Humphrey, has pointed out that, apart from some treaty law, traditional international law specifically recognised only one institution whose purpose was to protect individual human rights, namely, the customary rules of state responsibility for the treatment of *aliens*. As for their own *nationals*, states could treat them as they thought fit. But to this rule, surmises Professor Humphrey, there may have been one exception: 'If, it is said, a State treated its nationals in such a manner as to shock the conscience of mankind, other States could then intervene, if necessary by force, to protect the persecuted nationals. This is called humanitarian intervention.'[18]

This might form a useful working definition for our present purpose. Yet it will be noticed that Professor Humphrey writes in the past tense. This is because, by Article 2(4) of the UN Charter, member states are bound 'to refrain in their international relations from the threat or use of force . . .' – a categorical pledge that has been followed by three decades of General Assembly refinements and applications which clearly exclude any recourse today to humanitarian intervention.

The Charter has in fact lifted human rights out of the prohibition in the controversial seventh paragraph of Article 2, which states that the United Nations cannot intervene 'in matters which are essentially within the domestic jurisdiction of any State'. By their very nature, violations 'that shock the conscience of mankind' cannot be 'essentially within the domestic jurisdiction of any State'. Moreover, as we shall see later on, the concept of a consistent pattern of gross violations of human rights has now come under direct United Nations scrutiny. So a yet bigger hole has been driven through Article 2(7).

Some international lawyers have already begun to speak of the assimilation of the customary law regarding the treatment of aliens into the new law of the Charter regarding 'universal respect for, and observance of, human rights'. Sir Humphrey Waldock has said:

> The assimilation is logical enough so far as concerns the 'minimum standards' of treatment, that is, the scope of the fundamental rights and freedoms protected by international law. Human Rights, *ex hypothesi*, are rights which attach to all human beings equally, whatever their nationality.[19]

For the moment, however, we are looking at what humanitarian intervention meant – or was supposed to mean – in pre-Charter times. Confining our survey to the nineteenth century, the domination of Turkey over Eastern Europe up to the Balkan Wars of 1912–13 provided many motives and pretexts for West European interventions, both diplomatic and military. Undoubtedly, the rights of individuals were always in issue; but, once again, power relationships were always present too. Each intervention by a 'kind-hearted gunman' (as Ian Brownlie terms it) did not strictly terminate until the Peace Treaties set up a regime of defending minority rights in 1919, the topic of our next section. But several notorious cases have provided historians with cause for reflection and lawyers with cause for disputation. We can select only a few of them here and deal with them in the simplest terms.[20]

The first classical case was particularly noteworthy because it was pursued, in effect, to its logical conclusion. The sprawling Ottoman Empire so brutally oppressed its minorities that, in 1830, the Greeks appealed to Western powers. By the Treaty of London, Britain, France and Russia intervened by armed force. One result was that Greece attained its independence as a nation.

The Syrian case in 1860 – again in protest against Turkish misrule – brought five 'Christian' powers together in the Conference of Paris. They sent an expeditionary force of 6000 French troops to keep order – withdrawing them a year later. An interesting 'spin-off' here was the drafting of a constitution for Lebanon, providing for a Christian governor.

A third case, in 1866, was instructive in so far as there was no landing of troops. An appeal by the Cretans induced Austria, France, Italy, Prussia and Russia to propose a fact-finding International Commission of Enquiry to visit the island, thus creating a precedent for the United Nations a century later. Turkey's rejection of this proposal on grounds of domestic jurisdiction, however, might have been followed by military intervention again, had not Britain – not a party to the intervention – been able to persuade the Turkish government to promulgate a new constitution for the island and undertake certain human rights commitments.

The Bulgarian case in 1876 was perhaps *sui generis*. It was really the inspiration of one man – William Ewart Gladstone – summoned from his retirement as former Prime Minister, as H.A.L. Fisher phrased it, 'by the bitter cry of Bulgarian distress'. The diplomatic complications of the Balkan muddle we cannot enlarge on here, but we can continue in Dr Fisher's graphic words:

> The campaign which he then conducted in and out of Parliament is one of the outstanding physical and oratorical achievements in English history . . . That English voters could not be in-different to the general welfare of mankind was the main burden of his argument. 'Remember,' he said to the electors of Mid-lothian in a characteristic flight, 'that the sanctity of life in the hill villages of Afghanistan among the winter snows is as inviolable in the eyes of Almighty God as can be your own.' He had no fear of the big Bulgaria. With a sound instinct he declared that there could be no greater barrier against the advance of Russian influence in the Balkans than a nation of free men.[21]

Gladstone's vigorous championship of Bulgaria had a sequel in the Congress of Berlin, in 1878, following Russia's war with Turkey. A regime of Christian autonomy was established which guaranteed Bulgaria, while Montenegro, Serbia and Rumania became inde-

pendent states. Obligations were then assumed by Britain, France,
Germany, Italy and Russia – and later Hungary – to maintain
minimum human rights in Bosnia and Hercegovina, as well as
Bulgaria, after Turkey had rejected their proposals for a supervisory
International Commission.

The foregoing instances do not, of course, spell out the historical
significance of each intervention. There were others, not only in
Europe, but also in the Americas.[22] But they do raise some
provocative speculation. First, we notice that, apart from
Gladstone's lone campaign (which curiously combined a domestic
with a European appeal), the intervening powers always acted in
concert. They also employed diplomatic pressure before resorting to
force or threat of force. Their joint motive (Moslem Turkey being
the target government) was ostensibly 'Christian'.

Second, we notice that in each case the longer-term result of the
intervention was political. In other words, though protection of
human rights was the pretext, the situation to be remedied was a
political one. Can it be said that things are fundamentally different
in the twentieth century? Can individual human rights be protected
by outside intervention, even if collective, except through *internal*
political change? An answer will be explored as our study proceeds.

Third, we notice that these 'classical' interventions, by their
nature, were arbitrary, transient, and without continuing authority. It was the declared objective of the League of Nations
protective system, that followed the First World War, to remedy
these defects. 'Two lessons had been learnt from the history of
intervention on behalf of minority populations before the World
War,' remarks Julius Stone:

> The first was that to allow to individual States a right of direct
> political interference in the affairs of another was a dangerous
> policy from the point of view of European peace. The second was
> that, if there was to be any reality in the protection granted to
> minority populations, some form of permanent supervision was
> essential.[23]

Before we turn to the League's handling of minorities, however,
an important comment should be added on the vast jump across a
whole century that had to be made between these (now) illegal
interventions and interventions that the UN can, and often does,
take in defending and protecting human rights since the Charter
appeared. This point was clearly made during a conference of

international lawyers, cited earlier, at Charlottesville, Virginia, on
the Procedural Aspects of the Law on Humanitarian Intervention,
by Professor E. Frey-Wouters:

> The only real solution lies in a more responsible world com-
> munity with new institutions and procedures and a willingness to
> respond to these very tragic situations. For the time being,
> unilateral humanitarian measures by one State in the territory of
> another State should be permitted only in extreme crisis
> situations, and when the regional or international community is
> not able to respond. In those cases, the intervention should be
> authorized either by the parties directly involved in the situation
> or by the regional organisation or by the United Nations. The
> intervention should not involve the use of armed force and should
> be nonstrategic and strictly humanitarian.[24]

In the rapidly expanding field of human rights, as in so many of
the Charter's other global concerns, few people seem yet to have
grasped the fundamentally different character of the UN approach
from those of any previous epoch. The carry-over from the lingering
nationalistic anarchy of today to a more orderly and responsible
form of world co-operation between alleged 'sovereign' states is
unfortunately hard to discern at times.[25] Yet, slowly the international community of scholars and world civil servants is
beginning to endow the new order with the elements of fundamental change, while the UN system has been developing new
techniques for handling old problems that can truly be regarded as
revolutionary.

Diplomatic terminology has not, however, caught up with
reality. Phrases linger on the lips of foreign offices and state
departments that ring as hollow as the moralities they betray. The
international lawyers and political scientists who participated in the
Conference at Charlottesville could not accept the legality or
respectability of humanitarian intervention, because all the rules
had been changed since the term was coined as part of customary
international law. Harvard Law Professor R. R. Baxter, for
example, stated a plain historical fact when he suggested, with
cryptic reserve:

> I assume that humanitarian intervention, for better or for worse,
> is a short-term use of armed force by a government, in what
> would otherwise be a violation of the sovereignty of a foreign

State, for the protection from death or grave injury of nationals of the acting State – and incidentally, perhaps, nationals of other States – by their removal from the territory of the foreign State.[26]

The truth is that, for better or worse, these old-fashioned adventures no longer *work*. Looking back at the Bay of Pigs, as a relatively minor catastrophe, and the unspeakably disastrous 'intervention' in Vietnam, no-one in his senses today would place such disgraceful episodes in either a legal or a humanitarian category. The least said about the *Pueblo* affair, the better! We might still be confronted, alas, with another Entebbe commando raid as justifying the diplomatic formula: 'To save American – or Israeli – lives'!

As regards Entebbe, nobody believed for one moment that this hot-war Arab-Israeli confrontation was legalised by some nineteenth-century doctrine of humanitarian intervention, though some State Department lawyers remembered it. As regards the Dominican Republic landing (1965), I venture to repeat here what I have documented elsewhere, namely that: 'When troops suddenly landed, it was announced that they had come to remove endangered United States citizens; whereas the intervention had been planned behind the scenes in advance as a political move.'[27]

The Thirty-first General Assembly denounced on 17 December 1976 'any form of interference in the internal affairs of States, including the recruiting and sending of mercenaries and any act of military, political, economic *or other intervention*' [*Our italics*]. It also condemned all forms of 'coercion, subversion and defamation aimed at disrupting the political, social or economic order of other States or destabilizing the Governments seeking to free their economies from external control or manipulation'.

It is against this background of what has actually been *happening*, that the new order of things, 'struggling to be born', stands out in stark and welcome contrast. Even if the contentions in the preceding paragraphs can be disputed or contradicted on strictly legal or policy grounds, no one can deny that, over three decades, the UN's multiple system of peace-making has offered a rich variety of alternatives which, given time, make the subterfuges we have instanced appear as relics of a barbaric age. The gigantic Congo reconstruction operation, masterminded by Dag Hammarskjöld; the *casques bleues* in Golan; or the patient UN International Force in Cyprus (UNIFCYP) still standing between the Cypriots and the

Turks – always with the rival governments' consent – point to a widening range of peace-keeping techniques and programmes that have, in short, given the term 'humanitarian intervention' a new direction and purpose under the UN Charter, as the legitimate guardian of human rights.

Finally, on a more pragmatic, even if inconclusive note, the rights of the alien and non-citizen have not been neglected, though progress has been slow. Recent action by the General Assembly to protect the alien or non-citizen have taken various forms. We can conclude this survey of humanitarian intervention by selecting two current procedures. The first approach to offer legal protection to non-citizens, following up a report by ECOSOC on 18 May 1973, was a resolution which runs, in part, as follows:

> *Requests* the Sub-Commission on Prevention of Discrimination and Protection of Minorities to consider as a matter of priority, at its twenty-sixth session, the problem of the applicability of existing international provisions for the protection of human rights to individuals who are not citizens of the country in which they live, to consider what measures in the field of human rights, including the possibility of a declaration, would be desirable, and to submit appropriate recommendations . . .[28]

A second approach has been proceeding for some years in the International Law Commission, established by the General Assembly in 1947 to promote the codification and development of international law. Most of the Commission's work has taken the form of draft articles; international conferences are then convened by the General Assembly which have adopted Conventions on the basis of these draft articles. Under '*State responsibility*', the Commission is now making a study of the rules that govern the new legal relationships which might follow from an act of a state characterised as 'internationally wrongful'.[29] The Commission is attempting to codify the rules governing the responsibility of states for such internationally wrongful acts, and doubtless its recommendations will come before the General Assembly in about 1980 in the form of a Convention.

At its 1976 session the Commission included among its definition of an international crime 'a serious breach on a widespread scale of an international obligation of essential importance for safeguarding the human being, such as those prohibiting slavery, genocide and *apartheid*'. But other draft articles, on acts which would be considered under international law as merely wrongful (international delicts) include 'acts causing injury to the person or property of aliens'. In other words, a new branch of international law is slowly evolving.[30]

It seems likely, therefore, that this evolution will proceed on dual lines. For, in the meantime, the status of aliens and the necessity to take effective measures to promote and protect their fundamental rights is already being considered by the Commission on Human Rights, which started doing so in April 1972. Following violations of the human rights of aliens in certain parts of the world, the subject was also raised at the Sub-Commission on Prevention of Discrimination and Protection of Minorities, under the item 'Questions of the gross violation of human rights and fundamental freedoms'. The discussion led to the adoption of a resolution in which the Commission was recommended to consider the problem of the international legal protection of 'the human rights of individuals who are not citizens of the country in which they live' and to draw up a list of measures in the field of human rights. This action will probably be carried towards the presentation of a 'Declaration', possibly in 1978 or soon after.[31]

One of the acute difficulties in drafting such a Declaration, however, is that certain civil and political rights that attach to citizens, by definition, cannot be *identical* with those of non-citizens. Expulsion is one of these; so that an appropriate Article in the proposed draft has been put forward (in 1976) in these terms:

Article 7
1. No non-citizen shall be subjected to arbitrary expulsion or deportation.
2. A non-citizen may be expelled from the territory of a State only in pursuance of a decision reached in accordance with law and shall, except where compelling reasons of national security otherwise require, be allowed to submit reasons against his expulsion and to have his case reviewed by and be represented for the purpose before the competent authority or a person or persons especially designated by the competent authority.[32]

The proviso in Article 7(2), if the Declaration is eventually adopted by the UN General Assembly, will no doubt have some bearing on alien expulsion issues, such as the sharply controversial case that arose in early 1977, when the British Home Secretary made deportation orders against two American journalists, Mr

Philip Agee and Mr Mark Hosenball, under the 1971 Immigration Act, in spite of representations they have made to an independent panel, which had no juridical functions.

In a forthcoming study, *Human Rights and World Order*, the authors state that every individual is a potential alien. They itemise some of the ways in which aliens are handicapped in their legal rights and social opportunities, and point out that

> the access of aliens to health facilities and services is generally less than that of nationals, and housing often presents difficult problems. Even the lives of aliens may be threatened by mob actions, inspired by xenophobia; and in many communities alienage remains a stigma of disrespect, affecting many civil liberties.[33]

But they acknowledge the slow evolution, to which we have already drawn attention, in these terms:

> In a global society aspiring towards the utmost freedom of choice for individuals in matters of group affiliation, residence, movement, access to value processes, and so on, differentiation upon the ground of alienage is scarcely less invidious to human dignity values than discrimination based upon race, sex, and religion.

MINORITIES

What is a 'minority'? For our present purpose, we can assume as a working definition that a minority is a body of people bound together by a kindred consciousness that is rooted in a common ancestry, traditions, language, and culture or religion, which sets them off from the majority or the dominant people of the country in which they live.

Minorities have been with us a long time. Frequently, minorities are found along the frontiers of a state. When this borderland adjoins another state in which its minority forms the majority of the other state, a partial solution of the minority 'problem' might perhaps be found in territorial adjustments or exchange of populations by mutual consent. But numerous minorities live in 'islands' entirely surrounded by other peoples. Obviously no *territorial* settlement is feasible for them. For minority peoples who are so interspersed among the majority, it would be impracticable for them to govern themselves as a unit. The only possible solution is some kind of inter-state arrangement guaranteeing them the *right* to preserve their own language and traditions and enjoy equal civil rights with the majority. This, in essence, is the problem. For its solution in practical terms we might usefully look back over half a century.[34]

As a major issue of European foreign policies and of growing international concern, the protection of minorities became one of the first duties of the League of Nations after the First World War. 'It is in its manner of dealing with these problems that the settlement of 1919–20 was of outstanding merit,' stated a contemporary authority, Dr Julius Stone:

> Although certain minorities provisions of the Nineteenth Century are to be found in collective instruments, like the Paris and Berlin Acts, there was in general no stipulation for collective action by the Powers in case those provisions should not be observed. The right of intervention was a right vested in the Signatory Powers individually and not collectively.[35]

In this broad appraisal of progress in protection of minority rights under the League of Nations, we have come a long way from the hypocrisies and subterfuges portrayed in the previous section. We begin to move towards that new order of collective responsibility which we saw struggling to birth amidst the nineteenth-century anarchy of sovereign states. The three fundamental organs that the League brought to establish this new order were: (1) the League Council; (2) the Permanent Minorities Committee; and (3) the World Court.

The League's reputed failure to handle minorities' problems effectively was set in due perspective by an experienced official of the League, Mr F. P. Walters, whose two-volume classic, published after the Second World War, summed up the position as follows:

> The League Council took the first step in accepting yet another function, which was to provide it with much difficult work during the next fifteen years – that of protecting the rights of racial, religious, and linguistic minorities in Eastern and Central Europe. In many areas of mixed population a complete reversal had been effected by the Peace Treaties: the ruling power had passed from the race hitherto dominant – German, Austrian, Hungarians – to those hitherto largely treated as subject

peoples – Poles, Serbs, Croats, Slovenes, Czechs, Romanians. No human skill could draw frontiers which would not leave considerable minorities on either side . . . The new masters had had, in many cases, to bear much tyranny and wrong from those who were now their subjects. If they were tempted to pay off old scores, their action would be easy to understand: but its political dangers would be great.[36]

The Paris Peace Conference had devised a new form of treaty by which the new states that had set themselves up on the defeat of Germany and the Central Powers pledged themselves to grant fair and equal treatment to the minorities within their frontiers. Moreover, their solemn undertakings were declared to be 'a matter of international concern' and were placed under the guarantee of the League. This system was later extended by the Assembly to Finland, Albania, the Baltic States and Iraq, on their admission to the League.

In short, this series of treaties for the protection of minorities guaranteed protection of life and liberty, free exercise of religion and use of the mother-tongue, and the opportunity of education in that tongue, whenever the minority constituted a considerable proportion of the population. Nine European states were bound by these treaties, and five other countries which made minority declarations to the League Council, recognised that these stipulations constituted fundamental laws for them and that they represented obligations of *international concern*. Any violations could be brought to the attention of the Council of the League by any member of the Council.

Petitions could be addressed to the League and forwarded to the interested government for comments. Such petitions, together with the government's comments, were then sent to the members of the Council, and a small committee of the Council examined them. If this committee, or any other member of the Council, found that the matters deserved attention, they were then placed on the Council agenda. When one studies the systematic work done by the Minorities Section of the old League Secretariat, in assembling information, classifying petitions, or preparing speeches or reports, one gains a *déjà vu* awareness of the immensely important role of the present Division of Human Rights within today's UN Secretariat.

While it frequently happened that the questions were answered by the League Secretariat before coming on to the Council agenda, several dozen cases did, in fact, come eventually before the Council. Legal aspects of some of them were referred to the World Court for advisory opinions. For example, one of these involved the right of the Polish government to expel certain Polish citizens of German race from their farms in Western Poland; and another concerned the nationality of German residents in Poland. The opinions expressed by the Court in these two leading cases enabled the Council to reach a settlement. There was also a reference by the Council to the Court of a legal question concerning Greeks liable to expulsion from Constantinople. The Court's opinion was accepted by both Greece and Turkey. Other complaints before the Council concerned minority rights in Lithuania; and also a petition from a number of farmers of Hungarian origin regarding a Roumanian agrarian reform law; and so on.

It cannot be too strongly stressed, however, that the minorities provisions of the minor peace treaties in 1919–22 were not the *product* of the League of Nations, nor even mentioned in its Covenant, which was drafted as a distinct and separate legal instrument – though put at the front of the Versailles Treaty. They were sometimes the outcome of incredible and often reprehensible haggling in the 'expert' Committees of the Paris Conference.

One of the most distinguished Foreign Office participants, Harold Nicholson, published as Part Two of his well-known and fascinating account of the Conference, *Peacemaking 1919*, a detailed diary of day-to-day debates in one of those Committees.[37] Some of his frank and off-the-cuff entries reveal all too plainly how impossible became the self-imposed task of the League when the new frontiers of Europe had to be drawn under such conditions as are described in two typical extracts from Nicholson's diary:

> When in Prague, I had begged Smuts to urge on Masaryk not to claim that wretched Danubian island. He had done so. Masaryk had agreed that if they could obtain a bridgehead across the river at Pressburg they would abandon the Grosse Schütt. I begged Hardinge to bring this offer up before the Council . . . To my dismay, however, Pichon put up Laroche to say that he had heard from Benes that Smuts had 'completely misunderstood' old Masaryk.

> They all sit round the map. The appearance of a pie about to be distributed is thus enhanced. Lloyd George shows them [the

Italian delegates] what he suggests. They ask for Scala Nova as
well. 'Oh no!' says LL.G., 'you can't have that – it's full of
Greeks!' He goes on to point out that there are further Greeks at
Makri, and a whole wedge of them along the coast towards
Alexandretta. 'Oh, no,' I whisper to him, 'there are not many
Greeks there.' 'But yes,' he answers, 'don't you see it's coloured
green?' I then realise that he mistakes my map for an ethnological
map, and thinks the green means Greeks instead of valleys, and
the brown means Turks instead of mountains.

Close students of the 1919–20 Peace Settlement and its vast
documentation might be induced to forget that, from the confusion
and wirepulling and downright skullduggery of those five months of
torturous proceedings, some good did come. At least the foundations were laid for an intelligent approach to international affairs
that we take for granted today. Moreover, Nicholson's unofficial
daily account shows how desperately the 'staff of the Conference
strove both to meet President Wilson's high principles of international morality and to cope with sordid compromises amidst
the selfish pressures that descended upon them from the moment
they arrived in Paris'.

'We shall be looking at the question in the wrong perspective if we
imagine the Allies sitting down with a blank map of Europe', said
Professor Alfred Cobban, 'and a free hand in drawing up the new
frontiers. In many cases the claims had already been staked out and
occupied, and only military action on a large scale could have
ousted the new possessors.' As Harold Nicholson frequently con-
fesses, no human being could have drawn a clean line through those
myriad of ethnic coloured patches that dotted the map of Europe
from immemorial migrations and ancient resettlements. 'I see
nothing but blackness in the future,' he said, on reviewing the Peace
Treaties as a whole. Nonetheless, the invention of the Minorities
Treaties themselves, with all their imperfections, was a recognition
that the human rights of some 30 millions covered by them had
become international obligations. It was a big step forward.

The present author had a closer contact with some of those
obligations when, in 1929, I was appointed Organizing-Secretary of
the International Conference on Minorities of Language, Race and
Religion, held at the Caxton Hall, London, and presided over by
Lord Robert Cecil. This non-governmental conference was sponsored by the Women's International League, and it brought

together a group of well-known scholars, such as Professor Gilbert Murray and the Rt Hon. Philip Noel-Baker in England, and international lawyers who participated in the Conference from France, Poland, Belgium, Germany and other European countries, as well as some League of Nations officials actually dealing with minority problems.

One decision of that Conference was to submit to the 'Committee of Three' of the League Council at Geneva suggestions for improved procedures in the handling of complaints received from minority groups and individuals. More frequent resort to the jurisdiction of the World Court was advocated as an important asset in the new system so as to deal more effectively with the complicated legal points that were continually arising.[38]

The main purpose of the London Conference, however, was to enlighten and stimulate world public opinion on what those problems were. Many of them – as now – seemed quite hopeless of solution. I recall particularly the plight of the Macedonians (divided between Serbs, Albanians, Romanians and Greeks), who never achieved national status. Their publicity organ *La Macédoine* reached me regularly from their Paris office for some years. Unfortunately, one cannot pursue such reminiscences here, as more immediate issues claim our attention.

It would not be feasible, in this overall account, to deal at length with the position of national minorities today. In Chapter 5, however, the modern aspects of 'self-determination' will be explored further. The problem of minority rights is one of the most explosive issues in the modern world. Even in the older countries, secessionist movements among minorities have been gaining strength. In Northern Ireland the discrimination against a minority within a minority has produced a seemingly insoluble problem. The examples of Nigeria, East Pakistan and Cyprus, to name but three, show what havoc can result from minority conflicts in developing countries.

Some final observations might be attempted here on two long-standing 'classical' minority problems examined at the Paris Peace Conference, though neither managed to secure a stable existence: those of the Kurds and the Armenians. According to an authoritative monograph published by a British research organisation, the Minority Rights Group, the origin of the first problem lay in the fact that:

In the division of the Ottoman Empire after the First World War, the Kurds were offered the prospect of independence under the Treaty of Sèvres of 1920 but, mainly because of the rise of Kemal Ataturk, this was never implemented . . . Today the homeland of the Kurdish people lies in five different independent states: mainly in Turkey, Iraq and Iran, with enclaves in Syria and the U.S.S.R. In these states racial minorities, such as the Kurds, do not expect protective treatment, but they have had to put up with an increasing barrage of state nationalism, whether it be revolutionary or reactionary, monarchist or socialist, Iranian, Turkish or Arab.[39]

It is true that these states have made many public avowals about equality of opportunity for all citizens and races, but the Kurds have all along been sidetracked and oppressed by their respective rulers. Living for the most part in inaccessible mountain areas, the Kurds have suffered from the worst forms of administrative neglect and indolence from governments who despise their claims for autonomy. It is only in Iraq that the Kurdish movement has sought 'autonomy' or a wide degree of self-government, within the framework of the Iraqi State. In Turkey, Iran and Syria, the Kurds call mainly for 'national rights', in terms of language and culture. Kurdish nationalism is an answer to the denial of such rights, but, in practice, it provokes a hostile response.

A beginning might now exist, however, in Article 1 of the 1974 'Law for Autonomy' (in Iraq), which reads: 'The area of Kurdistan shall enjoy autonomy and be called the area whenever it is mentioned hereinafter'; and this 'area shall be so defined as to be populated by a majority of Kurds'. And Article 2 states that 'The Kurdish language shall be the official language, besides the Arabic language, in the area'; also that 'The Kurdish language shall be the language of education for Kurds in the area, but the teaching of Arabic shall be compulsory in all stages and institutions of education.'[40]

But are these new laws being carried out? Miss Leah Levin, of the United Nations Association's Committee on Human Rights in London, has been looking at the evidence and says:

Evidence of a deliberate policy of dispersal is also reflected by alterations in administrative boundaries; and the renaming of geographical areas, institutions, even streets, from Kurdish to

Arabic. The word Kurdistan is avoided in official publications; the preference is 'autonomous area'.[41]

And she concludes: 'It is clear that the enforced placing of Kurds among the Arab population and the thinning out of Kurdish areas are being arbitrarily pursued in the expectation of forcing the Kurds to integrate.'

How much worse the sufferings of the persecuted Armenian people have been is known to everyone. The Minority Rights Group has this to say:

> In the course of a quarter of a century – between 1895 and 1920 – the Armenian race lost a million and a half people by the gun or the bayonet, by deliberate starvation, and by privation and pestilence. About a third of all Armenians in the world died a gruesome, painful death. This national catastrophe is comparable to that suffered by the Jews under the Hitler regime.[42]

Bringing the story up to date, Mr Edward Mortimer, in *The Times* of 11 January 1977, reminds us that although the Peace Settlement of 1919 produced, on demise of the Turkish Empire, an Armenian Republic, it was conquered after only two years by the Bolsheviks and forcibly transformed into a Soviet Republic. Nevertheless, he writes, 'it seems that Soviet Armenia has remained a "national home", acknowledged even by the most capitalistic Armenians of the diaspora.'[43]

A bright light is, however, thrown by the above-mentioned MRG Report on the Armenians' present position, since it would appear that they 'are somewhat privileged compared with other Soviet nationalities, enjoying a reasonable standard of living, a health service highly acceptable by Near Eastern standards, and excellent educational facilities'. Moreover, they travel extensively abroad, and some even possess a Western nationality as well as their Soviet one. Consequently, both before and after 1917, Armenians have regarded Russia as their protector against Turkey, and today 'their underlying loyalty to and dependence on the Soviet Union is beyond doubt'.

Perhaps we can best leave our historical review there, and return in later chapters to consider how international minorities fare within the United Nations sytem, now that they are rooted in international law under Article 27 of the International Covenant on Civil and Political Rights, which reads as follows:

In those States in which ethnic, religious or linguistic minorities
exist, persons belonging to such minorities shall not be denied the
right, in community with the other members of their group, to
enjoy their own culture, to profess and practise their own religion,
or to use their own language.

MANDATES

Even if the protection of minorities was never mentioned in the
Covenant of the League of Nations, the mandatory system was
given ample space. As Article 22, it became the longest Article of all.
We need not reproduce the whole of it here, but its first three and
most weighty clauses are as follows:

Article 22 [Mandatories: Control of Colonies and Territories]
    To those colonies and territories which as a consequence of the
late war have ceased to be under the sovereignty of the states
which formerly governed them and which are inhabited by
peoples not yet able to stand by themselves under the strenuous
conditions of the modern world, there should be applied the
principle that the well-being and development of such peoples
form a sacred trust of civilization and that securities for the
performance of this trust should be embodied in this Covenant.
    The best method of giving practical effect to this principle is
that the tutelage of such peoples should be entrusted to advanced
nations who by reason of their resources, their experience or their
geographical position can best undertake this responsibility, and
who are willing to accept it, and that this tutelage should be
exercised by them as Mandatories on behalf of the League.
    The character of the mandate must differ according to the
stage of the development of the people, the geographical situation
of the territory, its economic conditions and other similar
circumstances.

The Article goes on to specify that 'communities formerly
belonging to the Turkish Empire have reached a stage of development where their existence as independent nations can be pro-
visionally recognized'; but that 'the wishes of these communities
must be a principal consideration in the selection of the Mandatory'. Other peoples, especially those of Central Africa, were
described as being

at such a stage that the Mandatory must be responsible for the administration of the territory under conditions which will guarantee freedom of conscience and religion, subject only to the maintenance of public order and morals, the prohibition of abuses such as the slave trade, the arms traffic, and the liquor traffic.

Equally forbidden were fortifications or military and naval bases and military training of the 'natives' for other than police purposes and the defence of territory.

'The German colonies in the Pacific and Africa,' General Smuts wrote in 1918, 'are inhabited by barbarians, who not only cannot possibly govern themselves, but to whom it would be impracticable to apply any idea of political self-determination in the European sense.' It would appear that South Africa's political leaders today feel the same way.

It is significant, therefore, since the evils of apartheid are still with us, that the League's Article 22 continues:

There are territories, such as South-West Africa and certain of the South Pacific Islands, which, owing to the sparseness of their population, or their small size . . . and other circumstances, can be best administered under the laws of the Mandatory as integral portions of its territory, subject to the safeguards above-mentioned in the interests of the indigenous population.

In every case, however, the Mandatory had to render to the League Council an annual report on the territory committed to its charge. The degree of authority or administration to be exercised by the Mandatory was to be defined in each case by the Council. Finally, a Permanent Mandates Commission was set up to examine the annual reports sent in by the Mandatories and to advise the Council on the observance of their mandates.

The mandatory system, in spite of its imperfections, was undoubtedly a hopeful advance in world responsibility. It marked an important step forward in the relations between the developed and backward peoples. Emergent racial problems were already being perceived by progressive thinkers as likely to become more acute during the century. President Wilson, more farsighted than most of his generation, had proposed that racial equality be included in the Covenant. Though he failed in this endeavour, he insisted, supported by General J. C. Smuts and Lord Robert Cecil, that territories given up by Germany and Turkey after the War should not be treated as spoils of war and annexed by the Allied Powers. Fortunately, the Peace Conference agreed with him that these territories should be administered 'as a sacred trust of civilization' under the care of the League itself and in the interests and the welfare of the 'native' peoples. Thus, when the mandatory system came into being, the colonial system began to disintegrate, though this was barely understood at the time. How many participants in anti-racialism and decolonisation programmes today recognise that their campaign really began with the League of Nations Covenant and that Woodrow Wilson's epoch-making Fourteen Points laid the foundation for this and many other human rights principles enshrined in that Covenant?[44]

According to the terms of Article 22, there were to be be set up three classes of Mandates. Further description of these would be irrelevant here – especially as the author has dealt with them elsewhere.[45] What is important to note is that the Permanent Mandates Commission was appointed by the Council to advise it on all relevant matters. This Commission was a highly efficient body, composed not of government representatives, but of eleven *independent* experts, the majority of whom were citizens of non-mandatory countries. It was presided over by that brilliant Swiss scholar, William Rappard. A representative of each Mandatory Power also attended its meetings when the report of his Government was being discussed, in order to give additional information. It became an increasing practice for the Mandatory Powers to send for this purpose actual or former administrators in the territories concerned. The Commission also drew up detailed questionnaires for the different territories. After a thorough examination of their reports it presented its observations to the Council of the League, who brought to the attention of the Mandatory Powers whatever suggestions it considered advisable.

A detailed account of how the Commission discharged its duties and the resistances it encountered from some of the Mandatory Powers cannot be pursued here; but no student of the Trusteeship Council's successes in 'decolonialisation' today can ignore the debt that the UN system owes to Professor Rappard's pioneering achievement in the 1920s and 1930s. One single example may not be without interest when we recall that, during its third session, Rappard's Commission had to give anxious attention to the rebellion of the tribe of Bondelzwarts in South-West Africa, a matter which later came before the Third and Fourth Annual Assemblies of the League – a small dark cloud on the horizon that has grown to the vast black rebellion today!

Apart from the regular examination of the reports of the Mandatory Powers, the Commission became increasingly a competent forum for exchanging experience and for establishing human rights standards between the colonial powers and their charges. When, later on, we review the freedom struggle proceeding now in Namibia (formerly South-West Africa), we may well conclude that the League's almost forgotten Commission did not labour in vain.

Seen at this distance of time, the Mandates system seems to have been a sensible and a practical device. But the Mandates Commission was kept very busy with all sorts of crises – such as the revolt of the Druzes (1925–7) in Syria and the mounting turmoil in Palestine, which became a full-scale war in 1948 when Britain gave up the Mandate. To some extent the system became, historically, the opening phase of today's 'self-government' and independence movements, for it led on to the independence of India and the African colonies one after another, following the Second World War – all except the paradox of a tragedy of errors when General Smuts's own country refused to let go the people of South-West Africa.

LABOUR STANDARDS

There was another very important Article of the Covenant dealing specifically with another aspect of human rights – labour rights. This was Article 23, which began

> *Article 23* [Social Activities]
> Subject to and in accordance with the provisions of international conventions existing or hereafter to be agreed upon, the members of the League –
> (a) Will endeavour to secure and maintain fair and humane conditions of labour for men, women and children, both in their own countries and in all countries to which their commercial and industrial relations extend, and for that purpose will establish and maintain the necessary international organizations. . . .

The Paris Conference had set up a fifteen-member Commission on Labour Legislation. Sitting for ten weeks under the chairmanship of Samuel Gompers of the American Federation of Labor, this Commission prepared a document that the full Conference approved on 11 April 1919. This document became Part XIII of the Treaty of Versailles. With some amendments, it remains to this day the basic charter of the International Labour Organisation (ILO).

The ILO was envisaged by its founders primarily as an organisation for raising standards by building up a code of 'international legislation' (to give it its widely accepted name). In the years between the two World Wars this was, in fact, the ILO's chief function, and one which it performed with conspicuous success. Despite the many new areas into which the ILO has extended its activities since the end of the Second World War, standard-setting in labour relations retains its vital importance. These international standards take the form of Conventions and Recommendations. It is enough to note here that, since its establishment, a total of nearly 150 Conventions and 160 Recommendations have been adopted. Taken together, these form a world-wide Labour Code, which now constitutes a heavily-annotated volume of labour 'rights' in all the official languages.

Although the ILO was the product of the social thought of the industrially developed countries of Europe and America, the objectives assigned to the new Organisation were not those of any particular society or time, for the ILO was conceived as the protector of the interests of working men and women everywhere. The universal nature of the goals set before the ILO more than a generation ago has enabled the Organisation to respond and adapt itself to the growing challenge of the developing world.[46]

During the Second World War the ILO (which had continued its basic operations) considered the policies and programmes which it would be called upon to pursue when peace came again, and how best to co-operate with the projected United Nations Organization. Hence, in Philadelphia in 1944, the International Labour Conference was convened and hammered out a new definition of its aims and purposes. This declaration of labour rights, called the Declaration of Philadelphia, has been annexed to the ILO Constitution. It reaffirms the ILO's basic principles: namely, that labour is not a commodity, that freedom of expression and of association are essential to progress, that poverty anywhere constitutes a danger to prosperity everywhere, and, finally, that the war on want must be carried on both within each nation and by concerted international effort.

The Declaration goes further than any later declaration by linking peace with human rights. It states that 'lasting peace can be established only if it is based on social justice'. It affirms, among other principles, that:

(a) All human beings, irrespective of race, creed, or sex, have the right to pursue both their material well-being and their spiritual development in conditions of freedom and dignity of economic security and equal opportunity.

(b) The attainment of the conditions in which this shall be possible must constitute the central aim of national and international policy.

How many enthusiasts for human rights today appreciate the foresight of a wartime Declaration which asserts that the principles it proclaimed

are fully applicable to all peoples everywhere and that, while the manner of their application must be determined with due regard to the stage of social and economic development reached by each people, their progressive application to peoples who are still dependent, as well as to those who have already achieved self-government, is a matter of concern to the whole civilized world?

Following up the 1944 Philadelphia Declaration, the Universal Declaration of 1948 spells out in concrete terms the human rights of labour, which it is the ILO's responsibility to protect and implement, in the following four Articles:

Article 22
Everyone, as a member of society, has the right to social security and is entitled to realization, through national effort and international co-operation and in accordance with the organization and resources of each State, of the economic, social and cultural rights indispensable for his dignity and the free development of his personality.

Article 23
(1) Everyone has the right to work, to free choice of employment, to just and favourable conditions of work and to protection against unemployment.

(2) Everyone, without any discrimination, has the right to equal pay for equal work.

(3) Everyone who works has the right to just and favourable

remuneration ensuring for himself and his family an existence worthy of human dignity, and supplemented, if necessary, by other means of social protection.

(4) Everyone has the right to form and to join trade unions for the protection of his interests.

Article 24

Everyone has the right to rest and leisure, including reasonable limitation of working hours and periodic holidays with pay.

Article 25

(1) Everyone has the right to a standard of living adequate for the health and well-being of himself and of his family, including food, clothing, housing and medical care and necessary social services, and the right to security in the event of unemployment, sickness, disability, widowhood, old age or other lack of livelihood in circumstances beyond his control.

(2) Motherhood and childhood are entitled to special care and assistance. All children, whether born in or out of wedlock, shall enjoy the same social protection.

But it is in the field of *implementation* that the ILO can be seen, after fifty-eight years of pioneering and experiment, to have cut new pathways in defending, rather than defining, human rights. Since the essential administrative machinery of the ILO has been described in the present author's ILO publication *Labour Faces the New Age*, two elements only need be stressed for the purposes of this chapter, namely, the importance of the Conventions and the value of the supervisory system the ILO has built over half a century of actual experience.

Each Convention is a specific legal instrument regulating some aspect of labour policy or human rights. It is framed as a model for national legislation, though member countries are not bound to ratify Conventions, even though they may have voted for their adoption. They are *obliged*, however, in accepting the ILO Constitution, to bring all Conventions approved by the Conference to the attention of their own legislative bodies. If a Convention is ratified, the ratifying country must report periodically to the ILO on the manner of its implementation. The total number of ratifications has topped the 4000 mark.

It should be added that the obligations of governments in regard to Recommendations are somewhat different from their commitments in regard to Conventions. Both types of instrument aim at effective *national* action; but, unlike a Convention, a Recommendation is not subject to ratification. Governments must, however, bring a Recommendation to the attention of their competent national authorities, who must in turn weigh the possibility of taking the necessary action to give effect to its provisions. Governments are also required to report from time to time on their position with respect to Recommendations and any unratified Conventions.

So much for setting the standards. Their enforcement is clearly a vital procedure. The reports submitted by the governments on the way in which they are giving effect to ratified Conventions and dealing with Recommendations and unratified Conventions are carefully examined by a special Committee of International Experts. This Committee prepares a report of its own for submission to the annual International Labour Conference, including a summary of other information received from governments.

A tripartite Conference Committee (governments, employers and workers) then examines both the information received and the report of the international experts.[47] It can invite representatives of governments to appear before it to answer specific criticism by the experts. Meetings of the Conference Committee are open to the public and its report to the plenary is a public document. Experience has shown that governments are usually anxious to avoid being criticised in the Committee's report. Once again, public opinion becomes an effective means of ensuring that governments live up to their pledges.

The ILO's enforcement machinery also provides for a government to complain if it believes that another government is not living up to a Convention. Complaints may also originate with the ILO's Governing Body or with a Conference delegate. The Governing Body may then appoint a Commission of Enquiry. Its report is published, and the government concerned has then to decide whether to accept the Commission's findings or to appeal to the International Court of Justice at The Hague. If a government fails to carry out any recommendations that have been made either by the Commission of Enquiry or by the World Court, the Governing Body may then make recommendations to the Conference on steps to ensure compliance.

Thus, it will be observed that the ILO, within its special competence in human rights, has already gone a long way to solve one of the most crucial and difficult problems involved in establishing world standards; namely, how to combine the precision necessary for formulating an international instrument with the flexibility essential for its application in countries of vastly different social structures and degrees of economic development.

It is not, indeed, fortuitous that the path-blazing experience of the International Labour Organisation should have been sketched at some length at the end of the first chapter of this book. The serious student of human rights, as he explores their ramifications in so many disparate fields, will find his mind returning again and again to a global experiment that has justified for a whole generation the faith and vision of men and women who sought unceasingly to practise what they preached and to get governments to do likewise.

2 1948–9 Breakthrough

For while the tired waves, vainly breaking,
Seem here no painful inch to gain,
Far back, through creeks and inlets making,
Comes silent, flooding in, the main.

– A. H. Clough

The Universal Declaration of Human Rights, proclaimed by the UN General Assembly on 10 December 1948 (observed as Human Rights Day) without a dissenting vote, has proved to be the starting point of a new legal order in the world. But this did not happen all at once.

Although as a 'declaration' it could not become legally binding on states, much if not all of it has since become part of what the late Wilfred Jenks called 'The Common Law of Mankind' – what in more prosaic language is generally termed customary law. More significant, perhaps, than these generalities, a major part of the Declaration has become part and parcel of the national constitutions of some thirty new states.

By the United Nations Charter of 1945 the peoples 'reaffirmed their faith in fundamental human rights and in the dignity and worth of the human person'. Up to that date all earlier 'rights' were the inchoate local beginnings of a global movement which sprang so quickly from the Universal Declaration of 1948 that its impact on contemporary life was barely understood. The Declaration was itself born of the escalating inhumanity of a catastrophe that had started with the 'defence' of Poland and ended (did it?) with the rain of atomic death over the unwarned civilians of Hiroshima.

The Universal Declaration was humanity's unanimous response to the Nazi death camps, the fleeing refugees, and tortured prisoners-of-war. But it was by no means a once-for-all reaction. In 1949, the century-old humanitarian law enshrined in the first Red Cross Convention was revised and widened to cover some of the shameful gaps the War had revealed, especially safeguards for civilians caught in armed conflicts. And the Universal Declaration itself began at once to proliferate further Declarations, Protocols,

45

and Conventions – a process that has grown faster of late. We shall review both the 1948 Declaration and the 1949 Conventions in this chapter.

The Universal Declaration itself was, in fact, conceived from the start as a global 'Bill of Rights', to be implemented by a legally enforceable Covenant. Actually, this became two: the Covenant on Economic, Social and Cultural Rights, and the Covenant on Civil and Political Rights – both of which came into force following thirty-five ratifications for each in 1976. So the international *law* of human rights is quite recent. Almost unnoticed by general press and mass media – preoccupied with news and photographs of violence, torture, exile, and with the deprivation or extinction of human rights – these two Covenants have at last laid down the *legal* foundation for a world order of human rights that had not existed before.

That this 1976 event should have received no, or only casual, notice in the world's press or parliaments is indicative of the malaise – almost entropy – into which public opinion had fallen, except when shocked or scandalised by some blatant violation of human rights. The 1976 event should not be underestimated, and its implications will be spelled out later on, especially in Chapter 7. Though, once again, the proof of the cooking will be in the eating. An American human rights specialist, Moses Moskovitz, rightly points out:

> By transforming international concern with human rights from a political principle into *legally binding* international obligations, the Covenants have laid the groundwork for the erection of international institutions and procedures to give concrete expression to these obligations. Without institutions functioning continuously in their service, even the most solemn obligations tend to sink to the level of pious benevolence.[1]

Perhaps a major cause of this apathy (apart from the extravagant claims of national sovereignty, dealt with in Chapter 5) lies in the fact that human rights activities, as the same author states,

> lack a sense of inter-relatedness and it is difficult to fit them into a clear and rational pattern. There is no way of studying the whole and the functioning of its parts in relation to objectives . . . In the absence of a definite body of doctrine, as well as of deeply rooted convictions, international human rights have been dealt with on

the basis of the shifts and vagaries of daily affairs and of evocations of daily events.

At least, it is the intention of the present study to contribute a little towards remedying that deficiency. Every historical legal system – from the Code of Hammurabi, through classical Roman Law and Civil Jurisprudence, to the English Common Law, and right up to the modern Law of Nations – has sought to establish its own special body of doctrine, its *raison d'être*. It is the academic lawyer's joy to sharpen his intellect on one phase or another of those solid doctrines. But the international law and practice of human rights, with its ever-expanding range of topics and depth of research – as these chapters will illustrate in small part – has not yet, as Moskovitz regrets, produced a consistent body of philosophy which can be accepted as a positive doctrine in the exact sense in which Hersch Lauterpacht used the term when he said, 'The orthodox positivist doctrine has been explicit in the affirmation that only States are subjects of international law'.[2]

One reason for this is the extreme difficulty the human rights specialist encounters in fixing clear definitions in this wide and expanding field. But a more fundamental cause is to be found in the quite recent discovery that the *individual* is no longer merely an object of the law of nations, but also its subject. As Lauterpacht has himself so neatly summed up this revolutionary change:

As a result of the Charter of the United Nations – as well as of other changes in international law – the individual has acquired a status and a stature which have transformed him from an object of international compassion into a subject of international right. For in so far as international law, as embodied in the Charter and elsewhere, recognises fundamental rights of the individual independent of the law of the State, to that extent it constitutes the individual a subject of the law of nations.[3]

A third and, in a way, startling innovation is the open acknowledgment that states – one's *own* government, for instance – can be *wrong*, can be delinquent, can be criminal, by modern standards of international behaviour. *Paterfamilias* can no longer be portrayed in the Divine image; he is no longer beyond reproach, but is a common jailbird! Who was it who first asserted that patriotism was the last resort of the scoundrel? How many critics of their own nation's foreign policy could go as far as Marc Bloch, the foremost

French medievalist and resistance leader (executed by the Nazis in 1944) who described in *L'Etrange Défaite* the internal reasons for the fall of France in 1940? He states:

> As a Frenchman I feel constrained, in speaking of my country, to say of her only what is good. It is a harsh duty that compels a man to make a public show of his mother's weaknesses when she is in misery and despair. As an historian, I know better than do most men how difficult it is to conduct such an analysis.

Professor Roberto Ago, engaged as Special Rapporteur of the International Law Commission on the task of defining 'internationally wrongful Acts of States', has stressed the need to distinguish a separate category of exceptionally serious wrongful acts which have become more and more evident since the end of the Second World War. 'Several factors have no doubt contributed to this more marked development,' he has stated:

> The terrible memory of the unprecedented ravages of the Second World War, the frightful cost of that war in human lives, in property and in wealth of every kind, the fear of a possible recurrence of the suffering endured earlier, and even of the disappearance of large fractions of mankind and of all traces of civilization, which would result from a new conflict in which the entire arsenal of weapons of mass destruction would be used, are all factors which have established in the consciousness of peoples a conviction of the paramount importance of prohibiting the use of force as a means of settling international disputes.[4]

Moreover, Professor Ago points out that the feeling of horror left by the systematic massacres of millions of human beings perpetrated by certain political regimes, the still-present memory of the deportation of entire populations, the outrage felt at the most brutal assaults on the human personality, have all pointed to the need to take steps to ensure that not only the internal law of states, but, above all, the law of the international community itself, 'should enunciate *imperative rules* guaranteeing that the essential rights of the human person will be safeguarded and respected'. All of this has, in fact, prompted the most vigorous international prohibition of crimes such as genocide, apartheid, and other inhuman practices. The Special Rapporteur concluded his submission to the International Law Commission as follows:

Thus, some new rules of international law have appeared, others are in the process of formation, and still others, which already existed, have taken on a new vigour and a more marked significance. These rules impose upon States obligations which are respected because of an increased collective interest on the part of the entire international community.

It is extraordinary how many times this term 'new rules' comes into contemporary discourse on human rights. We shall meet it frequently in subsequent chapters. In fact, there is probably no branch of international law that is bearing so much fresh fruit as this one. We meet it in the application of the Covenants; we meet it in the European Convention, the Geneva Conventions and their 1977 Protocols, and the Refugees Convention; we meet it in international court decisions at Strasbourg and national court decisions, influenced by the existence of so many international instruments binding on states today.

If this proliferation of new rules, touching the life and liberty of all citizens in all countries, is as bewildering as it is fascinating to the student of human rights, how much more challenging is it to the legal practitioner? As the Chairman of the English Bar, Peter Webster, QC, has pointed out:

Human Rights and Fundamental Freedoms are by definition supposed to be universal, both in their application and in the corresponding duties which all men owe to other individuals and to society. They are not the preserve of lawyers or the prerogative of any one political ideology, but the Rule of Law is the only instrument which can ensure that a fair balance will be struck – and maintained – between the necessarily conflicting interests of individuals and states.[5]

Mr Webster goes on to cite the recommendations of a report of the International Commission of Jurists in 1962 on 'The Responsibilities of Lawyers in a Changing World', to the effect that:

In a changing and interdependent world lawyers should give guidance and leadership in the creation of new legal concepts, institutions and techniques to enable a man to meet the challenges and the dangers of the times and to realise the aspirations of all people. The lawyer today should not content himself with the conduct of his practice and the administration of justice . . . if he is to fulfil his vocation as a lawyer he should take an active part in the process of change.

Since the Universal Declaration was the fountain-head of this outflowing of new rules of international law, we can now look at it afresh by reducing it to its simplest terms. This naturally leads to a summary glance also at the two major covenants that spring from it, though their implications must be left to be taken up in later chapters. Then, the 1949 Red Cross Conventions follow as a matter of date. And this introduces us, in turn, to some quite recent, though somewhat disturbing, new rules of what has been characterised as 'humanitarian law', which are now being extended to 'freedom-fighters'.

THE 1948 DECLARATION

The Declaration is introduced by a Preamble setting out the basic ideas, which are expanded later on in the main text (see Appendix I for full text). For instance, the Preamble says that 'the inherent dignity' of each member of the human family is the starting-point of the Declaration. So the *individual*, not the state or the government, is 'the foundation of freedom, justice and peace in the world'. Looked at historically, this is quite a startling proposition.

It goes on: 'disregard and contempt for human rights have resulted in barbarous acts which have outraged the conscience of mankind'. Because of this, it is essential 'that human rights should be protected by the rule of law'. These assertions are plainly a direct challenge to all states – and they are many – which are not providing their peoples with this protection, either by introducing necessary laws or establishing that machinery of justice which will enforce these laws equally among all their inhabitants.

The Preamble goes on to state that the Declaration is based on the Charter by which member states 'have pledged themselves to achieve, in co-operation with the United Nations, the promotion of universal respect for and observance of human rights and fundamental freedoms'. Yet it is not sufficient for the General Assembly merely to have proclaimed the Declaration as 'a common standard of achievement for all peoples and all nations'. Every individual in the world, and all governments and groups, are urged to strive, 'by teaching and education', to promote these rights in every way that is open to them. This is a most sweeping appeal. It leaves nobody any excuse to think that responsibility for observing the terms of the Declaration is a job to be left to somebody else. That is what is meant by 'universal'.

But one important question of drafting remained. General declarations, however emphatic they may be, do not legally commit governments until accepted by them in the form of an international treaty. Treaties may be broken, of course – and often are – but they do represent, up to this point of time, the strongest form of binding obligation on nations and on their governments. So it was agreed, even while the Declaration was being drafted, that a treaty to protect human rights should also be assembled and put before the world's governments for signature and ratification, embodying and amplifying the ideas of the Declaration. Thus, the full force of international law would be put behind the Declaration.

So an International Covenant on Human Rights was decided upon. Further discussion in the Commission on Human Rights showed, however, that it would be preferable to prepare two separate Covenants: one on civil and political rights, and the other on economic, social and cultural rights. Preliminary drafts were completed in 1954 and the Economic and Social Council passed them on to the Third (social affairs) Committee of the General Assembly for final drafting.

The General Assembly adopted them in 1966. Both Covenants, which are now ratified by the required number of states, are legally binding on states which are parties to them, and will be examined later on. Meantime, an examination of the chief articles of the Declaration will take us also into the subject-matter of these two Covenants.

Article 1 states quite simply that 'all human beings are born free and equal in dignity and rights'. Because of this, they 'should act towards one another in a spirit of brotherhood'. Thus, for the first time, an international instrument proclaims the principle of human brotherhood, enshrined for hundreds of years in the great religions and in the books of the philosophers. The two sentences of this Article hang together. They could quite well be reversed as follows: '*Because* all people on earth are brothers and sisters and form one human family, they must respect and help one another in every way they can.'

The second Article carries the premise further. It states, in part, that 'everyone is entitled to all the rights and freedoms set forth in this Declaration, without distinction of any kind'. Then it lists a number of categories in which people are frequently divided and insists that, because of the principle laid down in Article 1, these categories – race, colour, sex, language, religion and so on – must no longer affect any individual's rights. This is another way of saying that discrimination on the ground of any of these physical or social differences is prohibited. Nor have man's personal *rights* on this planet anything to do with his family or his ancestors, the colour of his skin, the language he speaks, his wealth or possessions, or his poverty in worldly goods. Though some governments do not live up to these standards, this principle of non-discrimination is beginning to be recognised everywhere.

Articles 3–11 centre upon the freedom of the individual and form the heart of the Declaration. Article 3 begins: 'Everyone has the right to life'. This may look a simple phrase, but it will become clearer during the course of the following paragraphs that the life of the individual involves an elaborate piece of social machinery to sustain it. It has, in fact, taken many centuries to establish this right to life.

Article 3 reads in its entirety: 'Everyone has the right to life, liberty and security of person.' But, when the social committee of the General Assembly came to analyse this Article in the draft Covenant some years later, the Committee spent over a dozen meetings deciding what the 'right to life' really means. Defining or defending the 'right to life' is by no means as easy as it seems to be at first sight.

The extraordinary thing about these debates was that all the national delegations agreed that the 'right to life' existed. What they differed about was: under what conditions could that 'right' be *taken away* by the state? In other words, on what grounds could the state legitimately deprive a person of his life – and yet observe the terms of the Declaration? In the course of these debates it was revealed that over twenty states had already abolished capital punishment by law, while another twenty or so never or rarely practised it; so these states had little difficulty in being categorical about the right to life.

The other states argued that it was impossible to postulate that basic right so boldly. It had to be hedged around with exceptions, because mankind was not yet perfect, and bad people – murderers in particular – had to be deterred by the. threat of death.[6]

Those debates make interesting reading for the serious student of social institutions. They covered many questions of philosophy, law and penal reform. At the end of it all, the Committee agreed on a form of words, which now appears as Article 6 of the political Covenant, the gist of which is as follows.

1. Every human being has the inherent right to life. This right shall be protected by law. No one shall be arbitrarily deprived of his life.
2. In countries which have not abolished the death penalty, sentence of death may be imposed only for the most serious crimes in accordance with law in force at the time of the commission of the crime . . .
. . .
4. Anyone sentenced to death shall have the right to seek pardon or commutation of the sentence. Amnesty, pardon or communtation of the sentence of death may be granted in all cases.
5. Sentence of death shall not be imposed for crimes committed by persons below eighteen years of age and shall not be carried out on pregnant women.
6. Nothing in this Article shall be invoked to delay or to prevent the abolition of capital punishment by any State Party to the Covenant.

It will be noted that, by the last sentence, the drafting Committee left the door open very diplomatically for any state to change its laws and abolish the penalty, and so get rid of the exceptions which form the bulk of the above text.

Yet two important matters still remained. The first was the need felt by many states to bring 'genocide' into the final text and outline procedures of punishment. So we can consider it briefly here. Genocide means 'race-killing' – that is, the intentional destruction of human *groups*. Genocide was, in fact, declared to be a crime under international law by the General Assembly in 1946, and a Convention was unanimously adopted by the Assembly two years later, at the same time as the Universal Declaration.

This Convention defines 'genocide' as the committing of acts with the object of destroying, *in whole or in part*, a national, ethnic, racial or religious group – that is to say, by aiming at the group as such, not at individuals as individuals. Acts constituting genocide are killing, causing serious bodily or mental harm, deliberately inflicting conditions of life calculated to bring about physical destruction of a group, imposing measures intended to prevent birth, and the forcible transfer of children. Conspiracy or incitement to commit it, are also punishable under this Convention.

Another important point about the Genocide Convention is that all who are guilty of genocide must be punished 'whether they are constitutionally responsible rulers, public officers or private individuals'. In other words, no one can hide behind his own government or use the excuse that he acted on 'superior orders', if his acts constitute the international crime of genocide.

This brings us back forcibly to Lauterpacht's point about the new status of the individual under international law. The political Covenant included, therefore, a direct reference to the earlier Genocide Convention, to the effect that 'when deprivation of life constitutes the crime of genocide, it is understood that nothing in this Article shall authorize any State Party . . . to derogate in any way from any obligation assumed under the provisions of the Convention on the Prevention and Punishment of the Crime of Genocide'.

The other matter which came out of this re-examination of the meaning of Article 3 of the Declaration rang a more positive note. The UN Assembly proposed in 1959 that a thorough study should be made of that big exception to the right to life – the death penalty – and the Secretariat was charged with preparing a detailed report on the pros and cons of this form of ultimate punishment. Questions were sent to all governments, and, on the basis of the replies from over sixty of them and from non-governmental organisations and expert lawyers and criminologists, a Report was issued in 1963, which, for the first time, brought together a worldwide survey of this important branch of criminal law.

A large number of other rights follow this basic right to life. These are set out in Articles 4–11. Naturally, slavery in *all* its forms (Article 4) can have no part in civilised society. As we noticed in Chapter 1, the history of the fight against slavery has been a continuous one with an important landmark in the League of Nations Slavery Convention of 1926.

Within the 'UN Family' the world struggle over human rights soon led to a powerful attack on what is called 'forced labour', a form of servitude imposed upon individuals by governments rather than by individuals. Here, the ILO had a direct part in investigating working conditions in various countries, leading up to the adoption in June 1957 of its further Convention on the Abolition of Forced Labour. Under this Convention, the states who are party to the Convention undertake to suppress any form of compulsory labour whether it is used as a means of political coercion or education, or as a method of mobilising labour for economic development.

Articles 5–11 bear mainly on the limitations on punishment for crime. 'No one shall be subjected to torture' (Article 5). 'Cruel, inhuman or degrading treatment or punishment' is outlawed. Articles 6–10 all seek to enforce the 'Rule of Law'. In Article 6: 'Everyone has the right to recognition everywhere as a person before the law'. The accused person must not be arrested 'arbitrarily' (Article 9). When he is brought before the court, he must have all the professional help he needs for his defence; and he is entitled to an 'independent and impartial' tribunal (Article 10). Article 11 lays down that punishment can only be meted out after a public trial and *after* the accused has been proved guilty 'according to law'. Even then, punishment must fit the crime – 'nor shall a heavier penalty be imposed than the one that was applicable at the time the penal offence was committed'. This is a warning against *ex post facto* law. And, most important, every individual 'has the right to be presumed innocent *until proved guilty*'.

Between Articles 12 and 21 the rights of the individual can be seen expanding into a series of concentric circles. For example, Article 12, which in effect lays down the rule that every man's home shall be 'his castle', is strengthened by Article 16, asserting his 'right to marry and to found a family'. As Article 12 points out, the 'protection of the law against such interference or attacks', could hardly be more essential to man's existence in society. Yet, this Article goes further and insists that his 'privacy' and his 'correspondence' – and that includes his telephone! – and even his 'honour and reputation' are to be protected from any intruder or outsider. Article 16 adds a certain element of 'sacredness', for it states that 'the family is the natural and fundamental group unit of society'. Hence, the family 'is entitled to protection by society and the State'. And in conformity with this principle of co-operation between the sexes: 'Men and women . . . are entitled to equal rights as to marriage'. Sex is never to be the test of civic rights.

For instance, in 1957, the Convention on the Nationality of Married Women was adopted. This Convention protects women from the automatic loss or acquisition of nationality because of marriage to a man of a different nationality. Later, a Convention on Consent to Marriage, Minimum Age for Marriage and Registration of Marriage was adopted in 1962 to eliminate such practices as child marriage and the inheritance of widows. This Convention also provides that no marriage can be legally entered into without the free consent of both spouses and that all marriages shall be officially registered.

It is not possible here to list all the subsequent Declarations and Conventions, but one other instrument can be added, and that is the Convention on the Political Rights of Women – to ensure that women obtain political opportunities and status equal to those enjoyed by men – adopted by the General Assembly in 1952.

Residence comes up again in Article 13. The modern citizen 'has the right to freedom of movement' not merely within his own state, but also 'to leave any country' and to return to his own country. This is a bold affirmation, in view of the suspicions and hostile attitudes which exist between nations today, but the point of Article 13 is that freedom of movement has at least been *proclaimed* as a universal right. (This was nearly three decades before the Helsinki accords!)

Article 14 deals with the 'right of asylum'; in other words, the right of every individual (except those accused of non-political crimes) who has fled from his own country because his political opinions may put his life in danger, to be protected by the land to which he has fled.

The United Nations has been studying statelessness and related questions since 1947. Several Conventions protecting the rights of refugees and stateless persons have been adopted, and a High Commissioner for Refugees appointed to assist refugees. In 1951, a Convention on the Status of Refugees was adopted; it entered into force in 1954, and some seventy states have ratified or acceded to it. Parties to this Convention undertake to give refugees the same treatment as nationals with regard to religion, access to courts, elementary education, social security, and so on. Provision is also made for issuing travel documents, to protect them from expulsion from the country of refuge.

A Convention relating to the Status of Stateless Persons came into force in 1960, after six Governments had ratified it or acceded to it. In 1976 a Declaration on Territorial Asylum was adopted by the General Assembly. But, unfortunately, in 1977 a Plenipotentiary Conference, convened to draft a Convention on the *Right* of Territorial Asylum, terminated without agreement. The reluctance of a number of governments to accept territorial asylum as a *legal* right had a great deal to do with the prevailing attitude towards so-called 'terrorists'.

Yet, in spite of this long delay in attempting to secure legal recognition of the rights of a man or woman seeking political asylum, the next Article, Article 15, insists that 'everyone has the right to a nationality'. The language is explicit. And, as a corollary, the second part of the Article states that no-one shall be 'deprived of his nationality', though he may change it if he desires.

Little need be said about Article 17, which states that 'everyone has the right to own property'. The gist of the right is to be found in the second sentence, which lays down that no one shall be *arbitrarily* deprived of his property. While Articles 18 and 19 both take us back to the objective in the Preamble of the Charter: 'to practise tolerance'. 'Freedom of thought, conscience, and religion' (Article 18) and 'freedom of opinion' (Article 19) deal with the freedom that exists inside us. But the second part of both Articles breaks new ground. For a personal belief to be truly 'free', it must be expressible publicly. Hence, the emphasis in Article 18 is clear: 'manifest his religion or belief in teaching, practice, worship and observance'. The point is taken further in Article 19, because everyone must enjoy 'without interference', the freedom 'to seek, receive and impart information and ideas through any media and regardless of frontiers'.

It will thus be observed that the simple, direct phrases of the Declaration go far beyond a prescription for individual freedom. They lay down the essential conditions of how a state should be organised, so that each of its citizens may 'count for one'.

The next two Articles follow on naturally from this concept. Article 20 affirms that anyone has a right to join any association or organisation, but no one can make him join it if he does not want to. In passing, we can note that the ILO adopted in 1948 the Freedom of Association and Protection of the Right to Organise Convention, and, in 1949, the Right to Organise and Collective Bargaining Convention. The ILO has continued with later Conventions, backed by the administrative machinery we noted in Chapter 1.

Article 21 reads like an essay in political democracy. The will of the people, says the article, is 'the basis of the authority of government'. Every people has the right to choose its own government. There should be free, secret and periodic elections on the basis of 'universal and equal suffrage.' Everyone has 'the right to take part in the government of his country' and 'the right of equal access to public service in his country'.

We now pass, in Articles 22–7, to Economic, Social, and Cultural Rights. What strikes us most about this group is that many of them are being taken for granted today in the advanced countries, but they are only beginning in the developing world. To begin with, Article 22 speaks of the 'right to social security'. Articles 23 and 24 bring us back to the rights of labour – free choice of employment, fair remuneration, trade unions, and a somewhat novel addition: 'the right to rest and leisure'.

Article 25 takes us back to the rights of the family – food, clothing, housing – and relates to the more detailed provisions adopted in 1959 in the Declaration of the Rights of the Child.

Behind Articles 26 and 27, we recognise UNESCO's widely flung activities on behalf of human rights in education: 'Education shall be free, at least in the elementary and fundamental stages', and 'elementary education shall be compulsory'. The main point of Article 27, that 'everyone has the right freely to participate in the cultural life of the community', is surely a corollary of the standard laid down in the previous Article that all 'education shall be directed to the full development of the human personality'. And could there be a more cogent summing-up of all that has gone before than that the objective of such education is that it 'shall promote understanding, tolerance and friendship among all nations, racial, or religious groups, and shall further the activities of the United Nations for the maintenance of peace'.

The last three Articles of the Declaration introduce no new rights, but call (Article 28) for a new international order based on the foregoing rights; while Article 29 stresses the phrase 'general welfare in a democratic society' sustained by the fact that 'everyone has *duties* to the community, in which alone the free and full development of his personality is possible'. And Article 30 is intended to deter any 'State, group, or person' from employing the words of the Declaration to defeat its objectives.

Yet one vital topic must be referred to before we pass from the 1948 Declaration, although there is not a word about it in the Declaration. When the two Covenants on Civil and Political Rights and Economic, Social and Cultural Rights came before the General Assembly and its Third Committee, an entirely new section was grafted on to the beginning of the original human rights stem. That addition – which has since had wide reverberations throughout the United Nations system – is expressed in these terms: 'All peoples have the right of self-determination'. This principle is an approach to human rights which takes us into the controversial but vastly important field of 'colonialism' – political, economic, military. The resultant all-too-often acrimonious debates in the General Assembly and other UN bodies over many years, are dealt with later in Chapter 5.

Perhaps it should be added that, although the Assembly decided in 1952 on two separate Covenants rather than one, to implement the terms of the original Declaration, the intervening years have never separated the two Covenants. In fact, they were adopted *simultaneously* in 1966, to show that they are both of one piece.

As continuous evidence of this 'inseparableness' of the two implementing instruments of the famous Declaration, we can select a few representative opinions from the significant debates in the Human Rights Commission in 1977. For instance, Mr V. C. Trivedi, from India, said that civil and political rights and economic, social and cultural rights were so inextricably interlinked that the only effective means of bringing about the realisation of political rights was to remove the obstacles which stand in the way of full and free enjoyment of economic rights. It was, therefore, imperative that concrete action should be taken to facilitate and promote the establishment of a new international economic order. It was only such action that would enable nations and individuals to secure better standards of life. Moreover, the increasing diversion of human and material resources from peaceful pursuits to an unproductive, wasteful and dangerous arms race heightened the current crisis in the world economy.

He was followed by Athanase Nanema of Upper Volta, who went further and stressed that civil and political rights would be without any real meaning without the realisation of economic, social and cultural rights. He admitted that Upper Volta was far from having realised full enjoyment of economic and social rights based on its own resources, so it had appealed to the international community for assistance. The economic Covenant, therefore, could not be viewed in the same abstract or legalistic terms as the political Covenant, since 'it is the duty of the industrialised countries to promote the realisation of the economic, social and cultural rights of the people everywhere in the world through a co-operation translated in terms of transfer of technology, investments and better terms of the exchange'.

As was to be expected, in the same debate, Mr Zorin for the

Soviet Union took the bull by the horns and insisted:

The realization of economic and social rights cannot be achieved in capitalist countries where millions of workers continued to be exploited and millions deprived of work. Shameless and cruel exploitation has transformed workers into mere commercial commodities in developed capitalist countries, while in developing countries, colonialism and neo-colonialism are preventing the vast majority of humanity from enjoying their basic rights.

This lengthy debate in 1977, welcoming the coming into force of the two Covenants a year earlier, might well be summarised by an observation of Mr Chávez-Godoy of Peru, who said that he did not know of any country where the well-being of the people and the enjoyment of their fundamental freedoms *preceded* their economic development and well-being. On the contrary, only economic development had permitted the enjoyment of human rights. The Commission on Human Rights, he concluded, had now the bigger task of finding the necessary means to eliminate the causes which frustrate development efforts, so as to make it possible for all the people to demand and enjoy all the human rights.

The foregoing few extracts reveal not only the growing edge of the human rights movement, after three decades, as a powerful living force; but, more significant, they reveal, too, how the wider programme of the total UN system has drawn its inspiration and incentives from the original Declaration as it faces today the contemporary challenges of world arms limitation and a new international economic order.

THE 1949 CONVENTIONS

Within a year of the Human Rights Declaration, a Convention that strictly bears the name of 'humanitarian law' came from outside the UN system, as such. At least, that is the appellation by which it is nowadays known, though the UN's own reports on this new branch of international law seem to prefer the term 'Respect for Human Rights in Armed Conflicts'. But, whatever its official name, its international instruments go much farther back in history – to 8 August 1864, in fact, when the First Geneva Convention was signed in Geneva Town Hall by some sixteen countries. That was the beginning of the International Red Cross. As the present author has described these events elsewhere, all that need be recalled now are the key dates and bare substance of the conventions as they evolved and were revised from Henri Dunant's dream in 1859 up to the new Geneva Protocols of 1977.[7]

Humanitarian law began, as all human rights law has done, from an abuse of the human person. Returning as an eye-witness from the horror and carnage of the Battle of Solferino in 1859, the redoubtable Swiss businessman and philanthropist Henri Dunant so challenged the whole senseless and savage slaughter on Europe's battlefields that, before he died as a Nobel Peace Prize Laureate in 1910, he had turned his country's flag inside out, as it were, so that a red cross on a white ground became the touchstone of the earth's care and compassion for the sick and wounded and imprisoned in war and peace alike. This was no act of religious symbolism, but rather a guarantee of the strict neutrality and impartiality of a global agency (still under the direction of Swiss citizens) which stood above the battle and administered succour to the individual in need, irrespective of his race or nation.

Henri Dunant's graphic account in his *Souvenir de Solférino* was translated into the principal European languages and sent by him to leading personalities in the different countries, while the press in Switzerland, England, France and Germany published long and, generally, favourable articles on Dunant's ideas of aid to the wounded, which appeared at the end of his book. Hence, public opinion was being mobilised from the start. But European political heads had to be converted – always the most difficult task in human rights! So Dunant trekked to Paris, Berlin and London. Slowly the idea of establishing the *neutrality* of army medical services – the very germ of the Red Cross – caught on. A Berlin Congress of savants and public officials unanimously voiced the hope that 'all Governments would recognise the *neutrality* of the wounded, as well as of military and civil volunteer surgeons and auxiliary medical personnel'.

Dunant had to fight strenuously for this cardinal principle of *neutrality*. The terms 'neutral' and 'neutrality' appear several times in the first Geneva Convention of 1864 as evidence of Dunant's persistence. For the very thought of neutrality was as repugnant to military minds then as it is today. Dunant was more concerned with the human being than with who was going to win any next war. He was the first to realise that 'neutrality' need not be a negative attitude – the indecision of the physical coward – but a *positive* attitude – the resolve of the morally courageous to preserve at all costs, at least within a limited area, what was once called the Truce of God. If Dunant had lost on this point, it is hardly possible to conceive of any Red Cross movement at all.

But all this had to go into an international treaty. In Geneva, a 'Committee of Five' decided to summon an international conference on 26 October 1863, 'for the purpose of putting M. Dunant's suggestions into operation . . . and, if necessary, to recommend the appropriate measures for their execution'. All European governments were invited to send delegates. Representatives from seventeen states attended. They voted resolutions recommending the creation in all countries of voluntary committees for the relief of the wounded. As this conference was an unofficial one, it requested the early convening of a Diplomatic Congress to agree on questions of international law raised by the problem of 'neutralising' the wounded. In accordance with these 1863 resolutions, committees were formed in almost every country in Europe, and the Geneva Committee was transformed into an International Committee, with General Dufour (formerly Chief of the Swiss armed forces) as President, Gustave Moynier as Vice-President, and Henri Dunant as Secretary. General Dufour had already issued such commands as the following to his troops: 'When the enemy is beaten, care for his wounded as if they were ours; show them all the consideration that is owing to misfortune. Disarm the prisoners, but do no harm to them.'

The new Committee sent a questionnaire to all European governments, asking them (1) to give their support to any Relief Committee set up in their own country; (2) to accept the principle of the neutralisation in wartime of field-hospitals and military hospitals and of army medical personnel; and (3) to adopt a distinctive emblem 'such as a white flag bearing a red cross'.[8]

The success of this diplomatic Conference, which produced the First Geneva Convention, undoubtedly owed most to the ability displayed by Dunant himself in assembling, just one year after the Geneva resolution had been voted, the leading plenipotentiaries of Europe. The eventual agreement was extremely simple. It was a businesslike document, and its four basic provisions were as follows:

(1) All establishments and hospitals for the treatment of wounded and sick soldiers and their personnel must be immune from capture and from acts of destruction.
(2) This protection also covers voluntary aid performed by civilians in favour of the wounded.

(3) Sick and wounded soldiers must be received and treated without regard to the side on which they have fought.

(4) A heraldic emblem – the red cross on a white field – should be employed for distinguishing hospitals, ambulances, and the personnel protected under the agreement.

On 22 August 1864, twelve representatives affixed their signatures to 'The Convention for the Welfare of Soldiers Wounded in Action'. In the year of its signing, the Convention was ratified by Belgium, Denmark, France, Italy, The Netherlands, Sweden, Norway, Spain and Switzerland. By 1867 all the Great Powers had followed suit, with the exception of the United States, which adhered fifteen years later. This First Convention is important because it contains the essence of the later ones. Being, in the true sense of the term, a *peace* treaty, and not a legalisation of future wars, the Geneva Convention did not share the fate of the thousands of 'peace' treaties which have paved mankind's bloody and tear-stained path all down the intervening years.

For a long time, the law of armed conflicts has developed as customary law. It is only since the second half of the nineteenth century that the multilateral treaty became an important instrument in this development. The Declaration of St Petersburg of 1868 was one of the first of these treaties. The law of armed conflicts covers, in fact, a range of subjects. There are, for instance, the relations between the parties to the conflict. Existing diplomatic relations will be severed; so what happens to the diplomatic premises? What is the fate of the treaty relations which existed between the parties? And so on. We are not concerned here with these questions, but with what is called 'international humanitarian law applicable in armed conflicts'. This deals with such matters as the use in combat of weapons and other means and methods of warfare and the treatment of war victims by the enemy.

A large part of humanitarian law applicable in armed conflicts has thus come to be incorporated in treaties. Historically, two lines can be discerned in this process of codification: one leading to what is commonly referred to as the 'Law of The Hague' and the other as the 'Law of Geneva'. These two bodies of law coincide to a large extent with the rules relating to the use of weapons and other means of warfare on the one hand, and, on the other hand, with the treatment of war victims who have fallen into the enemy's hands.[9]

It should be noted, however, that this distinction reflects a difference, not a division. Considerable parts of the law codified by The Hague Peace Conferences of 1899 and 1907 have been incorporated in the Geneva Conventions, viz., the treatment of prisoners-of-war in 1929 and relations with 'protected persons' in occupied territory in 1949. As explained below, recent conferences of governmental experts, held in Geneva in 1974-7 produced new instruments additional to the Geneva Conventions of 1949.

Thus, developments that had led up to the 1949 Diplomatic Conference resulted in much of Red Cross law being put under one cover, as it were. Four separate revised Conventions emerged from the 1949 Conference. Hence, when people speak of the Geneva Conventions today, they refer to these four international treaties which came into legal effect on 21 October 1950, and which now bind practically all the countries of the world. We now summarise their provisions briefly.

The *First Convention*, for improving the lot of the wounded in armies in the field, was signed, as we have seen, by twelve Governments in 1864, and within about twenty years it became almost universal by the accession of practically all the other governments of the world. This original Convention was amended and extended in 1906, 1929 and, finally, in 1949. It laid down, in short, that wounded or sick combatants must be collected and cared for; that ambulances and military hospitals should be recognised as neutral and, as such, respected by the belligerents as long as they accommodated wounded and sick; and, finally, that hospital and ambulance personnel should be considered as enjoying the same neutral status. This Convention dealt only with *soldiers*; but in the course of eighty-five years of applying it – through two World Wars – the Convention was revised by having the *Second Convention* added to it, concerned with *sailors*.

The first chapter of each of these 1949 Conventions is identical, being repeated word for word in all four. These 'General Rules', common to the four Conventions, lay down (in brief):

> Once armed conflict between states breaks out, the Conventions shall be applicable *in all circumstances*. In case of *civil war or internal strife*, certain humanitarian principles must always be observed. The taking of hostages, execution without regular trial, torture, and all cruel and degrading treatment are *prohibited at all times*. Reprisals on persons protected by the Conventions are forbidden. No one can renounce or be forced to renounce the protection

accorded him by the Conventions. Finally, protected persons must at all times be able to have resort to a Protecting Power (i.e. a neutral State) and to the International Committee of the Red Cross.

Of particular interest at present is Article 3 in all of the Conventions, which concerns 'civil war or internal strife'. It lays down that, in case of armed rebellion or civil strife within a country, states which are parties to the Convention must treat with humanity persons taking no active part in the actual fighting. This includes combatants who are put out of action through injury or sickness or are captured. They must be treated exactly as if they were prisoners-*of-war*. Nor must there be any discrimination as to race, colour, religion, sex, or otherwise, in dealing with captured rebels or civilians. The following acts against them are always prohibited by international law: violence to life, murder, mutilation, cruelty and torture, the taking of hostages, humiliating or degrading treatment, and extra-judicial trials or executions.

This Article is perhaps a most striking example of legal evolution. It stretches the old Conventions – going back to 1864, and all of them concerned with war between states – to cover *civil* war, as well as other conflicts which cannot be classed as *international* war. It was not easy to draw up provisions which would apply to civil war, without treading on the tender toes of various governments. The idea of extending the Conventions to cover domestic conflicts was at first considered to be legally impossible and quite incompatible with state sovereignty. So we might devote several paragraphs to showing how some of the difficulties were overcome and how 'humanitarian law' has gradually prevailed over the law of the jungle.

The Geneva Conventions, it was once rightly said, can bind only governments. Hence, an *illegal* rebel group may never be recognised as 'sovereign' by any of the signatory states, nor could it be itself *bound* by the Convention. Other critics feared that a government obliged to apply the Convention to a civil war would find its hands tied in suppressing the rebellion. They also thought that the Conventions would strengthen the position of insurgents, by 'legalising' them as belligerents. Then too, they asked: Who decides whether a conflict is or is not 'international', in the sense understood by the Convention? For the Convention to apply, is it sufficient for a small group of rebels to give itself the title of a rival government?

These misgivings were obviously not without foundation. It was remarkable, therefore, that the Geneva Conference of 1949 was able to agree upon a text which, without making *all* the provisions of the Geneva Conventions obligatory in civil war, at least imposed on all parties the duty of respecting Red Cross principles. Thus Article 3 has the great merit of saving human lives and of reducing uncertainties on both sides.

On the one hand, the rebels will be prompted to respect the Geneva Conventions, if only to show that they are *not criminals*, but are fighting as ordinary soldiers in a cause which they believe just. On the other hand, Article 3 in no way restricts the right of a government to prosecute and condemn rebels, in conformity with its domestic laws. If a government applies elementary principles of humanity to its thieves and murderers, giving them food and protection, should it have difficulty in applying to insurgents the same minimum legal safeguards, as provided in the Article? Thus, the 1949 Conventions laid the foundation for the far more complicated issues which faced the 'revision' Conference on Humanitarian Law which met in Geneva for four arduous sessions in 1974–7 to consider the rules applying to 'liberation movements'.

Before moving to that Conference, however, we might briefly complete our survey of the main provisions of the First and Second Conventions (those of Conventions Three and Four will follow). In identical terms they lay down that the wounded and sick of the armed forces and the shipwrecked must be respected and protected, *in all circumstances*. There must be no violence to their persons and they must be aided and cared for. The dead must be collected and their bodies protected against robbery. Bodies must be identified before burial and death confirmed, if possible, by medical examination.

Medical and religious personnel are likewise to be 'protected'. Such personnel must wear an armlet with a red cross, and carry an identity card; but they *may bear arms* for their own defence and that of the wounded. If medical and religious personnel fall into enemy hands, they are to be allowed to continue their duties towards the wounded and sick. But those retained are not to be considered as prisoners-of-war. As regards medical units, these cover all buildings or permanent installations (hospitals, stores, etc.) and mobile units (ambulances, tents, open-air installations, etc.) used *exclusively* in collecting and caring for the wounded and the sick. They must not be attacked or damaged, or prevented from operating.

Two new provisions open fresh ground and bring us closer to the theme of human rights in armed conflicts. They deal with the search for casualties and for the dead, their removal, and the recording and forwarding of information about them. Moreover, a valuable idea was embodied in the 1949 text that the wounded must be given at once the emergency treatment (ligatures, injections, etc.) they may require. Many lives have been saved by such immediate care.

The *Third Convention*, dealing with prisoners-of-war, also introduced important innovations and improvements. When studying this Convention, one is struck by the amount of detail it contains. This was because experience had shown that the prisoner, during his captivity, is exposed to all kinds of preventable suffering. That is why the Convention deals with every aspect of a prisoner's life behind the barbed wire, from the day of his capture right up to the day of his release. In these 142 Articles nothing has been forgotten which will enable the prisoners to lead a healthy and decent life. Alas, that so much care should be spent on mitigating evils that should have been prevented!

One of its first Articles lists the categories of persons entitled to the benefit of the Convention, not included in the previous Conventions. Particularly important are *partisans*, i.e. members of organised resistance movements in occupied territory. These, for the future, are given the same standing as militias and volunteer corps, and they must fulfil the same conditions. Other categories are specified, such as persons who accompany the armed forces without actually forming part of them. But to be entitled to prisoner-of-war status, persons who accompany the armed forces should have obtained authorisation to do so and be supplied with an identity card.

ARE FREEDOM-FIGHTERS CIVILIANS?

The *Fourth Convention* covers the 'Protection of Civilian Persons in Time of War'. A civilian is defined as a person who does not belong to the armed forces and takes no part in hostilities. Civilians may never be attacked; they shall be respected, protected, and at all times humanely treated.

When the Second World War broke out there was no law on behalf of *civilian* war victims, except under the humanitarian but incomplete The Hague 'rules of war'. Inhabitants of occupied countries, refugees and political deportees found themselves subjected to arbitrary treatment, culminating in the horrors of the concentration camps, without any effective *legal* rights under International Law. Now the Fourth Convention of 1949 gives legal protection to civilians in occupied countries. It adapts to civilians the principles laid down for the protection of military personnel in the other Geneva Conventions. Amongst other things, it prohibits mass deportations, the arbitrary arrest of individuals, and the taking and shooting of hostages. If detained, they must be treated in the same way as aliens in general. If security reasons make their detention imperative, they shall have a right to appeal, and to have their cases impartially reviewed.

When territory is occupied, the civilian population shall, as far as possible, be enabled to continue living as usual. Transfers of population are prohibited and every compulsory enlisting of manpower shall be subject to strict regulation. Workers may never be forced to do labour which would make them participate in military operations. The occupying power shall be especially responsible for the welfare of the children, the maintenance of the medical and health services, and the feeding of the population. In general, the civil authorities, administration and public and private institutions should continue to function as normally.

One particular Article of the Fourth Convention has come to the fore recently. Article 47, on the Inviolability of Rights, runs as follows:

> Protected persons who are in occupied territory shall not be deprived, in any case or in any manner whatsoever, of the benefits of the present Convention by any change introduced, as the result of the occupation of a territory, into the institutions or government of the said territory, nor by any agreement concluded between the authorities of the occupied territories and the Occupying Power, nor by any annexation by the latter of the whole or part of the occupied territory.

This Article, based on the UN Charter's prohibition of the use of force, is followed by Article 53, which reads:

> Any destruction by the Occupying Power of real or personal property belonging individually or collectively to private persons, or to the State, or to other public authorities, or to social or cooperative organizations, is prohibited, except where such

destruction is rendered absolutely necessary by military operations.

And the Diplomatic Conference 1977 adopted a further Article, 47 *bis*, on the protection of 'cultural objects and of places of worship', which supplements the responsibilities already assumed by UNESCO under its constitution, by the following provision:

> Without prejudice to the provisions of The Hague Convention on the Protection of Cultural Property in the Event of Armed Conflict of 14 May 1954, and other relevant international instruments, it is forbidden: to commit any acts of hostility directed against historic monuments, places of worship, or works of art which constitute the cultural heritage of peoples . . .

The special problem of Israel's breach of these provisions is dealt with later in Chapter 4. Meantime, it should be noted that all civilians have the right of free resort to the protecting power (i.e. neutral state) and to the International Committee of the Red Cross (ICRC). The representatives of the protecting power and of the International Committee shall be able to visit them freely in the occupied lands.

The ICRC is, in fact, a regular observer at the sessions of the Commission on Human Rights. The reasons for its presence may not be immediately apparent, since it cannot be denied that the Commission's discussions are carried out within a political framework removed from the strictly humanitarian concerns of the International Committee. However, a glance at the main items on the Human Rights Commission's agenda shows why the ICRC cannot stand aloof: e.g. territories occupied as a result of hostilities in the Middle East; southern Africa; Chile; Cyprus; protection of persons subjected to any form of detention; and other violations of human rights and fundamental freedoms throughout the world. The ICRC is present in all the afore-mentioned territories and countries.

Moreover, it is gravely concerned about the treatment of detainees and the recrudescence of torture in many countries. For a large number of political detainees ICRC delegates are the only link with their families and the outside world. It often occurs that, in the documentary material submitted by certain governments to the Commission, some reference is made to the Red Cross activities in their countries; yet it is quite out of the question that the ICRC might take sides in such discussions or at any time abandon its traditional principles of discretion. Nevertheless, the ICRC observers are able, as a general rule through personal contacts, to bring discreetly to mind the criteria adopted for visits by ICRC delegates to places of detention.

It will be noticed that, true to Dunant's inspired foresight over a century ago, the neutrality principle is seen at work by the presence in all armed conflicts of a 'Protecting Power'. But where, for one reason or another, no protecting power has been agreed upon by both sides, the Conventions provide a surrogate in the presence of the International Committee of the Red Cross.

We can select two recent cases of how this works in practice. The President of the International Committee of the Red Cross appealed in February 1977 to leaders of the opposing forces in the Rhodesia/Zimbabwe conflict to respect and to make their respective combatants apply in practice humanitarian laws in regard to the treatment of civilians caught in the fighting zones, and also of the wounded, the sick and prisoners-of-war. He sent his appeal to Joshua Nkomo and Robert Mugabe of the Patriotic Front, to Bishop Abel Muzorewa, to the Reverend Ndabaninghi Sithole and to Prime Minister Ian Smith, coupled with the request that the ICRC be granted all facilities for visiting prisoners and for providing humanitarian assistance to civilian victims. Specifically mentioned was the request to Mr Smith for visits to all nationalist fighters captured while bearing weapons and all other persons arrested in the conflict, in addition to the administrative detainees, already being visited by ICRC delegates over a number of years.

The appeal was also sent to the British authorities and to the heads of state of Angola, Botswana, Mozambique, Tanzania and Zambia, urging observance of such basic humanitarian principles as:

(1) Persons 'hors de combat' and those taking no direct part in hostilities are entitled to respect for their life, and for their physical and moral dignity. It is forbidden to kill or wound an enemy who is 'hors de combat' or who surrenders.

(2) Wounded and sick shall be collected and cared for by the party to the conflict which has them in its power. Protection also covers medical personnel, medical establishments, means of transport and equipment, and the Red Cross which is the emblem denoting such protection.

(3) Prisoners-of-war and civilians in the power of the adverse party are entitled to respect for their life, their dignity, their family rights and their convictions, and shall be protected from any act of violence.

(4) Parties to a conflict shall at all times distinguish between the civilian population and combatants, in order to spare the population and civilian property.

(5) *Parties to a conflict and their armed forces do not have an unlimited choice of methods of warfare.* Weapons or any methods of warfare likely to cause unnecessary losses or suffering are forbidden [*Our italics*].

A second current example comes from Israel and its illegally occupied territories in Palestine, Jordan, Egypt and Syria. Following a hunger strike by Arab civilian detainees in Ashkelon prison in March 1977, ICRC delegates paid two special visits to the prison, one to listen to what the strikers had to say, and the other to study with the prison authorities what humanitarian measures should be taken to meet the strikers' demands. There were then still outstanding a number of problems which had been reported at regular intervals by the delegates, one of these being overcrowding; other problems included medical, cultural and family questions.

For nearly ten years, in fact, delegates of the International Committee have regularly visited places of detention in Israel and its occupied territories. As in all other countries where the ICRC has access to prisons, the sole aim of these visits is to improve detention conditions, irrespective of the reasons for detention, and to co-operate with the detaining authorities to find solutions to penitentiary problems. In this connection, the hunger strike in Ashkelon shows how necessary and often urgent are the International Committee's constant efforts.

Locked away behind the concrete walls and barbed-wire of the maximum security prison of Ashkelon are some 400 Arab 'security prisoners' – most of them condemned to spend the rest of their lives in limbo, though most are native Palestinians from the occupied territories, while their homes and families are only a few miles away. To the Israelis they are simply terrorists and murderers, whose crimes are to be considered worse than those of ordinary criminals. The prisoners consider themselves, of course, to be freedom-fighters in a just war. Even behind bars they remain highly motivated and politicised. To give them prisoner-of-war status is out of the question, as far as Israel is concerned. This would be to recognise the legitimacy of the Palestinian organisations to which they belong.

Hence, a tantalising question remains to the end of this chapter: 'When is a civilian not a civilian?' Or, more directly, are freedom-fighters and members of 'liberation movements' civilians or soldiers? And 'guerrillas' – as they are called by their opponents – are they soldiers entitled to the protection of humanitarian law?

For four years (1974–7), a Conference on Humanitarian Law, convened by the International Committee of the Red Cross, struggled through some forty plenary meetings to come up with generally agreed answers to these questions and many similar ones. By the summer of 1977, it had reached a substantial area of agreement, which is in itself no small achievement of human rights in armed conflicts.

The last of the four annual sessions of the Diplomatic Conference on the Reaffirmation and Development of International Humanitarian Law Applicable in Armed Conflicts, to give it its full title, to which 155 States had been invited, opened in March 1977 in Geneva under the presidency of Mr Pierre Graber, Head of the Federal Political Department of Switzerland. It resulted in the adoption of two important Protocols, bringing international humanitarian law into line with world developments since the conclusion of the 1949 Conventions, whose provisions we have already outlined.

It would not be possible to summarise the scope or substance of this significant advance in humanitarian law – still subject to ratification by the states who are party to it. But attention can be drawn to a controversial innovation of worldwide significance concerning guerrilla fighters. They have been granted the rights of prisoners-of-war under a new Article, added to the 1949 Conventions. This Article 44 was accepted by 77 votes of the 109 nations present at the plenary session of the Conference (including that of the USA). There were 21 abstentions (including Britain) and only one against (Israel).

Under this provision, which is naturally considered a key article, guerrilla fighters and members of resistance movements captured in 'liberation wars' and in other _international_ conflicts are henceforth to enjoy, subject to certain conditions, the privileged status of combatant and prisoner-of-war, at present conferred on the soldiers of regular armies under the Geneva Conventions of 1949. This Article was the outcome of compromises reached after long negotiations that took place during the earlier sessions of 1975 and 1976.

It is symptomatic of the pathological climate that has dominated all activities in the Middle East for so long that the Israeli delegate, on the one hand, sweepingly described the decision as 'the end of humanitarian law'; 'this will encourage acts of terrorism. Anyone attacking a plane in a foreign country will get prisoner-of-war status,' he said. While the Palestine Liberation Organization representative, attending the Conference as an observer, on the other hand, expressed satisfaction at the acceptance of the new article and asserted that his only criticism was of a paragraph which stated that combatants must carry their arms openly during military action. 'But we take this as meaning that we must produce our weapons immediately before an action.' The article itself reads:

In order to promote the protection of the civilian population from the effects of hostilities, combatants are obligated to distinguish themselves from the civilian population while they are engaged in an attack or in a military operation preparatory to an attack.

The mercenary, however, received little sympathy from the big majority of governments assembled at Geneva. He was defined in a new article (no. 49) to Protocol I as a person who is specially recruited in order to fight in an armed conflict and does, in fact, take a direct part in the hostilities, but is motivated *essentially* by the desire for private gain, not being a national of a party to the conflict or a member of its armed forces.

Coming – almost like a tailpiece – at the very end of its four years of debate, the Diplomatic Conference decided by consensus that mercenaries taken in combat should *not* be accorded prisoner-of-war status. Nonetheless, the definition of a mercenary is designed to assure that members of regular armed forces and foreign military advisers cannot be considered as mercenaries. But though mercenaries are denied both combatant and prisoner-of-war status, the Conference made it clear that mercenaries must be treated humanely and cannot be punished without a fair trial.

Finally, it is far too late in the day for the United Nations system to stand aloof and detached from the day-to-day actions, good or bad, of the liberation movements. Let us glance, therefore, at a cogent statement by the Chairman of a Namibia Council mission to Geneva in April 1977, to elicit the help of the UN agencies: 'Often people ask "but what can the United Nations do?",' he said:

Well, the United Nations can do many things, but that depends on the political will of its members. In the case of our mission it is easily answered. The liberation movements will pursue the armed struggle. But the United Nations family can *play a supportive role* to their legitimate struggle by informing world public opinion about the issues involved, stimulating auxiliary support for the liberation movements and, particularly through the Specialised Agencies, ensuring concrete assistance to those movements now and when the armed struggle intensifies, as it inevitably must, if the illegal regimes continue in their intransigent attitudes.

It will be noted that the Namibian spokesman does not ask for (nor would he get) military help but, rather, the mobilisation of world public opinion in support of a legitimate liberation struggle. A step towards this was a United Nations conference sponsored by the Council for Namibia that same summer in Maputo, Mozambique, in support of the peoples of both Zimbabwe and Namibia for *self-determination*. But that is a question of some complexity, which we must take up in Chapter 5.

3 Mobilisation of Shame

Whoever has power is tempted to abuse it.

—*Montesquieu (1748)*

'We would desperately like to believe that all this is untrue', said the Reverend Theo Kotze, Director of the Christian Institute of South Africa, when listing the claims made by 115 prisoners that they were tortured by the South African police, and recording the stories of forty-nine people who have since *died* in police detention. His seventy-six-page report entitled 'Torture in South Africa' is a deeply disturbing document. But in its issue of 13 April 1977 the South Africa *Government Gazette* announced that the dossier had been banned as 'undesirable'. The careful factual way in which the document is presented without doubt brought about the banning order.[1]

There was another explanation, perhaps, for the list of deaths in detention, which covered the period from that of Looksmart Solwandle Ngudle on 5 September 1963, who was posthumously 'banned' after an inquest found that he died by 'suicide, hanging', to that of Samuel Malinga, who was being held under the Terrorism Act and died on 22 February 1977. The tortures as described in affidavits included electric shocks, kicking and compelling prisoners to lift weights while wearing shoes containing pebbles. One method of torture which portends a certain death, is the threat of being dropped from upstairs windows.

The information assembled in the document is drawn from parliamentary and press reports or surveys by the South African Institute of Race Relations. The names of thirty-seven individual blacks who had been allegedly tortured in 1973 were given to the Prime Minister by clergymen in Namibia. The reply was that the matter had been investigated and the allegations were found to be 'without foundation'. But the clergymen noted that Mr Vorster had done nothing at all about the allegations.

Steve Biko, aged thirty, the popular and vigorous founder of the South African 'black consciousness movement', who died in a prison cell in September 1977, was reported to be in a coma for several days before he died. So it was a little difficult for Police Minister James Kruger to maintain the legend that Biko had either committed suicide, as first announced, or succumbed to a week's hunger strike. Biko was the twenty-first person to die in police custody in eighteen months. We pursue further obscenities of South African police behaviour in our next chapter.

Geneva would appear to have become a focus of the earth-wide struggle against the perpetrators of crimes like these. For Geneva is not only the seat of the Human Rights Commission and its Sub-Commission, which are serviced by the Division of Human Rights of the UN Secretariat; non-governmental organisations of every shape and variety cluster around the major inter-governmental bodies and the inter-governmental conferences that have found in Calvin's City both a symbol and a habitation for humanity's vigilance against the callous cruelty of certain sovereign states. Under Article 71 of the Charter, several hundreds of international and national non-governmental organisations are brought into consultative status with the Economic and Social Council (ECOSOC) and are afforded various degrees of consultation with or representation on the official bodies.

Since the UN's own organs in the human rights field are frequently criticised or denigrated, not only by delinquent governments but by servile sections of the mass media, and are also blamed for their ineffectiveness and selective 'politicization', it would be useful to deal in this chapter with recent examples of how non-governmental groups have participated in that 'mobilisation of shame' which springs from individual and collective concern for the fate of the defenceless victims suffering under oppressive or careless governments. They are the auxiliaries of a universal movement. Following such a survey, we can move specifically into the area of systematised torture and illegal detention. For torture and detention are two sides of the same spurious coin.

A Special Committee of Non-Governmental Organisations on Human Rights, called by that name and under the chairmanship of Niall MacDermot, a distinguished English barrister, who is also Secretary-General of the International Commission of Jurists, meets regularly in Geneva, and comprises some sixty representatives of independent human rights and kindred organisations. Its agenda covers many crucial fields of investigation and its affiliated organisations are never without heavy case-loads. One of these – Amnesty International – we shall take up in some detail below, as well as the Committee's own campaign for a new set of rules for detainees.

Before looking at the more formal machinery, however, we might note that Geneva itself is continually the recipient of numerous appeals for public interest and support. Illustrative of this constant inflow there follow five quite different cases selected at random that arrived through the mail at NGO offices during the same week that the World Council of Churches issued the press bulletin featured at the beginning of this chapter. They are summarised below.

Case no. 1 comes from an American feminist group, Women's International Network, with headquarters in Lexington, Massachusetts, protesting against the genital mutilation of girls in Africa. They point out that these damaging operations are widely practised all over Africa by many different population groups and are documented in the medical and ethnographic literature of the World Health Organization (WHO). The most recent study was published in 1975 by Dr J. A. Verzin, MD, in the British journal *Tropical Doctor*, titled 'Sequelae of Female Circumcision'.

Women who are infibulated have to be cut open to allow intercourse and they have to be cut open further to permit delivery of a child. Some times they are closed up again after delivery. The decision rests with the husband, who has several wives. During their reproductive lives women are often subjected to these operations with each child. The mortality is high, but no records are kept anywhere. The severity of these inhuman and unnecessary operations or damage done to the girl seems to depend on the local custom, on the particular operator, on the tools used, or on the skill of the operator, mostly an old woman, often called 'midwife'.

Genital mutilation makes childbirth a great hazard for both mother and child, resulting in death for the mother and death or brain-damage for the child, especially where trained or medical help is not available, as in most of Africa. The Report adds that

> though Africans claim that these operations no longer exist except in remote rural areas, increasing numbers of women are coming to the hospitals seeking help, severely damaged by genital operations. African Health Departments do nothing about genital mutilation and information about reproduction and biological facts hardly exists.

Case no. 2 was actually detailed in the Geneva press, describing the mental pain and predicament of an Iranian resident, with a responsible post at the Geneva Institute of Advanced Studies and a French wife. His younger brother has for six years been incarcerated and tortured in the Ervine prison. This case had already been investigated by Amnesty International in 1973, and he is described as a non-violent protester against the Shah's *régime de fer et de sang*. A Swiss lawyer attended the trial, which condemned the young man to death – since commuted to imprisonment. His elder brother says that he is not 'recognisable' after six years in Iran's most notorious jail.

The Swiss Committee for the Defence of Political Prisoners in Iran have listed names and details of several *thousand* similar political prisoners incarcerated there, and they assert that the Teheran authorities are systematically inflicting the same form of 'moral torture' on the families, both in their own country and abroad.

Iranians have difficulty in obtaining passports, especially if they are released political prisoners, and members of their families too. Academic freedom is restricted and students and university teachers are kept under surveillance by SAVAK (National Security Organisation). A professor of literature was harassed, beaten, arrested and tortured because his courses had been deemed as not conforming with the 'ideology' of the Shah.[2]

Case no. 3 comes from Stuttgart through a Geneva postal address, and appeals for immediate action to support eighty political prisoners on hunger strike in West Germany (FRG), Austria and Holland, some of whom were nearing death. Their protest was against their solitary confinement, and they claimed prisoner-of-war status under the terms of the 1949 Convention, and appropriate treatment as such.

Case no. 4, again from a Geneva address, is captioned 'Camp VS 389/35' and includes, among others, an interview with Vladimir Balakhonov, who was a translator in the World Meteorological Organisation from 1969 to 1972, but had requested political asylum in Switzerland. He returned to the Soviet Union, however, quite voluntarily, to fetch his little daughter. ('For me the most precious being in the world.') He found himself, instead, arrested on the spot by the KGB on arrival, confined in Camp 35 in the Urals, then transferred to a psychiatric prison and, next, to another prison for three years – where he still is today.

He was tried by an ordinary court and sentenced to twelve years' imprisonment by virtue of Article 62 of the criminal code, which defines as treason 'flight abroad or refusal to return to the USSR'. We shall later on look at this monstrous legal catch-all in the light of the 1975 Helsinki accords. Meantime, in a message passed through friends to his supporters in Geneva, Balakhonov describes his condition as 'a proof of the inhuman character of the Soviet system, a system deprived of humanism, which destroys the individual in a cruel manner and without hesitation or regard for the sacredness and obligations of family ties'.

Case no. 5 announces that a Swiss weekly, *La Vie Protestante*, has taken the initiative in the fight against torture and has published a booklet proposing ways and means of actively opposing 'man's inhumanity to man'. Under the title 'A New Weapon against Torture', eighteen contributors from political, scientific and religious groups advocate the formation of a Permanent International Control Commission to visit places of detention at any time without prior notice. They propose strategies to fight torture and provide guidelines on how to contact national, international and religious bodies for assistance in cases of known torture. Above all, the various writers point out that global strategy is needed. They suggest that a start should be made by calling a convention of a small number of countries representing various ideological trends which will do the preparatory work for a larger assembly that can be charged with developing a global strategy.

THE FOURTH INTERNATIONAL

It must be emphasised that such fortuitous appeals as the foregoing examples are quite distinct from the tens of thousands of complaints ('communications' is the official word that squeamish governments prefer to call them) that arrive in the UN Secretariat and at the offices of the UN's specialised agencies under the prescribed legal procedures, and will be discussed hereafter. It is not really surprising, however, that it is the *non*-governmental groups who are steadily forming a global – even if not yet systematised – movement of investigation, protest and reform. For it is the world's *sovereign governments* who are now the criminals in the dock! This is quite a new departure in history; and 1000 years away from Henri Dunant's lonely protest in the 1860s or Gladstone's Midlothian campaign in the 1870s.

The fact that so many governments are under fire today – Amnesty International lists some sixty – has to be seen as a political event of crucial importance. And this for special reasons: (1) The sovereign state can no longer be regarded as sufficient in itself to protect the life and liberty of its citizens; (2) the international protection of human rights is no longer an expression of pious rhetoric, but an essential part of some tangible form of world authority – a speculation that we must postpone until the final chapter; and (3) the conferment of the Nobel Peace Prize upon Amnesty International in 1977 has, in Martin Ennals's words, linked peace with human rights for all time.

This Fourth International of protest and 'civil defence' (in the correct meaning of the term) looks back to a key date in 1961 when the most substantial and systematised of these volunteer efforts sprang into life, namely Amnesty International. How did it all begin? From the very beginning Amnesty International was visualised as a movement of committed *individuals* working on a voluntary basis to create a *practical* method to channel international goodwill into the vital struggle for individual human rights. And that is what it has remained.

Today there are over 100,000 members of Amnesty International in seventy-eight countries. In many of those countries small organised groups raise money, write letters to heads of state, send relief to the families of prisoners of conscience, circulate petitions among their friends, and give up their weekends to plan campaigns, translate reports and send messages of greeting to prisoners in distant countries, who may believe that they have been forgotten by the outside world. It is because of that tremendous reservoir of individual commitment on the part of so many people that Amnesty has become so well known and was awarded the Nobel Peace Prize.

On rare occasions it is one's privilege to meet in social or professional life a man or woman who can truly be described as 'the salt of the earth'. Such a personality was Peter Benenson, a London barrister, whose quiet and unassuming manner did not display the burning and passionate zeal that brought his name and influence into prison cells and torture chambers of despotic regimes across the globe. But when – as it would have done anyway – Benenson's dynamism ran into deliberate bureaucratic procrastinations and governmental obstruction, his sensitive nature could no longer accept this continued frustration and the calumnies at home, added to his most exhausting journeyings abroad, so that his health seriously suffered. However, his early leadership was fortunately succeeded by that of a much tougher and equally resolute fighter for human rights when Martin Ennals became Secretary-General in the late 1960s.

Martin Ennals soon found, as Benenson had done, that Amnesty International was one of the world's most denounced organisations. And he intends to keep it that way. 'In fact,' he says, 'it is an honour.' Nevertheless, he insists that, as far as it is allowed to do,

> Amnesty International intends to develop a rational dialogue with all governments and to persuade them to respect international standards for the protection of human rights. But at the same time it's obvious that when we talk about torture, about disappearances in police stations and about the incarceration of political prisoners, we are talking about an extremely delicate and sensitive matter. The easiest way for some governments to avoid any real dialogue is to claim (as loudly as possible) that our concern for human rights is politically biased. The discerning listener, however, soon realises that our information must be exceptionally accurate to cause such a fuss. On the whole all governments dislike criticism and reject it, but also like to maintain a good image and so are prepared to talk about human rights.[3]

The reports published by Amnesty International are the result of long and sometimes extremely difficult research work. The International Secretariat of the organisation in London numbers over 100 personnel, including a research department with expert staff. The researchers receive newspapers and periodicals in a variety of languages, consult specialists in law and medicine, correspond with other NGOs and with private individuals, such as lawyers and social workers, in many countries, and wherever possible undertake official missions to countries under investigation.

'Our dossiers provide the kind of specific data on which our entire credibility rests,' says Ennals:

> We can go to a Minister of Justice with the names, dates of birth, dates of arrest and charges against individuals and the exact addresses of the prisons in which they are being held. And we can ask 'Is this information correct?' If it is, then we can begin talking about very specific cases of violation of human rights. If it is not

correct, we are in a good position to ask detailed questions which lead to truth.

Perhaps the most widely known of Amnesty's actions is its claim that it has listed the names and details of some 5000 'prisoners of conscience'. By this term the organisation means persons imprisoned anywhere for their beliefs, colour, ethnic origin, language or religion, *provided they have neither used nor advocated violence*. Amnesty International recognises that they are unfortunately able to deal only with a small percentage of the hundreds of thousands of such prisoners in the world. But they do try to secure the release of each one about whom they can obtain sufficient information. 'We would like to point out,' says Ennals, 'that prisoners of conscience are *made*.'

Their very existence in any country whatsoever is a violation of the provisions of the Universal Declaration of Human Rights. A prisoner of conscience is *created* every time a man or woman is detained for his or her beliefs, every time a human being is arrested or imprisoned in order to silence ideas, to suppress a minority or to prevent legitimate freedom of expression and association.

As regards Amnesty's effectiveness and the impact that it has had on the release of prisoners, Ennals claims that

we can point to numerous instances in which, once attention was drawn to it, torture has actually stopped while it was in progress. Statistically, we can look at campaigns in which just under 50% of the cases taken up have been released. But it is not our policy to claim credit for releasing political prisoners – there are too many factors involved. Beyond that, however, I am inclined to think that despite the extremely gloomy picture of human rights in the world at present, we have been instrumental in helping to generate a counterbalancing force – a force of determination to see the jails opened, the instruments of torture destroyed and the dignity of the human person restored.

Certainly, Amnesty has not achieved its present stability without a fight. 'Martin Ennals's calming and good-tempered presence did much to salvage it from a chaotic end,' states a close observer, who records that in March 1966 the Amnesty offices were broken into and a number of files, as well as the index of London members, were, carried away. The burglary was shortly followed by allegations that the British Government had put pressure on Amnesty to moderate a critical report on the behaviour of the British authorities in Aden. There is no evidence at all that Amnesty succumbed.[4]

The same observer continues:

> Missions and ambassadors of Amnesty fly about the world, briefing people, talking, making suggestions, watching. Things happen; but the causal connexion is not examined. In 1975 Amnesty adopted 2,015 new cases of political prisoners; 1,688 prisoners were released during the year. Since Amnesty started, 9,000 people adopted by them have got out of jail. How many are actually free because of Amnesty intervention? Martin Ennals puts it neatly: 'The coincidence rate between the cases we take up and people released is simply high.'

Not least, having gathered over a million signatures from all over the world in support of an anti-torture resolution passed at the United Nations, a campaign formed itself in 1974 into a separate unit. On hearing of the arrest of a person in a country where there is a record of torturing detainees, the campaign goes into action with a machinery of telexes and telegrams and press releases. But the anti-torture campaign is only at its beginning.

ANATOMY OF TORTURE

In opening Amnesty's first International Conference on the Abolition of Torture in Paris in December 1973, Seán MacBride, SC, then Chairman of the International Executive Committee of Amnesty International, stated:

> There is no doubt that the practice of torture has been on the increase in recent years. There is no doubt that its use has been more widespread. There is no doubt that it is practised with the direct or implied permission of a large number of governments, many of whom consider themselves civilized. There is no doubt that, like a contagious disease, it spreads from one country to another, and, in many cases, is deliberately imported by the armed services of one country and taught to the services of another country.

Seán MacBride went on to add:

there can never be any justification for the use of torture. Some governments seek to justify it on the grounds that it is necessary in order to extract information from subversive organisations. But, in our view, torture is used more as a weapon to silence opposition and criticism than as a means of obtaining information. For whichever purpose it is used, it is a crime against humanity and involves the negation of all the principles set out in the Universal Declaration of Human Rights.

It is sometimes questioned why the United Nations' sophisticated apparatus of human rights, based on a Universal Declaration – which practically all national governments have, in principle, accepted – with its plethora of supporting declarations and covenants, nevertheless does so little to 'get things done'; while ordinary 'people's' organisations seem to be the pioneers and the real activists in getting visible results?

The first direct answer to this criticism – which really forms the central theme of this book – is that the UN system is at all times the invisible framework within which the growing range of voluntary effort becomes possible. Moreover, its own direct record of active achievement cannot be judged by the censorious editorials that so frequently greet some particularly horrendous violation.

A recent example of this double-think appeared in a London *Times* editorial headed 'Human Rights Commission Shirks Its Job'. This sums up its condemnation of a recent Commission meeting in Geneva 'without engendering any reactions' to the current massacres in Uganda, as follows: 'In short, the Human Rights Commission has little or nothing to do with rights, justice or human conscience'. Yet, unlike most newspaper indictments of the Commission, *The Times* (18 May 1977) does at least propose its own remedy a dozen lines further down in the same paragraph: 'But what matters now is getting rid of Amin and restoring the rule of law to Uganda'.

Exactly! But the Human Rights Commission – which, incidentally, did spend most of six days in February 1977 considering the massive confidential reports on Amin's bloodbath – was never set up to overthrow dictatorial governments and impose revolutionary changes on delinquent sovereign states. These ultimate remedies, which the press would like to see vigorously applied on selected occasions, are certainly not provided for in any of the declarations and covenants: they lie outside the UN's present machinery altogether. (We will attempt to set the record straight, in our next chapter, by dealing with some of the political and psychological obstacles that confront the serious contender for human rights, and which are either not seen or else appear diplomatically cloaked in the mass media.)

But another answer to the above criticism is implied in the first; that is to say, national governments, looking *outward*, and influenced by their global image and their dependence on one another, as well as by the commitments they have made in the UN Charter and numerous other engagements, constitute an international order of mutual convenience, rather than of right. But, looking *inward*, and obsessed with notions of superiority, sovereignty and security, they claim to be sole masters in their own house and makers of its rules. They resent the intervention of foreign governments or associations of foreign governments, brought together in UN organs or agencies in terms of international law.

For this reason, the non-governmental approach, given so little credence in 1945 and relegated discreetly to article 71 of the UN Charter, has grown in importance and influence over the years. The direct action of NGOs on their own governments and, increasingly, across the national frontiers has become a major element in foreign policy in the 1970s. It will grow stronger yet.

There is no doubt that NGOs are playing a special role in promoting international guidelines to prevent torture. This can take the form of working directly within the intergovernmental framework, as is the case of Amnesty International, or of setting standards applicable to certain professional or other groupings. This was demonstrated at the World Medical Association's Twenty-Ninth Assembly in October 1975 in Tokyo when it adopted the Declaration of Tokyo, containing stringent guidelines for medical doctors on the problems of torture. The World Health Organization submitted the draft of this declaration to the Fifth UN Congress on the Prevention of Crime and the Treatment of Offenders in Geneva that same year.

The Declaration of Tokyo states that 'the doctor shall not countenance, condone or participate in the practice of torture'. It forbids doctors 'to provide any premises, instruments, substances or knowledge to facilitate the practice of torture', as well as forbidding them to be present during any procedure at which torture is used or threatened. It also contains suggestions regarding the problem of hunger strikes and calls upon medical bodies and fellow-doctors to support their colleague, and his or her family, in the face of threats or reprisals resulting from a refusal to condone torture.

In this connection, the 1973 Amnesty Conference in Paris laid down certain guidelines; for example:

> By virtue of their profession, doctors have special duties to humanity which transcend other considerations. While this creates a responsibility for the individual doctor who is confronted with mental or physical ill-treatment, it also constitutes a collective responsibility for the whole medical profession. National and international medical bodies should become aware of these consequences for the profession, so that they can support and assist their individual members whenever they are confronted with torture procedures. A special load of responsibility and conflict of conscience can occur for doctors working in prisons and camps, as well as for medical personnel working in the armed forces and the police.

In the same field, the International Council of Nurses, in a policy statement in August 1975 on the role of the nurse in the case of detainees and prisoners, calls on nurses 'to take proper action when they have knowledge of physical or mental ill-treatment of detainees and prisoners', such as reporting the matter to appropriate national or international bodies. The statement reconfirmed that 'the nurse's first responsibility is towards her patients, notwithstanding considerations of national security and interest'. We revert later to some recent issues that have arisen regarding psychiatric hospitals.

At its April 1976 meeting the Inter-Parliamentary Council of the Inter-Parliamentary Union – a very influential non-governmental organisation – adopted a resolution, later approved by the IPU's Sixty-Third Inter-Parliamentary Conference that September, which marks a milestone in the protection of the human rights of *parliamentarians*. A list of imprisoned parliamentarians was sent to the IPU's many participants. A special committee has been set up to examine communications concerning parliamentarians 'who are or have been subjected to arbitrary actions during the exercise of the mandate entrusted to them by their voters, whether their Parliament is sitting, is in recess, or has been dissolved as the result of unconstitutional or extraordinary measures'.

In this swelling movement of public opinion, Amnesty's national sections play a continuous role by raising matters of vital concern with their relevant national bodies. Sometimes they initiate such developments, as in the case of a draft resolution concerning ethical guidelines for psychologists in relation to the problem of torture, proposed to the Twenty-First International Congress of Psychology in Paris in July 1976. This initiative was taken by professionals among Amnesty's members in Belgium and the Netherlands.

Most valuable, perhaps, for all concerned individuals and organisations who want to learn the facts is a documented 224-page *Amnesty International Report on Torture*, based on material collected by Amnesty's Secretariat in London. The authors have examined evidence of systematic brutality from more than sixty-five countries, analysed the legal remedies which exist in international law, described their use in the specific cases of Greece, Northern Ireland and the Middle East, and considered also the medical and psychological aspects of torture.

Before passing to the connection of torture with the cult and practice of violence, which has become the savage mask of our generation, we should perhaps notice a more hopeful link with the NGO activity featured above. This broader commitment was made on 2 November 1973, when the United Nations General Assembly unanimously passed a resolution rejecting all forms of torture and urging all governments to implement existing international conventions banning it. It was also decided to consider in more detail the remedies for torture and other inhuman and degrading treatment at a later session. The General Assembly in 1975 was even more categorical that torture must stop![5] It would seem, therefore, that non-governmental action, too, must now be focused on implementing this common commitment in terms of a legally binding International Convention – in the precise words of Seán MacBride, 'just as we abolished slavery'.

THE FACE OF VIOLENCE

This caption, taken from the title of an essay of the late Professor J. Bronowski, carries the thoughtful mind behind today's torture of individuals to the dark springs of human impulse leading to and conditioned by a violent society, a society at war with itself. Each of the three major investigations of gross and continuous violations of human rights now being conducted by the UN Commission (as detailed in our next chapter) have their roots in organised social

violence: namely, in Chile, in the ousting of a democratically
elected president by a fascist Junta; in Israel, in the occupation of
Arab territories by military force; and in South Africa, in the
suppression of the black majority by police power and vicious laws.

A comprehensive scientific study of the ever-mounting quantum
of torture today – which does not yet seem to have been attempted –
must be set squarely within the social violence of our time, in order
to be properly understood. Bronowski has put this point well:

> In this setting, the pervert and the possessed can again become
> instruments of power, as they did in the courts of Italy around the
> turn of 1500, in the lifetime of Leonardo and Machiavelli and the
> Borgias. The bootlegger, the condottiere and the Leader need
> such tools if they are to corrupt a following and bind it to them.
> The wish to hurt, the momentary intoxication with pain, is the
> loophole through which the pervert climbs into the minds of
> ordinary men.[6]

Perhaps de Sade was correct when he put this relationship into
one sentence: 'In a criminal society, one must be a criminal.' It is
beyond the purpose and scope of the present survey to explore these
deeper channels of social and individual psychology, though the
present author has made some observations in another work on the
bearing of 'the urge to punish' on the right to life.[7]

One conclusion might safely be drawn, however, from the results
of both the official and unofficial probings into torture at this time,
and that is that the element of punishment, with the normal
objective of correcting human behaviour, is secondary to the
purpose of *defending* or maintaining an imposed political regime. A
foremost sociologist, Professor Hamon of Brussels, in his classic study
La Responsabilité (1899), has called this 'the reflex action of defence'.

We are dealing basically, therefore, with a series of repugnant,
fearful, and isolated regimes. 'Not only did the [Greek] officers,'
states a recent Amnesty report, 'perceive themselves as isolated;
they also instilled these attitudes in their soldiers':

> Under the officers' tutelage the unit itself became increasingly
> segregated from the Junta's other security forces. The beatings of
> conscripts at KESA as part of their training was intended to
> reinforce that sense of separateness. Theofiloyannakos called the
> KESA training programme an 'initiation rite'. The metaphor is

an inviting one because entry into KESA was analogous to entry into a club.

Unwilling and resistant peoples choose to rebel in whatever ways are open to them rather than submit to their frightened and isolated oppressors. Torture has to be envisaged as an instrument of 'moral' defence and reaction against some threatened social and international change. Human rights are always political, where fear and insecurity reign outside.

In this context, the following findings of the Paris Conference in 1973 have particular relevance and they merit quoting at length:

Political stability and social or economic progress are two of the pretexts most frequently advanced to justify repression, of which torture often is a part. Each puts the planning of the State before the rights of the citizen. But experience from a number of countries shows that governments do not achieve stability through torture. On the contrary, violence tends to create counter-violence . . .

Torture is often a part of a more widely repressive policy. It tends to occur in societies where there are deep conflicts, where the judiciary is weak and dependent and where the press and other democratic forces are restricted.

Torture is spawned of fear and insecurity. With such a dubious parentage, torture and its evil twin, detention, can never prevail in the long-run as a viable instrument of government. A campaign was launched by Amnesty in June 1977 to persuade doctors to treat torturers as *diseased persons*. In fact, Amnesty published what is said to be the first medical examination of the symptoms and effects of torture. It convened a conference in London to discuss a booklet presenting the findings of a Danish team of doctors who have been examining the effects of torture. It was there argued that by discouraging doctors from helping or assisting in torture, the disease could be lessened.

In each of the three major areas of special enquiry that have taken up so much of the Human Rights Commission's time and energy these last several years, and been the topic of widespread public controversy, the dominating drives have constantly been fear and insecurity. Chile's military Junta has neither international respectability nor national security, so exists under a constant state of self-imposed siege. Israel's shaky governments enjoy neither peace nor stable frontiers, so draw nothing but hatred and menace from the 2 million Palestinians under their military occupation. South Africa, living on borrowed time, still contrives in vain to make apartheid a workable social system. As Lincoln long ago realised; 'no country can exist half-slave and half-free.' Time is running out for all three jailer-regimes.

Some passages from Simone Weil's poignant essay on *The Iliad* might well have been written, not in 1940 at the fall of France, but also as a commentary on the fragility of military force today:

> Perhaps all men, by the very act of being born, are destined to suffer violence; yet this is a truth to which circumstance shuts men's eyes. The strong are, as a matter of fact, never absolutely strong, nor are the weak absolutely weak, but neither is aware of this . . . The man who is the possessor of force seems to walk through a non-resistant element; . . . these men, wielding power, have no suspicion of the fact that the consequences of their deeds will at length come home to them – they too will bow the neck in their turn . . . Thus it happens that those who have force on loan from fate count on it too much and are destroyed.[8]

'FORCE ON LOAN FROM FATE'

A parallel has sometimes been drawn between the strategy employed by the 'colonels' who took over Greece in 1968 and General Pinochet's *golpe* in Chile in 1973. Both coups were planned in secret by a military caucus; both were ostensibly aimed at stopping Communism; both were aided and funded by outside allies. In Greece it was a secret NATO contingency plan named 'Prometheus' (as detailed in my *End of An Illusion*), while in Chile it was backed by the CIA and US multinationals, as revealed in subsequent Senate hearings. Both set up a military dictatorship, suspended the constitution, and shut down all the organs of democratic expression. Both imprisoned thousands of civilians and submitted their countries' leading citizens to imprisonment without trial and to systematic torture.

But the parallel – for the time being – has ceased to operate. This is because, in 1975, when the Chilean Junta was proclaiming its second anniversary, the Greek colonels were facing their judges in Athens, and the public trial of named torturers had begun in earnest. A recent editorial appraisal has set in due context the essence of the trials that we briefly summarise below. *The Times* stated on 18 April 1977:

> Amnesty International's report on torture in Greece, published at the weekend, is different from the usual run of that organization's reports. For once, instead of drawing attention to horrors currently practised by one of the world's too numerous repressive regimes, Amnesty has set itself the more cheerful but no less important task of following the procedure by which oppressors have been brought to justice in a free society after their oppressive regime had fallen.

> Amnesty's report analyses in considerable detail the trial of fourteen officers and eighteen soldiers of the military police (ESA), held in August-September, 1975. The report stresses that this trial is likely to have an international exemplary value because it 'established a truth and proved a point: torture *was* practised by the Junta's military police on a systematic scale as a means to enforce authority, and torture *can* be punished by the ordinary criminal process'.

Perhaps the most significant contribution to our present study of the Amnesty report is to remind us that, with the exception of the Scandinavians and the Dutch, both the West European and the American Governments, though well informed about the practice of torture in Greece, failed to respond adequately to the appeals of Greek democrats. They thus made themselves 'the Junta's silent partners in violating human rights'. It is true that expressions of concern for human rights by governments have since become more fashionable in the United States and Britain, but the important thing is to give them practical effect in terms of international action. It is because *governments* control, for the most part, the collective *actions* of the United Nations and most of its human rights units, that the present chapter has emphasised the overwhelming value of the non-governmental initiative and leadership. This has become one of the driving forces of the human rights movement in the later years of the twentieth century.

Amnesty's publication, *Torture in Greece* (1977) is one of the most moving documents of our time, and readers will not fail to look with horror at the photographs that appear between pp. 32 and 33 of the soldiers of all ranks who faced the Athens Permanent Court Martial on charges of torture committed during the seven years of dictatorship from 1967 to 1974. Here are the faces of scowling criminals who, as the report states, provide us with a disturbing insight into 'the inner clockwork of a torture state'.

Much could be said of the social and educational background of this bunch of perverts and neurotics who sought by military force and despotic means to rule a modern democracy. But one is strangely moved by a simple question from the father, a farmer, of one of the accused: 'We are a poor but decent family, and now I see him in the dock as a torturer. I want to ask the court to examine how a boy who everyone said was "a gem" became a torturer, who morally destroyed my family and my home?' Perhaps many other fathers are asking the same question in Chile today?

One ominous feature comes to the surface as the unofficial scrutiny proceeds in country after country, either through action by the churches, the trade unions, or through *ad hoc* investigations, and that is that the torturers' trade is not self-taught, but a common professional acquisition. It is not easy to get to all the facts nor the lines of transmission across the frontiers. For one thing governments have a strong distaste for unofficial meddling.

On 13 April 1977 six policemen without warrants broke into the Human Rights Commission offices of the National Council of Churches in Seoul and seized several bundles of files and documents related to the Commission's legal defence work. Arrests began the next morning. The group's determination at least to visit some of President Park's domestic opponents reportedly infuriated the US Ambassador Sneider, too. A career foreign service officer, he had been an advocate during his two and a half years of so-called 'quiet diplomacy', behind the scenes, to 'soften' Mr Park's policies. Guilty governments rely on diplomatic silence.

A 'Workshop on Torture in Greece and Portugal', held in London by Amnesty in November 1975, listened to direct evidence from the actual sufferers. The following revelations were made by the Portuguese participants:

Torture was most severe during the initial stages of the pre-trial period of detention (which usually lasted between 8 and 12 months) although it sometimes might continue even after sentencing. The most common method of torture was deprivation of sleep, usually for periods of five to eight days, although cases in which victims were kept awake for up to 18 days had also occurred. During the last three years of the old regime, virtually everybody arrested for political reasons had been subjected to the torture of sleeplessness by the PIDE (the security police).

The deprivation of sleep was the background of all other torture. Physical, psychological, electrical and chemical torture were additional. The torturers would record crying voices, including those of close relatives and play them back to the victim after days of sleeplessness. They would also subject victims, after days without sleep, to readings of jibberish by agents outside the cell.

Before leaving the satanic topic of torture and passing to its detestable twin, detention, some of the findings of the London 'workshop' can be cited to take one inside the 'clockwork of the torture state'. Given nearly half a century of dictatorship, the Portuguese PIDE worked within a firmly established and relatively insular political situation. Their methods of torture were largely self-taught and were applied as part of an overall repressive system which held the opposition in an iron grip. In Greece the military dictatorship, much younger and less stable than its Portuguese counterpart, was more sensitive to international pressure. With the military mainly in control of internal security, the methods used were generally of a more physical and primitive nature than those used by the PIDE. Partly as a result of the regime's instability, the Greek opposition appeared to be less organised than the Portuguese underground movements.

Nevertheless, the Greek and Portuguese experiences illustrate a pattern that is familiar to a large number of other countries. In the early repressive stages the military are usually the main agents in charge of internal security, whereas in more 'advanced' dictatorships the security police are usually the agents of repression. This is clearly the situation in the Soviet Union and other Communist countries.

The Greek experience revealed, so the 'workshop' participants asserted, a heavy dependence on the United States. But few hard facts have so far emerged to support this hypothesis. It was clear that more research is needed and, in particular, interviews with former interrogators. One of the former victims cited his experience on the prison ship *Elli* at the hands of a naval officer who boasted during sessions of torture that he had been trained to torture at a US Navy underwater destruction school. This experience was confirmed by other Greek participants. During the period 1967–71, when most of the interrogators were military officers of middle rank, some of them claimed to have received training at military schools in the USA. It was not clear whether this training was solely of a general military nature or whether it also included actual training in techniques of torture. It is known, however, that since 1947 thousands of Greek military officers have been trained in the United States.

The possible existence of training in torture in Communist countries should also be mentioned. One of the senior propaganda theoreticians in Greece spent some time in Eastern European countries studying psychological warfare. He became a professor at the War School in Athens and author of several books that describe methods of 'persuasion', which have since been used on Greek prisoners. Constantly disturbing evidence is emerging pointing at close international co-operation in teaching torture methods, which alone would seem to warrant substantial research into this whole criminal business.

LIBERTY OF THE PERSON

Few people realise, even today, how far many nations have progressed since the Universal Declaration laid down (in Article 9) that 'no one shall be subjected to arbitrary arrest, detention, or exile'. Set against their substantive achievement in guaranteeing the fundamental rights of their citizens, the record of the delinquent minority of states stands out in shameful contrast, as we shall examine below. It is in this field, perhaps, that the International Commission of Jurists has shown how a major non-governmental organisation can confront governments face-to-face as an indefatigable champion of individual freedom.

The International Covenant (Article 10) provides that all persons deprived of their liberty shall be *treated with humanity* and with respect for the inherent dignity of the human person. These principles have been recognised in the new constitutions of most countries. For example, the Constitution of Bahrain states that no person shall be subjected to physical or moral torture, or degrading treatment, and the law shall specify a penalty for persons guilty of such acts. In Iceland, the law stipulates that when a person is kept in detention steps must be taken to ensure that the person in custody is not subject to harsh or cruel treatment. The Constitution of Italy declares that any physical and mental violence to any person 'subjected to the restrictions of liberty' shall be punished. The Constitution of Kenya provides that no person shall be subject to torture, inhuman or degrading treatment. The Constitution of Kuwait declares that the infliction of physical or moral injury on an accused person is prohibited. The Constitution of the Philippines declares that no cruel or unusual punishment shall be inflicted. In Poland, it is provided that restrictions of individual rights must not exceed the necessary limits laid down for the proper punishment decided on by the courts; and that punishment should be executed in a humanitarian manner with respect for the human dignity of the sentenced person. The list of states who have translated these Covenant principles into their basic law is ever growing longer.

The International Covenant also provides that anyone arrested or detained on a criminal charge shall be brought promptly before a judge or other officer authorised by law to exercise judicial power (Article 9). By way of example, again, note may be taken that in many countries the law requires that the arrested person should be brought before a judicial authority shortly after his arrest in order to determine whether he should be kept for further detention.

In many countries the arrested person is to be taken immediately before a judge or a court. Thus, the Constitution of Cyprus stipulates that a person arrested shall be brought before a judge not later than twenty-four hours after arrest, if not released earlier. The criminal procedure of the Federal Republic of Germany specifies that any person held in custody, unless released by the police, must no later than the day after his apprehension be brought before a district court judge. The Regulations governing the Internal Security Forces of Lebanon stipulate that persons taken into police custody must appear before the competent judicial authorities within a certain time-limit. The criminal procedure of the Sudan provides that the person executing a warrant of arrest shall without unnecessary delay bring the person executing a warrant before the Magistrate specified in the warrant. And so on.

The relevant articles of this Covenant on Civil and Political Rights (see Appendix I) are in fact now part of the legal systems of most countries of the world. All in twenty years! What we are concerned with here, however, is how these principles are being abused and what remedies are being proposed, both on the official and non-official level, to prevent those abuses continuing.

We must first look at two exceptional and contrasting episodes – if 'episodes' is the right word – that occurred in the early months of

1977. They at least provided both diplomats and pressmen with material out of the run of routine debates on human rights! The first concerned the Soviet Union; the second the United Kingdom.

It is significant of the first episode, which took place during a March meeting of the Human Rights Commission in Geneva on the agenda item 'Question of the human rights of all persons subjected to any form of detention or imprisonment', that the Chairman of the Commission, Aleksander Buzović of Yugoslavia (as the record ran)

> welcomed, on behalf of the Commission, the representatives of the press media, who turned out in such a mass on the issue under discussion this morning, while on other issues, such as deprivation of basic human rights of 18 million Africans by the racist regime in South Africa, they hardly showed any interest.

It need hardly be added that the Geneva Correspondents' Association had their own views on the subject, and it required several closed but friendly meetings with the Commission's Chairman to 'clarify' the intent of his observations.

The episode itself, however, went far beyond this preliminary *contretemps*. It was introduced by the United States representative, Allard K. Lowenstein, who submitted to the Commission the draft text of a proposed telegram to be sent to the Government of the Soviet Union, which read as follows:

> The Commission on Human Rights, convened at its thirty-third session, mindful of its duty to promote and encourage human rights throughout the world, is concerned about recent reports of arrest and detention in the USSR of persons who have been active in the cause of promoting human rights. Desiring urgently to receive further information on this matter, the Commission would appreciate it if the Government of the USSR would provide information at the earliest opportunity on the circumstances surrounding the reported arrests and any further proceedings.

This draft proposal involved two days of public debate. At the very beginning Mr Lowenstein insisted that the United States' proposal could in no way be seen as an interference in the domestic affairs of another state. There had been several instances in the past when the Commission had seen fit to enquire into situations of human rights in other countries, including his own. . . .The United States proposal did not prejudge the problems in the Soviet Union, it merely sought information which would enable the Commission to form an objective opinion. The discussions should therefore be carried on in a spirit of détente and brotherhood.

Valerian Zorin of the USSR, however, was convinced that no one in the Commission – so he said – would consider the United States text as expressing 'a genuine concern for the promotion of human rights'. Worse, the proposal would ruin international co-operation and détente because it constituted a flagrant violation of the sovereignty of a state. Furthermore, the Commission should reject giving an arbitrary interpretation of reports concerning events in other countries. The USA had deliberately mixed press commentaries on certain individual cases with the official government policies. Mr Zorin was sufficiently precise to insist that people arrested in the Soviet Union 'were criminals whose conduct fell under the penal laws of the country'. To bring them to court was neither illegal nor constituted a violation of human rights.

He was followed by L. I. Maximov, representing the Byelorussian SSR, who asserted that the great revolution of the Soviet Union 'had ensured once and for all the enjoyment of economic and political rights by all the people'. What the Commission should concentrate upon was not to interfere in USSR domestic affairs under the fallacious pretext of concern over human rights, but to investigate and combat gross and mass violations of human rights. This was the case in southern Africa, in the occupied territories of the Middle East and also in Chile.

Quite apart from the opposition of other Communist countries, there was little backing for the US resolution, except of course from the West. For example, Judge Keba M'Baye of Senegal said that the Commission had a moral duty to act to ensure that human rights were respected, yet the Commission 'should act with circumspection' and not undertake a crusade each time it received information concerning alleged violations. Mr M'Baye appealed to the United States to withdraw its draft. Likewise, V. C. Trivedi of India, maintained that the Commission's main concern should relate to gross, mass and arrogant violations of human rights resulting from a government's official policies, as evidenced in southern Africa and the Arab lands occupied by Israel. International peace and co-operation and global détente were important elements of man's quest for a better life, freedom and happiness. He appealed to the US delegation not to press its proposal.

The view of the Canadian Parliament was that certain facts, since the signing of the final act of the Helsinki Conference, could no longer be considered 'as pertaining exclusively to the internal affairs of the signatory countries,' said Yvon Beaulne of Canada. The Commission could not remain silent because of legalistic reasons, while reports of violations of human rights continued to come to its knowledge.

The anticipated negative result of the debate – no doubt to the disappointment of President Carter's new policy – namely, that nothing should be done, did not preclude a reminder from the United Kingdom that the United States proposal was not unprecedented. Telegrams had been sent on other occasions to other governments including the United Kingdom government. Mr David Broad, for the UK, went on to say that the Soviet delegate should not take cover behind the doctrine of non-interference because, if all members of the United Nations were to invoke Article 2 (7) of the Charter whenever any human rights questions were raised in regard to their country, that would remove the constitutional basis for a great deal of the Commission's work. The Commission did not hesitate to set up a special committee to investigate violations in Chile. The Commission could not construct one set of rules for some states, and another set for others. That would be a surrender to power politics, and it would also be surrendering its moral credibility.

The second episode, to which we now turn, which was proceeding at Strasbourg at the same time as the foregoing debate in Geneva, brought the United Kingdom's own international record in a particularly sensitive area of human rights before a world-wide public. While a fuller comment on the purposes and constitution of the European 'system' of human rights must be deferred to later pages (Chapter 7), the essence of the *Ireland v. United Kingdom* case can be summarised in a few sentences. The long-term implications of this case will, however, be bound to bring about many changes not only in attitudes, but also in the slowly expanding mechanism of enforcement.

The case revolved around the use five years before (in 1971) of sensory deprivation methods by the security forces in Ulster for interrogating detainees. These methods were condemned outright as torture by the European Commission on Human Rights, under Article 3 of the European Convention, which reads: 'No one shall be subjected to torture or to inhuman or degrading treatment or punishment'.

The methods actually used in Northern Ireland in 1971 were hooding, electronic noise, prolonged periods of standing with fingers pressed against a wall, deprivation of sleep, and a diet of bread and water. The Commission considered that although the British Government had taken significant steps to abide by the Convention, the Irish Government was unable to accept that these measures gave satisfactory protection, so it had pressed its case.

The charges against Britain arose from actions of the security forces in August 1971, under a so-called 'Operation Demetrius', in which 354 people were arrested as a prelude to their internment. When some of them brought complaints of ill-treatment, the Irish Government in December 1971 made application to the European Commission, challenging under the Convention both the use of internment and the interrogation methods.

The Irish Government argued that the use of internment and detention was a breach of Article 5 of the Convention, which guarantees the right of liberty and security, that an individual should be told the reasons for his arrest and appear before a magistrate promptly. It was also alleged that Article 6, which guarantees a fair and public trial for any accused person, had been violated by the British Government. But the British Government argued the application of Article 15 of the Convention, which states: 'In time of war or other public emergency threatening the life of the nation, any High Contracting Party may take measures derogating from its obligations under this Convention to the extent strictly required by the exigencies of the situation, provided such measures are not inconsistent with its other obligations under international law.'

It can be seen at once from this bare outline of the main issues that a *cause célèbre* was in the making. The public were probably not aware that the European Commission of Human Rights had heard 119 witnesses before preparing a report that formed the basis of the court proceedings. That remarkable 'classified' document ran to 4500 pages, divided into fourteen volumes, and much of it remains a closely guarded secret. Among those who gave evidence on the operation of internment were General Sir Harry Tuzo, a former GOC in Northern Ireland, and Sir Graham Shillington, a former Chief Constable.

The British Attorney-General, Mr Samuel Silkin, QC, and a ten-man team of UK lawyers and officials came to Strasbourg to prepare and contest the case, which everyone knew could have serious repercussions on Britain's international standing. The Irish Attorney-General, Declan Costello, did not fail to point out that his opponents would have been in a stronger position if Britain had included the terms of the European Convention in a Bill of Rights.

Among the points that were most strongly contested was the continuing effort by the Irish to secure legal or disciplinary measures against British soldiers and policemen involved in the allegations, especially as the Irish delegation asked the Court either to order Britain to take measures against the individual men involved or to expand the Commission's original finding of torture to cover more than 200 cases of brutality, allegedly committed between 1971 and 1973.

Plainly, such a case, with so many related issues – military, political, legal, constitutional and international – cannot be evaluated in a few paragraphs. Nor can its impact on future British policy yet be estimated. The seventeen judges at Strasbourg closed their formal proceedings on 22 April 1977, thus concluding one of the bitterest public exchanges between two governments in the Court's five-year history. But on 18 January 1978 Britain was cleared by the European Court of Human Rights of the Irish Government charges that interrogation techniques on the terrorist suspects in Ulster amounted to *torture* in breach of the European Human Rights Convention. However, the seventeen judges ruled by sixteen to one that the techniques, used in August and October 1971 on 14 suspects, constituted a practice of 'inhuman and degrading treatment' in violation of Article 3 of the Convention. In a letter in *The Times* on 7 September 1976, the Secretary-General of the International Commission of Jurists, Mr Niall MacDermot, with others, had tendered some wise advice for the future, namely:

> that some of the other countries accused of permitting systematic torture will be prepared to take similar action and equally submit themselves to the jurisdiction of international inquiry bodies. Evidence recently submitted to the U.N. Sub-Commission on Human Rights suggests that these practices are still widespread, in spite of the universal support given to the General Assembly's Declaration on torture. We believe that torture will not be eradicated until there are effective investigative bodies both at the national and international level, and we hope that the United Kingdom Government will press for these, supported by its own experience in Northern Ireland.

JURISTS VERSUS GENERALS

There can be little doubt that the legal profession bears a special responsibility for the protection of every individual against torture or other cruel, inhuman or degrading treatment or punishment. Legislators are responsible for securing the prohibition of torture and a detainee's right to access to a lawyer upon detention and to other fair procedures. Members of an independent judiciary are responsible for the due process of law, to examine allegations of torture, and to exercise control over detaining authorities. And defence lawyers are responsible for exposing acts of torture that come to their knowledge. Academic lawyers and legal bodies also should take a leading role in improving the legal system and safeguarding it from such abuses as have been adumbrated above.

These are the objectives, in summary form, which the International Commission of Jurists has set before the distinguished judges and other jurists from around the world who comprise the Commission and its various national sections. Its main tasks were outlined in March 1969 in the first issue of its *Review*, as follows:

> On the one hand, the Commission must focus attention on the problems in regard to which lawyers can serve society and provide lawyers with the information and data that will enable them to make their contribution to society in their respective areas of influence. On the other, it must be the corporate voice of every branch of the legal profession in its unceasing search for a just society and a peaceful world.

The ICJ Secretariat-General has included Sir Leslie Munro of New Zealand, Seán MacBride, SC, of Ireland, and, at present, Niall MacDermot, QC, of the English Bar and a former government Minister. Its *Review* and other recurrent publications and studies, supported by numerous enquiries and investigations into actual local conditions, have provided governments and specialist institutions with factual surveys, as well as moral and intellectual leadership in the human rights movement of unique quality and persuasive power. At no time more than the present was this leadership more needed, for lawyers are themselves in the front line of attack by the torturers and tyrants.

The recent resignation of Dr Luis Requé as Executive Secretary of the Inter-American Commission on Human Rights is a case in point, and was a serious setback to the international implementation of human rights in the Western hemisphere. Under Dr Requé's guidance the Inter-American Commission had unearthed some remarkable findings about violations of human rights within the member states. It was normal practice for the Inter-American Commission to send a mission to the country concerned to investigate cases which appeared to merit it.

In recent years, however, it has become rare for any government to permit investigations of this kind and the Inter-American Commission has had to present its findings on the basis of the evidence which has reached it from outside the country. Findings of the Commission have revealed the torture and maltreatment of persons deprived of their liberty in Brazil; the execution, illegal detention or inhumane treatment of prisoners in Cuba; and the killing of over 100 Bolivian peasants by the army in putting down an anti-Government demonstration in 1974.

The most remarkable of its reports was on the violations on human rights in Chile since the military coup in September 1973. The report went into detail in explaining the overthrow of the Rule of Law in Chile and the violations of the Inter-American Declaration on Human Rights, including the systematic torture of prisoners and illegal killings by the authorities. When the Organization of American States failed to take any action on this report, and even decided to hold its June 1976 meeting in Chile, three members of the Inter-American Commission announced that they would not seek re-election.

Writing in the March 1969 issue of the *Review*, Seán MacBride had drawn attention to what he described as the 'Dangerous Swing Back to Militarism in Latin America'. The *de facto* military regimes in Latin America, he stated, gained a further foothold with the *coup d'état* that overthrew Fernando Belaúnde, President of Peru. It was soon followed by another in Panama against the President of the Republic, and a third in Brazil: 'An ostensibly democratic government (though it had come into power in circumstances that were hardly democratic) abruptly became an overt military dictatorship.'

But the overthrow of Argentina's constitutional president in 1966 was perhaps the first sad break in the century-long trend of most American nations towards constitutional government. Yet the cases of Peru, Panama and Brazil cannot be simply equated, since they are independent of one another, and their causes, arising from different situations, are distinct. Nevertheless, they do have one thing in common: in each case army officers assumed functions outside their field of competence and took over the entire administration of the state, usurping the powers of those who were in lawful authority.

In nearly every case the process has been the same. The president of the republic is overthrown by force and a military junta is formed. It promulgates a 'revolutionary law' and outlines a programme for governing the country. It grants itself powers which under the constitution are within the reserve of the executive and legislature. It allows itself the exercise of powers that become virtually unlimited, and it appoints one of its members head of state. Once the dictatorship has been installed, lip-service is paid to the independence of the judiciary.

It might be added that the implantations of military regimes in the soil of Latin America since 1966 is more disconcerting and alarming than the eruption of military controllers in Africa – in Uganda, Ethiopia, and elsewhere. In Africa, the army officers who have rapidly promoted and decorated themselves (from the rank of sergeant in Uganda and Zaire) to become dictators in their own lands, have few stable civilian rivals left and no mature administrative apparatus to take their place. But the countries of Latin America had steadily built up for over a century constitutional and social systems, often bearing a long tradition of democratic government and respect for the Rule of Law. The professional generals who have destroyed this slowly evolving structure of popular government – often with the clandestine backing and connivance of business and military assistance from the North – constitute a sophisticated power-complex defying outside pressures.

Amnesty International estimated in its most recent annual report that there were over 30,000 political prisoners in Chile, Argentina, Uruguay and Brazil alone. One result is that South American military leaders claim to have succeeded in crippling 'leftist extremism.' But, in the process, they have condoned murder, torture, secret arrest and other abuses of human rights. Repression designed to eliminate guerrillas has been turned against politicians, intellectuals, churchmen, journalists, students and foreigners who attract suspicion. The degree varies from country to country, but police sources, diplomats, international organisations and the victims all testify that basic rights are regularly violated by the police and the military in the six southernmost countries, namely,

Argentina, Chile, Uruguay, Brazil, Paraguay and Bolivia.

A new social phenomenon has therefore been developed by the military regimes of Latin America, to which no definite name has yet been given. 'Some call it fascism,' suggests the ICJ *Review*,

> but this is an inaccurate use of the term, as its ideology – so far as it has any – does not generally include either the corporatist or the racialist doctrines associated with fascism. It is, indeed, notable for the lack of any positive content in its philosophy. It is essentially negative. Its origins and its motivations are in the most literal sense counter-revolutionary. It seeks to maintain the capitalist economic system in its purest, almost nineteenth-century form. It represses all Marxist thought and all left-wing political activity.

Little by little a faceless system of power has gained ground. For it to do so, the democratic forms and procedures contained in the constitutions had to be abolished or their application suspended indefinitely. Repression has become a necessity in order to elim-inate, or at least neutralise, those social and political groups and trade unions which are the organised opponents of those in power.

Under these emergency measures there has been a continuous flow of repressive laws: legislative decrees, 'palace' decrees, military edicts and ordinances. These have created new political offences and military jurisdictions to try them, in place of the civilian courts of justice. Moreover, Argentina, Bolivia, Brazil, Chile and Peru have reintroduced the death penalty for political offences, although the constitutions of these countries prohibited the restoration of capital punishment.

Fortunately, however, the new Carter administration has been quietly mounting a drive to improve the machinery for the defence of human rights in the western hemisphere. He has recently urged each member government to pledge that it would allow the Inter-American Commission on Human Rights to investigate freely on its territory any allegations of human rights violations that it deemed worthy of probing. The United States will itself allow such access and will co-operate fully with any Commission investigations.

In face of the towering obstacles, lawyers nevertheless can and do find the ways, as well as the courage, to speak out as individuals or as a body. Many examples can be given of defence lawyers who contest evidence extracted from their clients by torture and of prominent jurists who denounce the gross violations of human rights in their own countries. Bar associations have intervened on behalf of persecuted colleagues. This intervention has often been successful; but in other cases their efforts have not only failed, but defence lawyers themselves have had to face the harsh consequences of their courageous actions, including detention, torture, and even death. The physical safety of independent members of the legal profession may become more precarious than that of anyone else in the community, once fundamental rights are violated; for, by the nature of their duties, lawyers are particularly vulnerable to these violations.

For example, in Franco's Spain, defence lawyer Carlos Garcia Valdes questioned his client before the Public Order Court in Madrid in January 1972 in order to establish whether his client's confession had been extracted under torture. He was charged with contempt of court and 'insult to the Spanish nation'. His conviction was reversed on appeal, but only after some 100 members of the Madrid Bar in an open letter to the President of the Supreme Court supported Señor Valdes's conduct and expressed their belief that 'Señor Garcia Valdes has fulfilled his duties as a defence lawyer throughout, and the fact that a lawyer can be persecuted in this context is a violation of the liberty and independence of the legal profession'.

In South Korea, Members of the Bar are frequently detained for questioning by the KCIA and the civilian police. Such periods of detention vary in time. The case of Attorney Kang, who was instructed to appear on behalf of the poet Kim Chi-Ha and nine Christian students in trials under the (now repealed) Emergency Regulations, is typical. On 9 July 1974, Attorney Kang criticised the court for not allowing him to make a full defence. He was arrested on a charge that he 'did defame the Constitution of the Republic of Korea'. Attorney Kang was sentenced to ten years' imprisonment, and a consecutive ten-year deprivation of civil rights. The effect of this sentence would be that he is prohibited from practising his profession until the year 1994, if the appeal fails.

In South Africa the case of Albie Sachs became well known. As advocate before the Supreme Court he conducted the defence in a large number of cases, some of them political, in which Africans were involved. In 1963 he was detained for 163 days, during which period he suffered psychological torture. Since then the South African authorities have become more sensitive about overtly harassing members of the legal profession; but their devoted work still meets with considerable obstruction from the judicial authorities.

From Egypt, however, comes an unprecedented move. A Cairo court in April 1975 ordered the Egyptian Minister of War to pay $75,000 in damages to lawyer Ali Greisha, who alleged that he had been tortured in the Cairo Military Prison in 1965, before being sentenced to twelve years' hard labour for 'anti-government activities'. The court further issued a recommendation that four former ministers of justice be tried on charges of having condoned torture and the degradation of Egyptian justice. Finally, the court asked President Sadat to order the demolition of the Cairo Military Prison, 'a monument to the humiliation of the Egyptian people'.

One function of the International Commission of Jurists is to monitor occurrences of this kind in whatever part of the world they take place. The ICJ also often acts as a kind of Honourable Opposition to the Human Rights Commission itself. For instance, one of its major concerns has been to try to ensure that the new UN machinery for investigating and dealing with alleged violations of human rights should be effective. This procedure for the first time in 1972 provided for complaints from individuals and non-governmental organisations to be investigated by the Sub-Commission, composed of independent members.

Some of the governments, however, are ostensibly appointing their own servants to the Sub-Commission, while complaints of gross infringements of rights are being shelved. The ICJ has therefore prepared a statement commenting on these subterfuges and delays, which was signed by over twenty other non-governmental organisations and presented to the Commission. At the same Sub-Commission meeting, the ICJ Secretary-General made an oral intervention in which he stressed, in particular, the intimidation of lawyers and the ill-treatment of suspects now taking place in a large numbers of countries. He affirmed the need for the judicial control of police and security forces, as instanced below.

The ICJ Commission's major interventions in the course of 1974, for example, concerned the trials in Greece, the consequences of military rule in Turkey, the torture of detainees and the suspension of *habeas corpus* in Brazil, the refusal of the governments of India and Bangladesh to return their prisoners-of-war, and the lawlessness and brutality of the regime in Uganda. Observers were sent to the trials in Athens on three separate occasions. The Secretary-General made a personal visit to Greece, during which he interviewed victims of torture and their wives, and visited exiles on Thermos Island. The ICJ press releases issued on his return attracted wide publicity.

Finally, we might observe that the International Commission of Jurists has been pressing for a long time for a more effective international legal instrument for 'the Protection of All Persons subjected to any Form of Detention or Imprisonment against Torture and other Cruel, Inhuman or Degrading Treatment or Punishment'. It points out that, without judicial supervision police and military forces often turn to these methods, and tend to become a law unto themselves, so that the basic rights of detainees remain unprotected. Torture occurs most frequently before the arrested persons are brought before any court, particularly when they are held for a long time incommunicado and without access to legal advisers.

The ICJ points out that various international instruments do already establish guidelines which can be used by national governments for this purpose. Those most directly applicable to the problem of the torture of detainees are the United Nations Standard Minimum Rules for the Treatment of Prisoners. The International Commission of Jurists' proposed amendments to the Minimum Rules would, first, make the Rules applicable to *all* prisoners, whether charged or not, and, second, incorporate in the Rules specific procedures designed to prevent the occurrence of torture.

It is not feasible here to itemise these rather lengthy technical proposals, but it would be appropriate to conclude this chapter by selecting just a few examples of the proposed amended texts which the ICJ has since 1977 presented to governments, NGOs, and the UN Human Rights Commission for eventual adoption:

No prisoner shall be subjected to torture or to cruel, inhuman or degrading treatment or punishment. Any official or other person who causes a prisoner to be subjected to torture or to cruel, inhuman or degrading treatment or punishment shall be subject to penal sanctions or disciplinary measures or both.

A prisoner or his relative or other person acting in his interest shall be entitled at any time to take proceedings before a judicial authority to challenge the legality of his arrest or detention and to obtain his release without delay if it is unlawful.

Any prisoner shall have an enforceable right to obtain

compensation from public funds for any material or moral damage he may have suffered on account of torture or cruel, inhuman or degrading treatment or punishment to which he was subjected while in detention.

An untried prisoner shall be entitled to communicate with and receive visits from his legal adviser and to prepare and hand to him confidential instructions . . . Interviews between the prisoner and his legal adviser may be within sight but not within hearing of a police or institution official.

No prisoner shall be subjected to physical or mental compulsion, torture, violence, threats or inducements of any kind, deceit, trickery, misleading suggestions, protracted questioning, hypnosis, administration of drugs or any other means which tend to impair or weaken his freedom of action or decision, his memory or his judgment, or to violate his dignity.

4 Raising a Double Standard

When the relations of my country with other nations are involved, I cannot yield to them. My politics have always stopped at the water's edge.
— *Henry Cabot Lodge (1914)*

What difference does party make when mankind is involved?
— *Woodrow Wilson (1919)*

No one talked of 'politicization' (with an American "z") until the mid-1960s, when the Human Rights Commision began to nail specific violations to specific doors of specific countries. This was bound to happen, sooner or later. And the states caught *in flagrante delicto* began to protest vociferously.

The basic reason is inescapable: human rights, by definition, belong to human beings. It is the state that must observe and protect them, or become delinquent. In that sense, all human rights are political. Hence, most of this chapter will be directly concerned with political issues. But a second reason has slowly emerged – as we noted in Chapter 1 – since the days when 'rights' were considered as the property only of individual citizens. State rights, always with us in one form or another, have recently invaded the realm of human rights and assumed the legal shape of 'collective' rights at the head of human rights instruments – a relatively new phase we shall pursue in Chapter 5. But a third reason is almost paradoxical: state rights attract a fierce native loyalty – sometimes blind and self-defeating – from nationals of that state, which often destroys or debases the rights of other individuals within its borders.

This chapter will be mainly devoted to enlarging on this last reason, as it applies to four countries in particular: South Africa, Chile, Israel and the Soviet Union. For those governments have attracted most critical notice and aroused most public controversy since 'politicization' became a convenient escape-hatch for delinquent states.

We cannot overlook the callous indifference shown in history by

the winners to the losers, by majorities to minorities, unless
restrained by effective law. A quite opposite view of the American
Revolution from the 'self-evident' Jeffersonian stance was expressed
by a contemporary poet, Charles Wesley, who in *Hymns on Patriotism*
opined that some quarter of a million pro-British 'loyalists' had fled
as exiles or refugees from the new American government:

> Where all are patriots, not one
> Will make the sufferer's cause his own
> Or succour our distress;
> Zealous for liberty and right,
> Humans, they cast out of their sight
> The sons of wretchedness.

Happily, two centuries later, even winners are developing more
concern for the feelings and the needs of losers. In a leading article
on 'Human Rights and Foreign Policy', the *New York Times* of 12
January 1977 stated:

> We shall soon have an Administration in Washington that is
> pledged to give human rights a central place in its foreign policy.
> We welcome that change from recent practice, understanding
> that it raises some extraordinarily difficult questions . . . But we
> should recognize that many of the most humane leaders of poor
> nations often cannot understand a concern for political rights that
> is greater than concern about poverty, and they suspect our
> motives.

The foregoing leader then raises a crucial point in the current
debate about 'double standards' today. It agrees that normally a
'single standard' is best for everyone, but it questions whether
'double standards' have not also their proper place in some human
rights contexts. In the United States, inaction over rights is all too
often justified by arguing that

> overriding interests were at stake (as in the case of South Korea or
> Iran); that the issue would politicize an otherwise nonpolitical
> forum (such as the World Bank); that applying sanctions against
> a government would penalize its least advantaged citizens (as in
> South Africa); or that pressure would be only counterproductive
> (as in the effort to require the release of Soviet Jews as the price of
> trade). These tactical questions deserve careful consideration.

They certainly do. But in this chapter we are examining the

'double standard' syndrome more as a matter of global strategy. Its use is more widespread than is often suspected, and it takes on a variety of forms. For instance, in Washington, human rights considerations have recently become an integral part of the process by which the United States allocates aid to other countries. Under the authority of laws enacted over the last few years, Congressional committees regularly scrutinise the political situations in countries receiving US aid. Congress has the option of limiting or even eliminating assistance altogether if it determines that a recipient government engages in a 'consistent pattern of gross violations of internationally recognized human rights' (which is the UN term).

'SELECTIVITY' IN ACTION

Examples of this are increasing all the time. A ceiling of $145 million was placed on aid to South Korea during 1974 because of alleged human rights violations within that country. In the same year, a limit of $25 million was placed on military assistance to Chile, a ceiling which was to continue until at least the end of September 1977. These precedents are based on the broad authority contained in two major laws: the International Development and Food Assistance Act of 1975 and the International Security Assistance and Arms Export Control Act of 1976. These Acts provide guidelines for nearly all US military support, development aid and agricultural assistance.

Perhaps the most ironic case of deliberate 'politicization' in recent years was the United States' own ill-conceived campaign – a backlash of the Nixon-Kissinger-Meany regime – that inflicted such calumny and financial straits on the International Labour Organisation, the world's leading champion of labour rights for over fifty years. Underlying the surface issue of whether or not the US would quit the ILO was an Arab-sponsored resolution passed by the Conference in 1974 calling for ILO action against Israel for alleged 'racism and violations of trade-union rights' in the occupied Arab territories. As a result of the combined voting strength of the Arab and other Third World countries plus the Soviet 'bloc' in the ILO's Conference of member states in 1977, the Communist and Third World countries rejected a high-level compromise proposal that the rules be amended to screen out such politically motivated re-solutions unrelated to the ILO's activities or bypassing its con-

stitutional procedures. They also refused to consider a routine ILO
report on Israel's responsibility to safeguard workers' rights in the
occupied territories under Convention no. 111, which Israel had
ratified. This was intended to be a direct affront to the United
States.

The ILO's governing body had recommended a tough United
States-sponsored proposal for this change, as a necessary step away
from the 'politicization' trend that the USA had denounced when it
gave notice of its intention to withdraw from the ILO, unless the
situation changed. Money-power is surely the worst form of
'politicization', when it is deliberately used to control the programmes of international bodies! The real scandal of deploying a
super-power's giant strength against these precious non-political
services – the ILO and UNESCO in particular – lies in the fact that
it ignores the only *political* change that matters, although it has been
shouted from the house-tops in vain for ten years by a hundred or
more General Assembly and Security Council resolutions – to put it
bluntly: *Get the Israeli invaders out of the occupied territories!*

Meantime, the damage has been done, and the United States
deserted the ILO on 5 November 1977, to the consternation of the
Western world. Yet it is no fault of the Specialised Agencies that 3
million Palestinians have been deprived of their rights to a
homeland. Nevertheless, the very existence of these essential UN
services is put in constant jeopardy by a super-power's politicising.
The majority of the nations who make up that nebulous 'tyranny of
the majority' are so poor and undernourished (and certainly
inexperienced in diplomatic manoeuvring) that their total financial
contribution to the UN's vital service agencies is infinitesimal. But it
is to *their* welfare and development that the 'advanced' nations have
solemnly committed themselves on a score of occasions and by the
principles of the UN Charter.

Nonetheless, a strong case can be made out, pending basic
political changes being carried out by the UN's political organs, to
safeguard the Specialised Agencies from 'politicization' from *all*
outside elements. Francis Blanchard, the Director-General of the
ILO, told an ECOSOC meeting that he regretted 'a trend which is
gaining ground in all the Specialised Agencies and which the press
sums up in one word – the growing 'politicization' of the United
Nations'. He rightly pointed out that:

While the Specialized Agencies are well fitted to deal with

questions within their sphere of competence, the Specialized Agencies are neither competent nor fitted to deal with major political questions which concern such matters as the maintenance of peace, and which are linked to situations outside their sphere of competence. Surely everyone realises that the consensus reached on the aims and work of the Specialized Agencies would be in serious danger if those agencies gave in to the temptation of dealing with questions outside their competence?[1]

In passing, it should be borne in mind that 'selectivity' is often related not only to a national but also to a cultural background. For example, a very challenging viewpoint comes from an Asian correspondent in Hong Kong. 'Asian perceptions of human rights', suggests Robert Shaplen in the *Herald Tribune*, 1 July 1977, are quite different from Western democratic ones. Not only are authoritarian limits on human freedom more generally accepted, but cultural, religious, familial and economic heritages and circumstances tend to preclude an active popular interest in the subject comparable to that in the West. He adds this cogent point: 'The high historic threshold of pain and suffering in Asia, unfortunately, has something to do with this.'

Some other forms of 'selectivity' by governments have evoked protests from non-governmental opinion. This was evidenced at an international consultation of church leaders from Asia, Australia, Europe and North America which appealed to the South Korean government for amnesty for eighteen imprisoned Koreans who had issued a declaration calling for the restoration of democratic government in South Korea. The consultation, initiated by the National Council of Churches in Korea in November 1976, declared: 'Christians cannot give their support uncritically to a Government for the sake of security alone. We believe that democratic governments that build trust are the best guarantee of people's welfare and national security.'

The main issue is by no means clear-cut. Selective morality is the general rule in foreign policy. On the very same day in December 1976 that the Inter-Parliamentary Union, concerned at the fate of Chilean MPs who were detained or had disappeared, had recommended to all its seventy national groups 'that Parliaments refrain from passing laws aimed at granting military or financial aid to the Chilean Junta', the World Bank President, Robert McNamara, supporting a $25-million loan to Pinochet's government, insisted that 'the Bank will run into problems if it begins to allow political judgements on various governments to influence its lending policies . . . loans should be approved or rejected on economic criteria alone'.

It would be easy to add to the contradictions inherent in day-to-day foreign policy, but difficult to pinpoint generally acceptable criteria for recognising human rights. According to an independent opinion from Japan, that of a leading businessman Jiro Tokuyama of the Numura Research Institute,

> The particular interpretation of human rights advanced by President Carter is very much American. Only about two dozen of the 147 nations that now belong to the United Nations enjoy anything even approximately resembling individual freedom as it is defined in the U.S. . . . President Park of South Korea, for example, has argued that keeping 35 million people free from Communist rule is the most effective protection of human rights possible in his country [*Newsweek*, 9 May 1977].

This sweeping generalisation is a long way from an important new voice coming from the Third World itself that was heard at a high-level symposium of jurists held in Vienna in April 1977 – that of the former Chief Justice of Tanzania, Professor P. Telford Georges. It conveys a much-needed caution against too complacent an acceptance of Western superiority. The one-party states of Africa may present a problem to the Western mind, but there has recently been a spill-over of the international human rights movement, and consequently jurists are revising their criteria. Professor Georges, now in Trinidad, told his white colleagues:

> The West in general, and the International Commission of Jurists in particular, have been quite misguided in asserting so confidently that human rights are incompatible with one-party political systems . . . Because one-party States happen to suit the Africans, it would be quite wrong to conclude that Africans are not therefore interested in human rights. Africans had strong customary laws about, for instance, wrongful seizure of property, and clear conceptions of guilt and innocence. Given time, one-party States can provide the indispensable stability that could allow human rights to be institutionalised and consolidated [*The Observer*, 24 April 1977].

BLACK HOLE OF AFRICA

South Africa has been the country under United Nations investigation for the longest time – in fact, from the formation of the
United Nations itself. For the Union of South Africa, as it then was,
rejected from the start the UN's request to turn over its mandated
territory of South-West Africa to the supervision of the Trusteeship
Council as a trust territory. To that rejection was soon added the
abomination of *apartheid*.

South Africa can hardly be said today – except by a few Empire
loyalists – to be a 'politicized' problem at all, though Prime Minister
Vorster declared that the World Court's adverse judgement in 1971
was a 'political' decision. On the contrary, it is a straight issue of
human rights: South Africa *v.* the United Nations. South Africa has
few friends in the world beyond those sections of the commercial
community who insist on trading illegally with it, in spite of
repeated General Assembly denunciations and Security Council
sanctions. Alongside South Africa we can, of course, place Southern
Rhodesia. But our stress in this chapter must be on South Africa as
the fountainhead of, in UN terms, 'the flagrant denial of human
rights to the African population and the brutal and inhuman
treatment of political prisoners in that part of the world'.

The Working Group of Experts charged with the investigation of
human rights in southern Africa was originally established in 1967
by the Commission on Human Rights to examine charges of torture
and ill-treatment of prisoners – detainees in police custody – in the
Republic of South Africa. ECOSOC then asked the Group to
investigate infringements of trade-union rights in South Africa. (We
shall come to these later.) This mandate was later extended by
resolutions of the Council and the Commission on Human Rights,
which, in 1975, decided that the Group should survey further the
policy of apartheid and racial discrimination in Namibia and
Southern Rhodesia, as well as the private jail and farm jail systems,
the 'homelands' policy and its effects on the right of self-
determination. So, for over a decade, a careful and exacting
investigation of all aspects of human rights has been pursued in
Southern Africa, reporting regularly to the principal UN organs, for
the whole world to know.

In the course of these ten years, thousands of witnesses have
been interviewed by the Group, innumerable reports have been

assembled on a vast range of topics. Dozens of governments in Africa and beyond have co-operated, and an increasing list of violations of human rights law has been itemised and recorded. Nothing like this supreme international effort has ever been conceived or accomplished before. There is no going back.

It is not always realised that UN investigations of this order of magnitude proceed on the strict basis of international law, and not on political grounds. In preparing their periodical reports the Working Group has acted on various international instruments establishing standards on human rights within its purview, including the UN Charter, the Universal Declaration and the Nuremberg principles, as well as major International Covenants on economic and political rights and the Optional Protocol which entered into force on 23 March 1976. To these must be added the International Covenant on the Suppression and Punishment of the Crime of Apartheid which came into force on 18 July 1976.

The quality and representative climate of this august Group is obvious from its current membership, namely: Kéba M'Baye (Senegal), Chief Justice of the Supreme Court (Chairman); Branimir Janković (Yugoslavia), Professor of International Law, Belgrade; Amjad Ali (India), Member of Parliament, New Delhi; Annan Arkyin Cato (Ghana), Counsellor, Ghana Mission to the UN; Humberto Diaz Casanueva (Chile), Professor of Spanish American Literature, Columbia University; and Felix Ermacora (Austria), Professor of Public Law, Vienna.

What do their reports consistently reveal? We can begin with the 16 June 1976 incident, when an estimated 30,000 schoolchildren gathered in their home town Soweto carrying banners with slogans: 'Afrikaans is Terrorism', 'Afrikaans–dangerous drug for our people'. A police contingent confronted 10,000 of them in Orlando West. When tear-gas failed to disperse them, the police opened fire. Within hours, road-blocks had been set up, but the police were unable to patrol the township. So, army helicopters, anti-terrorist police in camouflage uniforms and carrying submachine guns, and fourteen 'Hippo' armoured personnel carriers were called in. By 26 June, 176 people, many of them children, had been killed, according to official figures.

The violence had spread by 18 June to seven other African townships on the Rand. All African schools in the Transvaal had been closed, as well as the universities of the north (where students had tried to burn down the Afrikaans department), and Zululand, where young people had set fire to a Dutch Reformed Church, two liquor shops, the clubhouse, a school and the Indian shopping complex. The Minister of Justice banned all outdoor meetings. All boarding schools in the homeland of Bophuthatswana were also closed because of 'unrest in several schools'. This was a children's crusade for freedom and justice. It failed.

In the nationwide security clampdown of the next few days, the Minister of Justice admitted that 1298 people had been arrested as a result of the riots. On 17 September, when uprisings were by no means over, a UN report thus summarised the destruction and violence:

> The Government commission inquiring into the black unrest was told in Pretoria by a police officer that between 16 June and 30 August, the police fired 16,000 rounds of ammunition from rifles, revolvers, pistols, machine carbines and shotguns. Total casualties were: 120 blacks shot dead by the police, 50 killed by stabbing, shootings, assaults, stoning and fires; and two whites killed by blacks. A further 1,000 blacks were injured by shots, knives and in assaults.[2]

That was one notorious incident – or a series – widely covered by the world's press. But the Working Group's probings reveal a deliberately callous and humiliating legal system imposed on twenty million Africans and coloureds, dominated by less than four million whites. Hardly noticed, for too long, by Western media, because the hardships of these people were far beyond the West's experience, the daily torment of twenty million black and coloured people continued in silence year after year, until, only recently, these enormities began to crowd the front pages.

One of the bitterest hardships imposed over the last thirty years on the victims of apartheid (i.e. separate development) are the passbook laws. Blacks and coloureds consider South Africa's passbook system one of the most humiliating of discriminations. A total of 216,112 black men and 33,918 black women were arrested in South Africa in 1976 alone for passbooks irregularities or for being in areas not authorised in their books.

A network of pass laws under the Urban Areas and Masters and Servants Acts compels each 'native' to carry up to a dozen different passes. Being illiterate, many blacks may not be able to read them. The 'regular' ones include:

1 a residential or site permit
2 a lodger's permit
3 a night pass after 11 p.m.
4 a permit to seek work
5 a copy of contract with employer
6 a casual labourer's licence (if that is his work)
7 a registration certificate, if no contract of service
8 a temporary visitor's permit
9 an exemption certificate, if he is *not* required
   to carry a pass.

Although the 'citizens' of Transkei now carry their 'national' passports, restrictions governing the new document are the same as for the old. As they did with the pass*book*s, employers sign the pass*port*s every month – the white regime's guarantee that the documents are valid. Yet, once outside the Transkei borders, the 'citizens' find themselves foreigners within their own country – South Africa! Transkei was separate-development multiplied.

Apartheid has been described historically as an 'accumulative and purposeful system of racial containment'. Its components fall into four distinctive categories: (a) racial prejudice and discrimination; (b) racial segregation and separation; (c) economic exploitation of natural and human resources; and (d) legal oppression and police terror. Its proponents would have the world believe that genuine apartheid is merely 'racial separation', terror being simply a means to perfect the end! But, in reality, it is the terror, whatever the intentions of its perpetrators, that has become the true apartheid – perhaps its most indestructible component – and on which it must depend for its continuance.[3]

Racial prejudice is an attitude, a sentiment; but racial *discrimination* is an act, taken to the disadvantage of its victim. In Africa, apartheid has served three main social objectives:

1 to sustain among Europeans a communal sense of superiority;
2 to denigrate the capabilities of Africans; and
3 to protect the status and jobs of Europeans on the basis of colour.

It would be impossible to summarise, under the Terrorism and Anti-Communism Acts, the implications of thirty years of consistent terrorism, inflicted *on* the black people in their own land by the white architects of this police state. From the UN contemporary investigations we can, however, record a few factual revelations that must stand for the rest.

All the most influential leaders of the African people are today in jail – the leaders who might be expected, by education and experience, to form a parliamentary partnership with the whites in a democratic transition. Reviewing the events of just one year, 1975/76, the UN Working Group discovered that quite a number of persons detained during that period had already served jail sentences for political reasons. Among such detainees were Judson Kuzwayo, former member of the African National Congress, who had already served a ten-year sentence in the *huis clos* of Robben Island; two former members of the Pan-African Congress, who had also served sentences on Robben Island; Moses Ndulula, aged 80, a former member of the Pan-African Congress, who was released from Robben Island in 1971, and later re-arrested; and Mzimkulu Gwentshe, who had twice served terms of detention without trial under the vicious Terrorism Act. (He has since, in fact, issued summonses against the Minister of Justice for maltreatment while under detention.) In October 1977, the independent South African Institute of Race Relations reported that there were currently 662 persons detained without trial in South Africa, whose names and other personal details it knew.

The Working Group also noted that a very high proportion of school and university staff and students had been arrested in recent months. Among such student and university staff detainees were Sabelo Neko, twenty-one, a student from Soweto; seven Soweto high-school students, arrested on their way to Botswana for the Easter weekend; eight members of the South African Students' Movement; eight members of the University of the North (six staff and two students); and one staff member of the University of Zululand and another of the University of Lesotho, Botswana and Swaziland.

Since June 1976 the number of persons known to have been detained under South Africa's 'security' legislation was over 300. Another 5200 people had been arrested on 'criminal' charges arising from demonstrations. While some of them were later released and others brought to trial, many are still under detention for an indeterminate period *without being charged*. Most are believed to be held in solitary confinement, and they are often subject to the most inhuman tortures, as shown by the death under detention of a young black leader, Mapetha Mohapi.

Another feature of the detentions in September 1976 was the number of journalists arrested – reported as thirteen – most of them black and most of them reporters whose accounts had been a main source for newspapers nationally and internationally reporting on police repression in the black townships. Among those named in the press have been Steven Biko of King Williams Town, a director of the Spro-Cas black community programme (whose brutal murder a year later scandalised the civilised world);[4] Mrs Winnie Mandela, wife of ANC leader Nelson Mandela (serving a life-sentence on Robben Island) who is a leader of the Soweto Parents' Association; and also Joe Thloloe, president of the Union of Black Journalists. We have listed these few specific names because the Human Rights Commission is frequently assailed for pronouncing 'blanket' verdicts against delinquent countries.

In Geneva in June 1977 the international trade union movement struck back at Vorster's professional bullies on a scale never before attempted by workers' organisations. The Second International Trade Union Conference against Apartheid heard representatives of the International Confederation of Free Trade Unions, the World Federation of Trade Unions, the World Confederation of Labour, and the Organisation of African Unity, as well as representatives of southern African liberation movements and trade union organisations.

The Canadian Chairman reminded the Conference of the thirty-year-old Philadelphia Declaration of 1944, which redefined the aims of the post-war ILO, namely that 'all human beings, irrespective of race, creed or sex, have the right to pursue both their material well-being and their spiritual development in conditions of freedom and dignity, of economic security and equal opportunity'. How disgracefully this objective had been abused by the inhuman policy of apartheid was obvious, he said. The ILO had therefore devoted itself to the implementation of a programme to eliminate apartheid in labour matters in South Africa. The workers' delegates at the Conference and their trade union colleagues pledged themselves unanimously in these terms:

[The Conference]
Declares its unflinching support and lasting solidarity with the workers and people of South Africa, Namibia and Zimbabwe; Condemns in the strongest terms the continued arrogance in maintaining white supremacy by the racist minority régime of Vorster in South Africa . . . to enhance its repressive and oppressive measures against the majority people in defiance of

international opinion, while accelerating the totally unaccept-
able system of Bantustanisation, leading to making the African
majority people foreigners in their own land . . .

Denounces the role of the multinational companies collaborating with the racist régime in South Africa, aimed at protecting
interests and preventing the total abolition of the apartheid
system . . .

Calls on governments for action through the United Nations:
(1) to impose mandatory economic sanctions;
(2) to take immediate measures for an effective international
    arms embargo on South Africa;
(3) to initiate and intensify anti-apartheid action in all United
    Nations specialised agencies and inter-governmental organ-
    isations and to increase aid to the oppressed peoples of South
    Africa in co-operation with the international trade union
    movement . . .

If it is sometimes thought that these strongly worded but little-
publicised protests of organised labour across the world are over-
sentimental, then we can perhaps recall the more sober language of
the World Court in its 1971 Namibia judgement:

It was undisputed that the official governmental policy pursued
by South Africa in Namibia was to achieve a complete physical
separation of races and ethnic groups. This meant the enforcement of distinctions, exclusions, restrictions and limitations
exclusively based on grounds of race, colour, descent or national
or ethnic origin, which constituted a denial of fundamental
human rights. This the Court viewed as a flagrant violation of the
purposes and principles of the Charter of the United Nations.

It is to be noted, however, that the anti-apartheid movement has
been stressing more and more the scandal inherent in the economic
and financial support given to the Vorster regime from *behind*
certain governments, whose official spokesmen at UN meetings give
lip-service to this mounting public pressure. Addressing the 1977
Human Rights Commission, Ambassador Leslie O. Harriman of
Nigeria, who is Chairman of the Special Committee against
Apartheid, drew attention to this 'complicity' by relating how the
children of Soweto were murdered by FN rifles and Israeli guns
which had been licensed by a Belgian firm for manufacture in South
Africa. They were subjected to tear-gas attacks from Alouette

helicopters of the South African Air Force, purchased from France. Police officers flew over Soweto in Super-Frelon helicopters, also purchased from France. Tear-gas and ammunition were manufactured in factories set up with the collaboration of a British multinational corporation. Police reinforcements were flown to Cape Town in troop transports sold to South Africa by the United States.

These killings in South Africa should therefore weigh heavily on the conscience of many governments and many private companies. Mr Harriman urged that all such evidence of foreign involvement be investigated and publicised, particularly because, with the assistance of some Western Powers, the South African regime had been able to develop its capability to manufacture atomic bombs. The most sinister aspect of this clandestine assistance to South Africa was that some Western Powers had prevented an effective arms embargo by the misuse of their veto power in the Security Council and that they had continued to supply spare parts.

Finally, the preparatory committee of the proposed World Conference to Combat Racism and Racial Discrimination had agreed on the programme for a Conference to be held either in Geneva or some African country in mid-1978, including the identification of major *obstacles* encountered at the global, regional and national levels in combating racism and apartheid, and an evaluation of the methods so far employed for combating racism, as well as the formulation of effective ways and means for securing the full eradication of racism and apartheid.

The UN Secretary-General, Kurt Waldheim, summed up the present debate when he said:

> What we have today in South Africa is a dangerous confrontation of races, caused by the exclusion of the black population from the political life of the country and by the imprisonment, detention and banning of many of their acknowledged leaders. In my view the earlier Security Council recommendation for a National Convention remains valid today, offering a constructive approach for a peaceful and lasting solution.

Meantime, an outflanking movement (a more appropriate term than 'attack') had been happily evident in negotiations between five Western powers – Britain, the United States, France, West Germany and Canada – and Prime Minister Vorster over the liberation of South-West Africa. The near likelihood of an independent Namibia, under the transitional administration of the United Nations itself, would be a major influence in establishing democracy in Southern Rhodesia, too, and also a step towards the gigantic change-over required of South Africa itself.

It is significant that, appearing before the UN's Special Committee of 24 on Decolonisation in June 1977, was Garfield Todd, who had been Prime Minister of Southern Rhodesia during the 1950s. He stated that there seemed to him to be two possibilities before that territory: Mr Ian Smith could be induced to transfer power from whites to the people as a whole without further fighting, or the guerrilla war would continue until 'the gun' brought about the same shift of power. If the peaceful transfer of power could be made now, he said, a democratic state could be set up; but if the war continued until Smith was forced to surrender, so much damage would have been done to the institutions of government and to the economy that a totalitarian regime might well result. It will be noticed, again, that – as with Chile and Israel – it is a *political* charge alone that can remedy human rights violations.

With Mr Vorster's belated and reluctant agreement with the West in the summer of 1977 to abandon his own plan for establishing an ethnically based black government in South-West Africa under continued South African remote control, a faint light began to appear at the end of the tunnel – or rather at the edges of the black hole of southern Africa. This change meant moving, instead, toward an acceptance of free elections under United Nations supervision. Has the vast edifice of apartheid and racialism in southern Africa begun to crack, at last, and give way – even slowly – to justice and humanity?

CHILE UNDER THE JUNTA

The foregoing section on southern Africa has shown that working groups set up by the Human Rights Commission can deal only with investigating the gross violations of human rights, under the strict legal limits imposed by the General Assembly's guidelines. The fact that the remedies to be applied have to operate in the political sphere need not politicise individual rights as such, for these remain universal, no less than individual. The same rules apply to the parallel specialist groups on Chile and Israel. No doubt further specialist groups – one to investigate Uganda, for example – will appear as the General Assembly authorises them.[5] We can best liken this normal UN practice to that of the British Royal Commissions, with their specific objectives, impartiality of membership and investigatory procedures – but without the power to make recommendations. The Human Rights Commission does do that, however, on the basis of the reports of the specialist groups.

This thoroughness has certainly been true of the Chile Working Group, though the Chilean observer on the Human Rights Commission habitually insisted that its case had nevertheless been 'politicized'. Some members of the Commission have, on the one hand, added a new term of opprobrium to the Human Rights vocabulary and speak of the 'fascisization' of Chile. But its supporting countries, on the other hand, have deplored what they regard as 'singling out particular nations' in this way for condemnation. Human rights should somehow be kept general!

Carlos Giambruno of Uruguay, addressing the Third Committee of the General Assembly on 19 November 1976, said that a distinction had to be made between protection of human rights, as such, and the use of this subject to attack specific countries. In Latin America, it had been necessary to resist the acts of terrorist organisations which had aimed at the destruction of certain countries. And he added: 'If the Covenants on Human Rights are used to interfere in the internal affairs of countries or to promote terror, this would be contrary to the cause of human rights. Our efforts should not be focused on certain countries.' Humanitarian concern must come into play without political colouring. 'We are losing sight of the main objective,' he concluded.

To the present author, the destruction of human rights (and human beings) in Chile brings a particularly poignant memory of a labour-relations study tour of the country that he undertook in 1972, some twelve months before President Allende's assassination. Interviewing, as he did, heads of universities and colleges, trade-union leaders (many of whom have since 'disappeared'!), newspaper editors, factory managers and civic leaders, all the way down from the world-famous Chuquicamata copper mines in the north to the scattered farmlands of the centre and south, the giant struggle to survive of Allende's democratically elected Popular Unity Government was all too evident. No appraisal of what has happened in Chile since 11 September 1973, when Pinochet's military thugs shot Allende down in his own office and instituted a reign of terror, is possible without looking, however briefly, at the motivation and causes of this long-premeditated *golpe* to overthrow the leading democracy in South America.

In a masterly two-hour speech before the UN General Assembly in December 1972, Salvador Allende appealed for world understanding and moral support for the plight of Chile – 'a nation of close to ten million people which, in one generation, has produced two Nobel Prize-winners for literature, Gabriela Mistral and Pablo Neruda, both children of modest workers; a land whose history, soil and people have merged in a great sense of national identity'.

Chile, however, was a country whose backward economy had been taken over by foreign capitalist enterprises; external debt had swollen to over 4000 million dollars, the service of which represented more than 30 per cent of the country's exports. It was an economy extremely sensitive to outside events, chronically inflationary, where millions of people had been forced to live in circumstances of exploitation, misery and unemployment.

'Today,' Allende continued,

> my country is confronted with problems that are of the permanent concern of this Assembly of Nations; namely, the struggle for well-being and intellectual progress, and the defence of national dignity. The prospect that faces my country, as in the case of so many others of the Third World, is the familiar model of adapting an alien pattern of modernisation. The prospect before us is the same that we had always been forced to accept in our state of colonisation or dependency. We, the underdeveloped countries, are asked to agree to being condemned to a second-class, eternally subordinate status. This is the pattern which the working class of Chile, upon becoming arbiter of its own future, has decided to reject, striving instead for a rapid, self-determined and independent development and the revolutionary organisation of traditional structures.[6]

Allende then explained that, through a coherent programme, the old structure based on the exploitation of the worker and the domination of the means of production by a minority was now being superseded:

> Its place is being taken by a new structure directed by the workers which, in serving the interests of the majority, is laying the foundations for a pattern of growth which spells genuine development. The workers are replacing the privileged groups

politically and economically, both in the work places and in the communes and the State itself. This is the revolutionary content of the process now being experienced by my country today: the replacement of the capitalist system and the opening of a way towards socialism.

Yet no political prisoners were in jail under Allende, except where found guilty by a civil court of specific acts of violence.

Allende then passed to the crux of this 'genuine development' of Chile:

the nationalisation of our basic resources constitutes an historic act of reclamation. Our economy can no longer tolerate the state of subordination implied in the concentration of more than 80 per cent of our exports in the hands of a small group of foreign companies, that have always placed their own interests before the needs of the countries in which they are making exorbitant profits... The nation's recovery of its basic resources and the freeing of our country from its subordination to foreign Powers constitute the culmination of a long historic process to win political and social freedoms. The Chilean people's traditions, personality and revolutionary consciousness have enabled them to push forward towards socialism, while strengthening civic freedoms, both collective and individual, and respecting cultural and ideological pluralism. Ours is a continuing struggle for the institution of social freedoms and economic democracy through the full exercise of political freedom.

As I listened to this superb feat of impassioned oratory, which was followed by a standing ovation from the Assembly, my mind went back to the sprawling waterless shanty-towns and the thousands of little bootblack boys who eked out a meagre living on the streets of Santiago, for whom this socially-conscious medical doctor and former Minister of Health, was pleading. No delegate could have failed to notice that this declaration of political faith – a point he enlarged upon in his press conference under close questioning – ousted the unqualified label of 'Marxist', for any serious student of politics. Karl Marx would have turned in his grave if he had listened to Allende advocating social pluralism.

In another clearly anti-Marxist declaration, Allende said in Santiago on 21 May 1972:

We do not envisage the way of the Chilean revolution as the destruction of the State apparatus. What our people have built during many generations of struggle will enable us to use the conditions created by our history to replace the fundamentally capitalist institutions of our time by others better adapted to the new social reality.

Yet the press has desecrated Allende's regime and his grave with the opprobrium 'Marxist', one of the most dishonest trap-words of present-day polemics. This dubious label has politicised every genuine political and social reform in modern times.

What has since happened in Chile under its usurpers can be set against Allende's assertion that 'Our nation's democratic will has taken up the challenge to carry through this revolutionary process within the framework of a law-abiding and highly institutionalised State, which has been flexible to change and today faces the need to adapt to the new socio-economic reality.' His apologia was clear and frank: 'We have nationalised our basic resources. We have nationalised copper. We have done so by a unanimous decision of Parliament, in which the Government parties are in the minority. We want everybody to understand this clearly: we have *not* confiscated the great foreign copper-mining companies.'

At his UN press conference in December 1972, Allende emphasised that his enemies were not the American people, but the American business corporations that had robbed his own people of their birthright. Multinational corporations had pushed their home governments to interfere in Chile's life and to boycott his country, while international banks under United States pressures were deliberately destroying Chile's trading prospects. Within these foreign corporations, Chileans had never got the top jobs. His Government had never expelled foreign administrators and experts; they were taken back home by the corporations themselves in revenge for Chile's perfectly correct legal action. This had left the nationalised industries without trained personnel at the top. Allende declared specifically that he was *not* 'a Marxist politician', though there were Marxists in his Government. Marxism was *not* in his programme. His methods were modelled pragmatically on 'the integrity of history'. He rejected political 'dogmatism'. His policy was 'non-sectarian'. He repeated emphatically: 'My Government is *not* a Marxist government; Chile is not Cuba, but Chile!'[7]

But the dead weight of the US-based multinationals, the well-financed intrigues of the CIA, the 'Paris Club' of international banks and the secret military plots were dead set on 'disestablishing' this courageous innovator. All this massive intervention has been the subject since 1975 of US Senate investigations and many well-documented books – but far too late! Allende's defeat and destruction ushered in parallel regimes of military dictatorship across Chile's borders, as we have already noticed in these pages. Hence, ample space has been devoted above to expose the political origins of human rights violations in Chile. As in Greece, it is a *political* change that is awaited.

On 11 September 1973 darkness fell. The state of siege – a state of war against the whole Chilean people – still continues; though, under world-wide pressure, Pinochet promises 'democracy' *after* 1985! In Pinochet's Chile you can be arrested at home, at work, on the street, in a bus, or in a coffee shop. You can be picked up because you are a relative or friend of a political prisoner or suspect. Arrests are often made on the basis of anonymous denunciations and weeks or months pass before the authorities even acknowledge that a detention has been made. At four o'clock in the morning 300 workers and their families in one village were awakened by one of Pinochet's press gangs; the young men were marched off and shipped across the country to military training camps.

A not-so-subtle web of surveillance and police control has entangled the schools, the shanty-towns, factories, farms and public administration. 'We will continue to maintain the intelligence services,' Pinochet has stated, 'because it is the only way to provide tranquillity for the citizenry.'

Personal connections are no guarantee of lenient treatment. For example, Cardinal Silva Henriquez, now a refugee in Washington, told his bishops that the Minister of the Interior had refused to release the cardinal's cousin, Marina Marshall Silva, a middle-aged woman with a conservative political background, from four months' imprisonment, until the Church had agreed to expel a worker-priest who had fallen into official disgrace.

Monthly arrests started at several thousands. They still continue. An unknown number of detainees are still awaiting trial. Even those who dare to provide medical assistance for torture victims have been tortured themselves. Dr Hector Garcia, for example, Director of the Red Cross Hospital in Buin, was arrested and twenty-four hours later shot. More recently, Dr Sheila Cassidy's case received wide publicity, after it had come before an investigating group of the

Human Rights Commission and details were included in the official report, mentioned below.

Sheila Cassidy's torture in Chile led to the withdrawal of the British Ambassador from Santiago. Nor was she the first British subject to suffer in this way. At least five other holders of British passports have been tortured in Chile since the military dictatorship took over, according to Amnesty International. A Roman Catholic priest, Father Michael Woodward, was tortured to death on the prison ship *Lebu* in Valparaiso harbour. Brian Pollitt, son of a former general secretary of the British Communist Party, and a university lecturer in Concepción, was burned all over his body with lighted cigarettes. He now lives in Australia.[8]

Another notorious case was that of Mrs Inez Beausire, wife of a Bristol engineer, who was tortured along with two of her children, William and Diana, because another of her daughters was living in hiding with Andres Pascal Allende, a leader of the underground Movement of the Revolutionary Left. The irony of this event is that Andres's famous uncle had the utmost difficulty in controlling the illegal actions of MIR, who were on the extreme left of his coalition Government. Another young Anglo-Chilean with a British passport was Santiago Bell, who now lives in Cambridge. He was badly tortured and still suffers severely from the after-effects.

Though the Chilean government has continued to deny that it uses torture, the evidence to the contrary is overwhelming. Among those who have concluded that torture is used systematically in Chile are at least four international commissions of inquiry, two Chilean church bodies, a delegation of American professors of medicine, a judge of the West German Supreme Court, and the Cardinal Archbishop of Santiago, who has publicly denounced the use of 'physical and moral pressure' during interrogation. Many of the 12,000 or more Chileans now living as exiles in Western Europe were tortured before they were allowed to leave the country. Amnesty International's signed statements from more than 300 of them make convincing but appalling reading.

All the basic rights and freedoms guaranteed under the 1926 Constitution have been suspended or severely eroded by decree laws. Decree Law no. 4 appointed military commanders to provinces and departments covering the whole country, who can govern by means of local ordinances (*bandos*). All political parties are suspended and those of left-wing tendency declared illegal. No political activity of any kind is allowed. No one may demonstrate, even in favour of the Government. No free assembly may take place.

One half of Chile's union leaders were removed from their posts. Many have been killed, or have disappeared since the military took power, according to a report by the three-man Commission set up by the ILO in agreement with Chile's rulers. After a whole year's investigation, including a visit to Chile, the Commission said that a large number of union leaders had been eliminated through their death, execution, detention, dismissal, resignation, exile or disappearance; and it drew up a list in 1975 of 110 persons alleged to have been killed and 1200 reported still then under arrest.

Academic freedom has been abolished. The universities have been brought under control of the military. Some departments, including departments of sociology, have been closed on the grounds that the teaching was 'subversive', and degrees conferred by them have been retrospectively annulled. Many institutes and other centres of learning have been closed. Teaching and administrative staffs have been widely dismissed. Government informers are installed in the classrooms. Students were required to re-register and many have since been eliminated on political grounds. [9]

A nationwide youth organisation run by the government has added to the control over all schools and has given the military the capacity to regiment the country's youth. (We have seen this procedure before – the Second World War was the result.) Private houses are searched by the military or police at any hour without a search warrant. The DINA vans circulated through the streets for suspects.[10] Freedom of movement is severely restricted, internally as well as externally. This Tom-Thumb Hitler can take no chances. But the thousands of exiles are steadily forming a broad-based political opposition in North America and Europe.

From the beginning, church groups and foreign observers have reported constantly on the details of how government interrogators use torture in questioning political opponents. But the UN Working Group's report has since exposed the full horror of Pinochet's fascist hell. Some parts of this sombre factual enquiry read singularly like *The Gulag Archipelago*:

> Apart from being subjected to all sorts of brutalities, intimidation and ill-treatment, detainees were held in overcrowded places lacking basic facilities; they were denied adequate food and, in places like Dawson Island – situated near the Antarctic – exposed to unbearably cold winds, though they were without adequate

clothing or blankets. They were forced to work, often in conditions of extreme hardship, and they were psychologically terrorized by uncertainty as to their future and the fate of their relatives. Although their health was in a number of instances seriously affected, they were not afforded proper medical care.[11]

The Mexican Government, openly sympathetic to the Allende cause, has provided political asylum for more than 1500 Chileans, including Señora Hortensia Bussi de Allende, the late President's widow. 'Women that I have treated have been in terrible physical and psychological condition,' testified a leading Mexican gynaecologist: 'Some were repeatedly raped by guards in the prison camps and they're completely shattered by the experience.' Many of the children also required medical attention on their arrival in Mexico.

Following a full five-day debate at the UN 32-nation Human Rights Commission in Geneva in the summer of 1975, the Junta undertook to admit the UN investigating mission. But then withdrew permission.[12] Defying the Junta's later efforts to paralyse it, the United Nations team completed its first round of testimony-taking in September 1975, and continued hearing witnesses in 1976 and 1977. This five-member mission, headed by Ghulan Ali Allana of Pakistan, former Chairman of the Human Rights Commission, rejected Chilean attempts to halt the team's activities when barred from conducting an on-the-spot investigation. Rejecting, too, Santiago's demand that the mission stop its work on grounds of bias and that the mission was a 'Communist tool', and also rebutting Pinochet's contention that the mission was hearing witnesses who had fled long ago, the Group stated that of its Caracas witnesses alone, 'many had left Chile in recent months, and some of them in the last few weeks'.

The Working Group's periodical reports have described in detail the different types of torture which have been used, the places where it is being carried out, and the names of the seventy-seven most notorious torturers, including one known as Oswaldo Romo, who usually 'boasted to his victims of his prowess as a torturer and an extractor of information'. Among others specifically named are several naval officers.

Among the most common forms of torture used are electric shocks to sensitive parts of the body, including the genitals; rape and sexual abuse; the introduction of objects like sticks, bottlenecks and even guitar shafts into the vagina or the anus; and beatings, usually with heavy objects such as guns, wooden or metal sticks, and chains. One report describes as particularly revolting the *Pau de Arará* where the prisoner is suspended by his hands and feet from a bar, and tortured in that position. The report concludes:

> The fact that massive torture methods appear to be taught and learnt by investigating officers, whether members of the armed forces or not, as a technique or a new science, merely from the standpoint of their effectiveness and without consideration of any human standards, is ominous and calls for strong reprobation.

Although the actual names are generally excluded from this 100-page basic document presented to the Human Rights Commission and made available to the press (including some ten pages devoted to Dr Cassidy's testimony alone), the following two typical excerpts must stand for the rest of Chile's living hell.

A student leader who spent fourteen months in detention was rearrested at his home and beaten in front of the entire family. He was not informed of the charges. The torture to which this witness was subjected included beatings with rifle butts; he was made to kneel with hands behind his neck with head lowered, each finger tied to a finger of the other hand; his hands were then tied to his feet with a rope and he was made to walk on his knees for five or six metres to enter the compound where torturers were waiting. He was then stripped and enclosed in two sacks, both wet, down to the waist; the hair of his beard was pulled out through one bag and he was simultaneously held and bashed against the wall. At the same time his feet, hands, knees, body and testicles were subjected to heavy blows; then his feet were untied and he had to stand up and his genitals were kicked; when he fell down the kicks and blows continued. Electrodes were put on his temples, chest, genitals, behind the ears, feet, wrists. He was hung up from a crane above a drum full of water and submerged time and again. Finally, he was put into an empty drum, the lid was put on and it was taken to the top of a small hill and rolled down. This produced the effect of being hit simultaneously thousands of times and a deafening noise as if his head would burst. He lost consciousness and was put incommunicado in a cell for twenty to thirty days, but made what he considered to be a heroic statement during interrogation, as a result of which he was made to run naked at night before a jeep on the front of which was a soldier with a pointed bayonet.

An unmarried student stated that she was arrested by four armed civilians in her home at 3 a.m. Her detention lasted two months. She was blindfolded, stripped and searched, including the vagina. Interrogation started the same night. She was put into a room with thirty women and two young children next to the torture room; there was no water and they were not allowed to go to the toilet, so the smell was terrible; their hunger was so great that one woman tried to eat the cement from the walls. This witness was submitted six or seven times to the electric shock treatment, particularly to the nipples and vagina, for periods lasting from half an hour to four hours. She was raped many times and at one time tied naked and blindfolded to a narrow table, while people came into the room and made fun of her, smacked her and pinched her breasts. The ringleader said 'Volodia' would be coming into the act to do his bit; and then there was a dog on her body. This greatly amused her torturers.[13]

Among the documents annexed to this 100-page Satanic record is a sanctimonious letter dated 11 November 1975 from General Augusto Pinochet addressed to Cardinal Silva Henriquez, Archbishop of Santiago, commanding the Archbishop to close down the Peace Committee, which the Christian community had set up:

> I wish to convey to Your Eminence the deep concern caused to me by a campaign, which has reached levels that cannot be ignored, the evident purpose of which is to produce the erroneous impression that there are disagreements between the Roman, Apostolic and Catholic Church and the Government of Chile.
> . . .
> In view of these considerations, and after a sober analysis of the public occurrences and their repercussions both inside and outside the country, we took it upon ourselves to seek the roots of some of these occurrences and we found them in the Comité Pro-Paz. As a result, we have come to the conclusion that the aforesaid body is a medium used by the Marxist-Leninists to create problems that jeopardize public order . . . The dissolution of the aforesaid Committee would thus be a positive step towards the avoidance of greater ills.

It should not be imagined, of course, that the elevated line of defence inherent in this piece of hypocrisy does not also run through the many protests that the Pinochet government has made replying to the solid factual indictment drawn up by the United Nations and the world community at large. But what was becoming clear in 1977 were some minor improvements in the human rights situation, as a result of this massive world pressure. These have not, however, greatly impressed the bulk of the UN membership or the international jurists. For example, on 11 September 1975 the Junta had issued Executive Decree no 1181 as proof of 'progress' in the restoration of human rights. On examination, this new decree is seen to be an absurd piece of window-dressing aimed at deluding the United Nations and public opinion.

One of the most vigorous defenders of the Junta was Ambassador Sergio Diez, who told the Third Committee of the General Assembly, in November 1976, that in 1973, almost immediately after the change of Government, 'a sustained campaign of vilification had been launched against Chile'.

Turning to the actual report of the Working Group, the Chile spokesman said that almost all of the reported witnesses were political adversaries of the Government, leaders of the former Government, ex-convicts, persons condemned to deportation, and persons who had sought asylum for fear of being tried or imprisoned in Chile for their extremist and terrorist activities. Their impartiality was therefore very doubtful. Moreover, their statements were not new to the Government of Chile. They had been made on previous occasions for the political purpose of contributing to the overthrow of the Government of Chile, as well as in messages (again, totally irrelevant) broadcast from Moscow, Berlin, Prague, Havana and North Korea. Furthermore, some of the statements dealt with events which had taken place shortly after 11 September 1973, and had no bearing on the present situation in Chile.

The Ambassador directed his main attack, however, against the methods and procedures of the Group. Concerning trade-union liquidation, the Government had dissolved the Central Unica de Trabajadores because it had been a political organisation. Its last two presidents had been members of the Communist Party and at the same time, Ministers of Labour and Social Welfare. It therefore seemed paradoxical that Chile was accused of destroying that absolutist trade-union dictatorship. (The ILO's independent investigation took quite a different view, since a score of well-known trade-union leaders had completely 'disappeared'.) By various decrees, which the Working Group could have consulted, six trade-union federations had been authorised since 11 September 1973.

Point by point, the Ambassador thus took the Group's findings to task. Coming to the fundamental question of the allegations of maltreatment and torture in Chile, he pointed out, first of all, that the relevant (i.e. selected) parts of the Working Group's report had been made available to the Chilean press. His Government had been accused of all kinds of acts of torture and incredible stories had been invented, which could only have come from the minds of sick persons. The Government had issued strict instructions to prevent such acts and had increased the penalties for abuse of power. It was actively concerned to punish the guilty, in keeping with its Christian and moral convictions. But it was impossible to reply to vague accusations which lacked any sound foundation.

Concerning missing persons, it must be explained that in Chile a person could move from one place to another without reporting that he had changed his residence. It was therefore almost impossible to ascertain where a person was! More than 2500 persons had disappeared in Chile every year, for many years past. The High Commissioner for Refugees himself estimated that there were 10,000 Chileans in Argentina alone. (A shocking self-admission!) Between Chile and Argentina there were only a dozen frontier posts. Neither Argentina nor Chile had the money or the inclination to turn the Andes into a Berlin Wall. Strangely, the Ambassador had nothing to say about the list of 119 named persons published in the world's press.

An organisation called Relatives of Missing Detainees has since made dozens of appeals for the missing and swamped the Government, visiting dignitaries and international human rights organisations with information on their cases. But, in September 1977, a spokesman said that the campaign had been fruitless. None of the missing persons had been found, and no criminal charges had been brought against the secret police where the courts had established that the missing were in their custody. So twenty-six members of the organisation staged a ten-day hunger strike inside the Santiago offices of the United Nations. The strike ended after Pinochet promised Secretary-General Kurt Waldheim that he would provide information on the relatives. But, so far, the pledge has not been kept.

Three significant trends became apparent, however, during 1977:

1 The combined pressure of United Nations and massive outside public protests was obviously becoming more effective. The Junta were now living in a fish-bowl. As *The Times* laconically stated:

United Nations Resolutions may be brushed aside as supported in some cases by countries with even worse records in human rights, but other warning signals must be taken seriously. Foreign investment is flowing in much more slowly than expected by those who believe that businessmen like nothing better than a tightly repressed country with high unemployment. [6 June 1977]

2 The Inter-American Commission on Human Rights of the 25-nation Organization of American States published as late as May 1977 a 90-page report accusing Chile of *continuing* to carry out arbitrary arrests, torture and murder of Chilean citizens suspected of being its enemies. It listed 109 persons who had disappeared – about 20 per cent of all those known to have been detained by the authorities. Since August 1976, however, it also recorded that there had been a pronounced decline in the number of new detainees and disappearances; but 'these have not ceased'. There can be little doubt that Chile has since attempted to modify some of its extreme actions under the glare of neighbouring Latin-American opinion.

3 More and more political prisoners were being released during 1977. Some were even exchanged – in a flamboyant gesture – if they were notorious Communists, for political prisoners in the Soviet Union and East Germany! UN Secretariat officials have always been in favour of 'quiet diplomacy' as being more effective, in the long run, for getting results. Speaking at a public meeting at the Athenée Hall, Geneva, on 21 June 1977, Dr Marc Schreiber, former Director of the Division of Human Rights, which had been instrumental in compiling and servicing those many detailed indictments, claimed that five political groups (presumably former parties in Allende's admininstration) had come to him personally to say that the growing international campaign had already saved a hundred lives and spared a thousand other human beings from torture.[14]

Towards the end of 1977 UN pressure on Pinochet became so insistent that he announced the immediate holding of a national plebiscite with compulsory voting and confined to a single ambiguous question as to whether the Chilean people backed his government. With his chief opponents dead or in exile and no organised opposition permitted, nobody outside Chile was surprised at the announcement of a 75 per cent vote, but it enabled Pinochet to declare that no further UN commission or investigations would be tolerated by the Junta.

'ISRAEL AND TORTURE'

The above three-word headline is taken directly from the leading article of London's *Sunday Times*, which on 19 June 1977 broke through the silence barrier with which the press of Britain and America have muffled the ugly practices going on in the occupied territories ever since Israel quadrupled its geographical size in 1967 by invading its four Arab neighbours, Jordan, Egypt, Syria and Palestine.

Because our survey is concerned with the human rights of the conquered peoples, a factual recital of Israel's pretexts or reasons for the unilateral invasion at 7 a.m. on 5 June 1967 and for its continued occupation since then of the lands it overran – in spite of every appeal of commonsense and self-interest – would be out of place in this book. However, since the present chapter focuses its attention on 'politicization', and Israel and its supporters have complained of that more than anybody else, our enquiry can best proceed along these lines:

1 What are the human rights charges against Israel?
2 What political responses are involved?
3 What are the foreseeable remedies?

First, then, we turn to the allegations in the *Sunday Times*, which were carried across the earth in many other mass media and later debated in parliaments and public assemblies. Not that any of these allegations were new. They had all been exposed a hundred times before at numerous United Nations discussions and in UN documents, and had been itemised by name and date and occasion in the detailed reports of the Special Committee that the UN General Assembly set up in 1968, whose findings form the basis of this section.[15] What the *Sunday Times* did was to release information which respectable newspapers in the West had tried for too long to forget – while condemning, paradoxically enough, the UN Human Rights Commission as 'a farce of a body' because it had attacked Israel for seven years while remaining 'shatteringly silent' over Uganda, a few months earlier.

This strong 'Israel and Torture' article was followed by four and a half pages of detailed personal testimony and collateral evidence, elicited by a team of experienced researchers who had been moving around inside Palestine for over six months. (A privilege denied to the United Nations investigating teams!) They reached the general conclusion: 'Torture of Arab prisoners is so widespread and systematic that it cannot be dismissed as "rogue cops" exceeding orders'; it is 'sanctioned as deliberate policy'. In other words, the UN's consistent condemnation of Israel's illegal occupation is indeed politicised – but by the government of Israel itself.

In a cleverly documented reply to the newspaper some weeks later, the Israeli Embassy in London rebutted several of the specific cases listed by the researchers and concluded its defence by stating that, 'if clear evidence is produced', the Israeli Government would undertake to make every effort to investigate such complaints and to prosecute any policeman, soldier or security official involved. But no such evidence, they claimed, *had* been produced. This published reply was phrased in the same terms as Chile's frequent rejoinders; and it followed the pattern that the Israeli representatives, without visible success, have consistently taken at the Human Rights Commission in Geneva and before the General Assembly in New York, ever since 1967; namely, a blanket denial. Unhappily, across the painful years since 1967, the ever-mounting pressure on Israel to get out of the occupied territories has been resisted on the following political grounds: (a) We are a democracy, unlike the Arabs; (b) Jews in Arab lands are badly treated; (c) we hold on to the captured territories for our security; (d) the Arabs are much better off economically under Israeli rule than they were before; and (e) the Palestine Arabs are terrorists and not fit to become our neighbours. The steady movement of the Arab states over the last ten years to comply with the provisions of the famous Security Council's unanimous resolution '242' has not been met with parallel concessions by Israel's government.

What is consistently ignored in this context is that the occupation itself is illegal *ab initio* and a flagrant denial of the principles of the UN Charter and the Universal Declaration of Human Rights, as well as of international law in general. The Israelis cannot be right, whatever arguments they employ, so long as their occupation of the Arab lands continues to affront civilised mankind and the rights of the inhabitants. It is the Israelis who have 'politicized' the problem, not the Human Rights Commission.

It would be invidious now to travel back over these ten evasive terrible years, with which we are dealing in this chapter or to show what they have cost in human suffering and bitter deprivation of land and property for the Palestinians, let alone in fear and insecurity for the Israelis themselves. It is easy to forget the long-drawn-out agony of the two million or more refugees left over from the earlier 1948 War, when the Israeli state was founded through admittedly terrorist activities, with a bare majority of votes at the United Nations. (Britain abstained.) But 1967 brought further cruel displacements of the former residents of the newly overrun territories. For example, though pressed by the United Nations Secretary-General, following the 1967 War, to allow the 150,000 *new* refugees who had fled to Jordan, to return to their homes on the West Bank, the Israeli government permitted only 14,000 to do so. It refused to allow former residents of East Jerusalem to return at all, so as to Judaise the Holy City. Margaret Arakie, a British worker over many years with the United Nations Relief and Works Agency (UNRWA) writes: 'Those who had crossed westwards over the River Jordan joined their hapless brother refugees – some 580,000 of them – to live under military government, as the second-class Arab citizens of Israel had been living for nineteen years.'[16]

The legal separation of the two races and their distinct religions (at least in modern practical terms) has been aggravated by the separation of the families of the conquered. In simple human terms, the Commissioner-General of UNRWA pointed out that as a result of the 1967 much-lauded 'victory':

> The disruption of the lives and careers of countless persons, the anxiety caused by the sudden loss of earnings and remittances from abroad, the personal tragedies resulting from the separation of husbands and wives, parents and children, are only some of the problems which confront the former Arab inhabitants of Palestine.

President Pompidou was not the first (or last) Western observer of this deliberate separation of races to have remarked during a visit to the United States in February 1970, that Israel is 'a racist and religious state'. So this issue was not new when US Ambassador Moynihan contested it at the UN General Assembly in November 1975. The old British Defence Regulations are still the legal basis for the military government under which the subjugated Arabs in Israel have lived since the establishment of the state. Israel has, in fact, continued solely for the Arabs the laws of mandatory Palestine, including the Defence (Emergency) Regulations of 1945, drafted when Britain, at war with Nazi Germany, faced the eruption of widespread Jewish terrorism in Palestine. At that time the Jewish community of Palestine and its leading lawyers had protested against the inhumanity of these regulations and their violation of elementary human rights, that contradicted 'the most fundamental principles of law, justice and jurisprudence'.

Yet, this is the 'law' by virtue of which Israel, as an occupying power, is carrying on its government in the occupied territories and by means of measures such as the demolition of houses, deportation of individuals and imposition of curfews, allegedly under the authority of the same obsolete Defence (Emergency) Regulations of 1945. The Government of Jordan, however, has questioned the validity of the Defence (Emergency) Regulations being imposed as far as the West Bank is concerned. Such measures are illegal, Jordan has told the Human Rights Commission, because they did not form part of Jordanian law in 1967. Hence Israel, as an occupying power, does not have the right at all under the 1949 Convention to promulgate such laws – in fact, Israel has not 'promulgated' the harsh regulations made under them, but just acted on them!

The territories occupied by Israel as a result of the June 1967 hostilities fall legally within the domestic jurisdiction of three foreign States, the UN report reminds us, because this situation is governed by the Geneva Conventions, to which Israel *is a party*, and which should regulate the way in which, as occupying power, she should exercise her authority in the occupied territories. The proper law to be applied in the West Bank by Israel should be the Jordanian law existing at the time of occupation, and not the British emergency regulations. This is one instance among many of the basic illegality of Israel's oppressive regime throughout the areas it still controls by military force. In other words, human rights *cannot* be protected so long as the occupation remains. This is a wholly politicised situation, imposed by Israel and nobody else.

As a result of the further Israeli expansion and her occupation of the old city of Jerusalem in 1967, more expulsions and displacements of the rightful inhabitants of the city took place, as we have noted above. Since then, the 'Judaisation' of the Holy City has never ceased, despite recurring United Nations resolutions: the blowing-up of houses, the forceful eviction of families from their homes, the detention of those who resisted, and the expulsion of 'undesirables', all continue; and the Grand Mufti of the Moslems in Jerusalem, the Arab Mayor of the City and many other religious and administrative leaders of the City were expelled and have never been allowed back. Mr M. A. Nowar, the Jordanian Ambassador to Britain, has protested in these terms:

Jerusalem is a unique and most precious city in the world for Christians, Moslems and Jews. Israelis alone have no claim to it. They took it by force, unified it by force and are Judaizing it through occupation . . . King Husain has declared the following: 'Whatever the solution, the Jews of Israel need to be reminded that an Israeli empire is impossible . . . No temporal kingdom, even if founded in the name of religion, will succeed in imposing itself against the will of people indigenous to the soil, upon a people in their own homeland' [*The Times*, 17 January 1974].

It is not surprising that under a resolution entitled 'Respect for and implementation of Human Rights in occupied territories', the UN General Assembly in 1968 appointed a Special Committee to investigate Israeli Practices Affecting the Human Rights of the Population of the Occupied Territories.

In presenting its first report in October 1970 the Special Committee stated that a major obstacle that it faced at the very outset was the refusal of the Government of Israel to co-operate with it. The Committee was therefore not in a position to visit the occupied territories for a more thorough verification of the allegations made before it. However, the Committee felt that it has achieved its purpose of ascertaining whether or not the policies and practices condemned in Assembly resolutions were actually in existence in the occupied territories. Later annual reports by the same Special Committee have summarised the mass of documentary material presented to it in support of the allegations that the government of Israel 'has consistently engaged in policies and practices in violation of the human rights of the population of the occupied territories'.

The Committee has held hearings in London, Beirut, Damascus, Amman, Cairo, Geneva and New York, recording the evidence of persons with first-hand experience of specific breaches of human rights. It has also examined statements made by members of the Israeli government and other political leaders, relevant to these allegations. 'The Committee has thereby created a basis upon which a responsible opinion can be given,' they state. The evidence has revealed 'the grim situation of the refugees living inside the occupied territories'. The Special Committee visited some of the refugee camps *outside* the occupied territories 'and was deeply moved by the unhappy plight of their occupants'. Not all the efforts of the relief organisations that minister to the needs of these refugees 'can restore to them the conditions of social stability and economic security from which they have been dislodged by war. The Special Committee is of the opinion that there is an urgent need for the improvement of the lot of these refugees and displaced persons'. The Committee commended the United Nations Relief and Works Agency and the other organisations, 'whose devotion to the cause of humanity is universally recognized'. It felt, however, that the activities of these organisations, in particular UNRWA, should be intensified to ensure for the refugees a greater measure of the essential amenities of life.

The Committee put it on record, too, that

> the Fourth Geneva Convention of 1949 may be considered as the expression of the international community's sense of revulsion at the treatment accorded to Jews who came under the Nazi régime during time of war and occupation and who were subjected to indignities, abuses and deprivations in gross denial of human rights. Since the adoption of that Convention, the irony of history has made the June 1967 war between Israel and its neighbouring Arab countries, and the aftermath of that war, the first occasion on which the value of the Convention itself and the genuineness of individual nations' adherence to it could be put to the test.[17]

The International Committee of the Red Cross, as noted in an earlier chapter, was the organ with responsibility for ensuring the observance of the relevant Geneva Conventions; but it was placed in the predicament of having to fulfil its traditional role as the neutral instrument for the observance of the humanitarian rules of war, while avoiding involvement in acrimonious controversy through the disclosure of violations of those rules which had come to its knowledge.

Among the many witnesses from Israel itself who corroborated the general evidence of systematic violations of human rights was a representative of the Israel League for Human and Civil Rights, Mr Joseph Abileah, who was authorised by the League's executive to testify before the Committee. His memorandum referred to specific instances of breaches of human rights, such as collective punishments, the blowing-up of houses, administrative detention, expulsions and torture and killing during curfew, and he supported these allegations with statistics and the names of the persons affected. In an effort to eliminate any possibility of political prejudice or any other form of bias on the part of the Israel League for Human and

Civil Rights, the Committee subjected Mr Abileah to an exhaustive cross-examination, which left no doubt in the minds of the Committee as to his credibility. No Arab, of course, sits on this Committee.

One by one, year by year, since 1969, the Committee has heard the evidence of the Israeli lawyers and other legal witnesses professionally in contact with persons who complained of ill-treatment while in custody often citing cases of deliberate torture. Since the Government of Israel frequently insists that the International Red Cross officials do have access to prisons, it is noteworthy that the Committee explains that the ICRC cannot, by its statutes, divulge the evidence that it has collected of these violations:

> The International Committee of the Red Cross would risk forfeiting the prerogative it now enjoys to prisoners-of-war and persons detained under military occupation, if it revealed information which has come into its possession in the course of its humanitarian mandate and which had been made available to it in confidence.

This factor has made the work of direct investigation by a neutral UN body all the more necessary, since the Israeli authorities cannot hide behind the anonymity of the Red Cross. In September 1977, Israel's Attorney-General was still using the spurious catchwords 'because of security' to prevent access of the Red Cross to the interrogation centres, which the ICRC had never been permitted to visit.

In a long, critical article entitled 'The U.N.'s Double Standard on Human Rights', William Korey, the Director of the B'nai B'rith International Council, makes the assertion that 'the Commission on Human Rights succumbed to the thrust of the Afro-Asian bloc', by appointing the Special Committee to enquire into Israeli malpractices. In other words: 'the powerful Arab bloc has succeeded in adding Israel to the targeted southern African areas as appropriate for formal inquiry'. And he adds: 'Clearly, the machinery for human rights implementation is restricted to those areas in which the new majority has a direct political interest. The far broader gamut of human rights issues embracing all sectors of the globe is treated with deliberate neglect'.[18] These last words are true to form, but are refuted by every page of the present book.

What he fails to say is that Israel was 'added' to the Commission's special investigations because two million Palestinians were added to Israel! It was not the Arabs but the Israelis who sparked the inquiry. It was the Commission's constitutional duty to undertake the investigation, Arabs or no Arabs. Whatever religious 'claims' may have been acquired by certain primitive tribes to the possession of lands some 3000 years ago, mankind has learnt by painful necessity that the rule of law in the twentieth century is the only possible basis of human survival.

The official inquiry has been conducted legally under a General Assembly Resolution[19] that specifies the types of violations on which evidence is sought, namely.

(a) The establishment of Israeli settlements in the occupied territories and the moving into the occupied territories of an alien population, contrary to the provisions of the Geneva Convention of 12 August 1949;

(b) The annexation of any part of the territories occupied by Israel since 5 June 1967;

(c) The exploitation and the looting of the resources of the occupied territories;

(d) The changes in the physical character or demographic composition of these territories, including the transfer or deportation of population thereof or demolition of houses and towns therein;

(e) The pillaging of the archaeological and cultural heritage of the occupied territories; and

(f) the interference in the freedom of worship in the holy places of the occupied territories.

The Commission's annual reports to the Assembly are accepted by an overwhelming vote each time. There is no 'automatic majority' at the UN on anything. But the myth lingers and is cultivated.[20] This 'double standard' syndrome is exploited – still true to form – in order to blame the UN Commission ('if you have a bad case, curse your judge!'); but nowhere is it proposed that a democratic Westernised state like Israel should, on that account alone, adhere to the rule of law, cease its occupation of its neighbours' lands, and so set an *example* which would raise the Commission – and Israel – in the world's esteem.

Mr Korey himself recognises the need for a more positive Western leadership at the Human Rights Commission, where the United States – backed usually by Britain – characteristically assumes a negative stance, unless a Cold War issue rears its ugly head. He states:

> What becomes the principal task of those committed to human rights, in view of existing flawed structural realities, is resistance to any erosion of the basic norms already established by the U.N. . . . The task will require the United States to press its Western allies, all too often inclined to withdraw or abstain, to join in the battle for preserving human rights.

We agree. And if Israel is a 'Western ally', surely the same rule applies? But these fine sentiments are very far removed from the invective and uncompromising fanaticism that Israeli spokesmen bring to these debates. No-one who has listened, time and time again, in one or another of the UN forums, to these vehement outpourings of undisguised hatred of their Palestinian neighbours can have any doubt that only the combined and consistent pressures of the United States and the other 'Western allies' can break this vicious circle.

The essentially political issue of Israel's return of her 1967 military acquisitions to the lawful owners is obviously too complex to be carried further here, but it should finally be noted that, especially in the United States, the unquestioned and unyielding support hitherto given to Israeli policy-makers has at last begun to crack. Israel's endemic fear and insecurity, the tragic mobilisation of her youth and resources for defence – she has a bigger GNP percentage defence budget than any other nation – added to the impact of both the Arab oil-monopoly, her territorial losses in the Yom Kippur War, and the new initiative coming from Washington, have given belated second thoughts to many of her erstwhile backers, at home and abroad. American Jews are becoming Americans first. The errors of the Israeli politicians in preferring territory to justice can no longer be condoned.

William Frankel writes of the United States:

> The life of the Jewish community revolves round the fund-raising for Israel while, collectively and individually, Jews act as a pressure group for Israel – a factor which is part of the American political tradition. But a minority rejects the concept of Jewish nationalism and therefore the idea of a Jewish state.[21]

That minority is growing. What is abundantly clear by this time is that no Jewish State can survive, unless justice is done to the

Palestinians. The future of Israel and of human rights in Palestine are bound up together; they both await the overall *political* solution pressed again and again by East and West alike within the UN system and its many Resolutions. Only then will politicisation yield to security and peace.

Everybody now recognises that the Israeli-Palestinian issue moved onto a new level of discourse and action in November 1977. Although it is far too soon to assess the impact of President Sadat's act of superb courage and political sagacity in appealing to the world's conscience from the rostrum of the Knesset itself, life for both Israelis and Palestinians will 'never be the same again'. The only comment that would be appropriate here in terms of the foregoing analysis is that an overall territorial settlement within the context of United Nations peacemaking and peacekeeping procedures (presumably through a reconvened Geneva Conference) offers the only tangible hope not only for Israel's future security but for the restoration of the human rights of the Palestinian people as well.

THE SOVIET ENIGMA

Even more predictably than in the foregoing section, every attempt to explain or appraise with some faint hope of impartiality the human rights situation in the Soviet Union, or in other Communist countries, is certain to be immediately countered by an opposite explanation or blank disavowal. If the general press is any criterion, then the Cold War that has plagued West-Soviet relations for three decades had become a phoney war by the time the Helsinki Agreement was signed in 1975. The first irony of Helsinki and its recall conference at Belgrade in 1977 was that the original purpose of the event had little to do with human rights, as such, but most to do with strengthening Security and Co-operation in Europe. That was its declared objective. The second irony was that, when human rights (only one of Helsinki's ten principles) were discovered in Basket Three, they were seized upon by the West's hardliners as a weapon to fight the Russians. The deeper tragedy of this ideological distortion of purpose of an historic declaration is that the sword has turned out to be double-edged, and the chief sufferers have been the 'dissidents' themselves. This was indeed a double standard!

Since we have already, in this book, given detailed instances of

Soviet intransigence in coping with human rights in principle and of individual sufferers under Communist regimes, we can best examine the intangibles of human rights in Communist countries on the basis of three propositions, as follows:

First, their approach to human rights is conditioned by the external realities of an arms race and the concomitant military alliances;

Second, political rights are subordinated to economic and social rights;

Third, the West's past and present record in human rights blocks their effective influence in Eastern Europe.

These are bold and disconcerting propositions. But they are, unfortunately, substantiated by looking at some individual cases which we shall consider first. For example, *A Chronicle of Current Events* is published in English by Amnesty International and was initially produced in 1968 as a bi-monthly journal by members of the Soviet Civil Rights Movement. They created this *Samizdat* journal with the intention of publicising events related to Soviet citizens' efforts to exercise their fundamental human liberties. On the title page of every issue there appears the Russian text of Article 19 of the Universal Declaration of Human Rights, which calls for universal freedom of opinion and expression. The Soviet authors are convinced that such universal guarantees of human rights should be firmly adhered to in their own country and elsewhere. They also feel that it is essential that truthful information about violations of basic human rights in the Soviet Union should be available to all who are interested. So the *Chronicles* consist almost entirely of accounts of such violations.

Although the Constitition of the USSR (Article 125) guarantees 'freedom of the press', the Soviet state officially reserves for itself and for officially approved organisations the right to decide what may or may not appear in print. In the past decade and a half many Soviet citizens whose writings have not been published through official channels have reproduced their work in *samizdat* form. *Samizdat* ('self-published') writings circulate from hand to hand, often being retyped on the chain-letter principle.

The *Chronicles* have maintained a high standard of accuracy. The editors openly acknowledge when a piece of information has not been verified. In February 1971, Amnesty began publishing English translations of the *Chronicles* as they appeared. Amnesty has no control over the actual writing of the *Chronicles*, so cannot guarantee the veracity of all its contents; but it continues to regard each *Chronicle of Current Events* as an authentic and reliable source of information on matters of direct concern to the worldwide observance of the Universal Declaration.

It is impossible even to bring into a connected summary the many different types of cases printed in recent issues; but one can select at random two or three divergent case histories which are quite unconnected, except by the human tragedy they reveal.

The first case deals with what, in the West, we would call 'academic freedom'. The astro-physicist K. A. Lyubarsky appealing in a letter to the Executive Council of the World Federation of Scientific Workers and to the Executive Committee of the International Association for Cultural Freedom (Paris), describes the effect of the camp routine and conditions on the professional future of prisoners who are scholars. 'We are not merely temporarily deprived of freedom. We are deprived forever of our profession, of the work we love'.

In a labour camp, writes Lyubarsky, it is strictly forbidden to receive any scientific literature, even highly specialised scientific literature, which has been published abroad. Literature published in the USSR can be obtained from mail-order shops, but only recently-published books in little demand are actually available from these sources. Private individuals are categorically forbidden to send any literature. Private letters from colleagues – especially from those abroad – containing scientific information, are delayed by the censors for many months, and often withheld altogether. Academics, mostly no longer young, are subjected in the camps to hard physical labour, which they are not used to, and which leaves them neither the strength nor the time for intellectual work. Lyubarsky therefore calls on the Federation and the International Association, and on scientists all over the world, to obtain for Soviet political prisoners 'the right of free access to academic literature and the right to academic contacts'; and he also calls on scholars to send scientific material to their political-prisoner colleagues.

We can next group together a number of discriminatory *extrajudicial* persecutions inflicted in 1974 on several innocent believers of the Lithuanian Catholic Church. The education department in Vilnius forced a day-nursery worker, Miss Aldona Matusevičiute, to resign 'at her own request', as she was suspected of belonging to a Catholic order of nuns. For the same reason, Miss Monika Gavenaite was dismissed from the publishing house Sviesa

(Light) in Kaunas, also 'at her own request'. Miss Marite Medauskaite, a typist in a finance department, was dismissed from her job in April 1974, on suspicion of being a nun.

Even the manageress of a chemist's shop in Ignalina, Miss Albina Meskenaite, who attended the funeral of a priest, the pastor of Melagenai parish, lost her job. After an investigation of the matter in the district Soviet executive committee (at which the chairwoman said that people with a non-Communist ideology could not be the heads of civic institutions) Meskenaite was dismissed by the pharmaceutical board. She was told that she would not get another job in her profession in Ignalina district. And, finally, Zenonas Mistautas, a student at the polytechnic in Siauliai, was deprived of his grant and, in January 1974, his marks were downgraded on the order of the polytechnic's director 'for non-fulfilment of social obligations he had accepted and for failure to give a lecture on atheism.'

Yet, to the Western mind, Russia has always been an enigma. Dr Donald Coggan, the Archbishop of Canterbury, on his return from a twelve-day official visit to Russia and Armenia in October 1977, said that he considered it quite possible 'that the climate was easier than it was some years ago for men of religious faith in both Russia and Armenia' [*Ecumenical Press Service*, Geneva].

Among the 40,000 appeals that reach the UN Secretary-General each year from all over the world, the persecution of the Crimean Tatars frequently finds a special place. The pathetic details that are contained in these appeals can be instanced by the following statement to the USSR Ministry of Internal Affairs, sent on 23 April 1974, by the wife of Reshat Dzhemilev Roza of Tashkent:

My husband Reshat Dzhemilev was sentenced on 21 April 1973 by the Tashkent city court to three years of imprisonment in strict-regime camps on charges of violating article 191–4 of the Uzbek Criminal Code . . . He has been sent to camp UYa 288/7 in Krasnoyarsk territory to serve his sentence. This creates great difficulties for his family. We cannot make use of the right guaranteed by law of three meetings a year with our convicted relative. One visit alone to this distant camp costs two months' salary. I have three children and my monthly wage of 100 roubles is not enough even to feed my family . . .

Citizens convicted for taking part in the national movement of the

Crimean Tatar people for return to their Homeland in the Crimea have deliberately been sent to distant camps, as a result of which the right to three meetings with the convicted prisoner turns into a hollow mockery.

Most Soviet 'prisoners of conscience', according to Amnesty International, are imprisoned for violations of six articles of Soviet criminal law. Article 64 defines as an act of treason, as we noticed above, 'flight abroad or refusal to return from abroad to the USSR'; Article 70 deals with 'agitation or propaganda carried on for the purpose of subverting or weakening the Soviet regime'; Article 72 is directed to the 'commission of especially dangerous crimes against the State and participation in anti-Soviet organisations'; Article 142 proscribes 'the violation of laws on the separation of church and state and of school and church'; Article 190 prohibits 'circulation of fabrications known to be false which defame the Soviet State and Social System'; and Article 227 punishes 'the organising or directing of a group whose activity, carried on under the appearance of preaching religious beliefs, causes harm to citizens' health or other infringements of the rights of citizens.' The new Soviet Constitution, promulgated at the end of 1977, would not seem to have affected these crimes either in substance or procedure.

Furthermore, there are several hundred political dissidents confined in mental hospitals in Russia, held for months or years without open trial and with no legal redress, but who are perfectly sane. Psychiatrists are collaborating with the secret police to commit them on trumped-up medical reports. Yet, although it would appear that the psychiatric community has acknowledged abuses of psychiatry, the vote of 90 to 88, which passed the motion of condemnation against the Soviet Union at the World Psychiatric Conference in September 1977 barely shows majority support for the motion. One reason for this may be that the human rights of individuals are regularly violated in psychiatric institutions throughout the world. But no one who reads page after page of these pathetic records of discrimination and persecution can avoid two conclusions: (1) The truth is out – nobody, not even in the Soviet Union, can hide the ugly realities any more; (2) Behind all this is a frightened and apprehensive Government, unable to take any chances with anyone, however non-political. We are still living in the days of the Tzars. But time need not be devoted here in assessing how much of the cruelties of Dostoievsky's Old Russia linger on or whether the 'nature' of Communism is inimical to human rights.

What we are facing today is the systematic violation of human rights as an ideological or political principle.

The Western press has gloated over individual cases *ad nauseam*: usually concerning prominent Soviet scientists or academicians, like Andrei Sakharov and Vladimir Bukovsky. There is no call to amplify this selective press campaign here – since it is in intent primarily anti-Soviet, and human rights are a useful handle. We might rather ask how far this tidal wave of Western indignation has successfully swept up the Gulf of Finland all the way from Helsinki to the beaches of Leningrad itself? Or, how far it has failed in its purpose?

The answer is, alas, that this rising tide of Western moral protest—so loaded with political overtones—has encountered several unexpected mudbanks that have fundamentally retarded this massing of shame against the Soviet Union, and even turned it back. The Soviet Union's specialist on US affairs, Georgi Arbatov, wrote in a major *Pravda* commentary on 3 August 1977 that the political atmosphere between the two countries had changed for the worse:

> This is a direct result of the anti-Soviet propaganda campaigns which are being carried on one after another in the United States and also of the attempts and interference in the internal affairs of the USSR and other Socialist countries under the pretext of 'defence of human rights'.

Setting aside such imponderables as the 'nature' of Communism or the built-in defences endemic to a closed political system, two of these barrages have already been repeatedly stressed in this book. The first is what can be described as the stark reality of the present phoney war between the 'West' and the 'East', abetted and bolstered by a suicidal arms race of gigantic proportions that has turned Europe into a Berlin Wall of nuclear weapons. The second is the attempt, on the part of Israel, to transfer millions of Soviet citizens to fill the vacant lots in the occupied territories, backed by the serried ranks of self-proclaimed champions of Israel like Senator Jackson, who actually campaigned to trade Russian emigrants for US commercial favours. He lost, both ways. So the 'dissidents' question has never been a clear-cut issue.[22]

Both the foregoing elements – and there are others – of a concerted, or even unconscious, US policy of not-so-brotherly persuasion, have so far proved to be a diplomatic failure. They have muddied already dirty waters and served only to harden the Russian soul. Every session of the Human Rights Commission has heard the Soviet voice insisting (a) that there are no gross and consistent violations of human rights in Russia, as in many other countries, only individual cases of 'criminal acts' in breach of the ordinary law protecting the state; and (b) that the Western charges are an illegal and provocative attempt to interfere with Soviet internal affairs, contrary to international law and the UN Charter and opposed to détente.

Towards the end of 1977 a significant dialogue began to develop in the general press. What *The Times*'s leading article of 11 July 1977 described as a 'Russian counter-attack on human rights' emerged in response to President Carter's initial series of well-publicised appeals. This riposte certainly calls for careful reflection because, for one thing, it reveals the fallacies of unilateral attacks by means of a human rights 'weapon' on the Soviet system from the outside.

Most important, it lends added value to the United Nations' more tactful and less spectacular *multinational* approach to delinquent states. The same *Times* article goes into the nature of this counter-attack in some detail, as the following excerpts reveal:

> The Soviet Union is showing more and more heart-warming concern for Red Indians and Jews in the United States, Roman Catholics in Northern Ireland, pickets at Grunwick, and the unemployed millions in the West . . . In the United States, says *Tass*, the trial of two Red Indian Leaders shows that the authorities are attempting 'to make short work of the leadership of the indigenous population of America, who are speaking out more and more actively in defence of their rights'. *Tass* is also indignant about '158 million people for whom personal police files have been made, as well as thousands of people in jails on charges of dissent, and millions of Americans whose telephone conversations are bugged by United States special services in direct violation of the Constitution'.

> Drawing its information from Western sources, the East German press has similarly documented that, 'if dependants are taken into account', some forty million Americans suffer from unemployment and that in Detroit 50,000 elderly people live below the poverty line. Moreover, twenty million American children grow up without adequate medical and social care, and thirteen million American

families live in inadequate or indecent housing conditions.

In Washington D.C., states the *Neues Deutschland* (9 June, 1977), thirty to thirty-five families are ejected from their homes every working day; five million American children do not go to school; 1798 serious crimes are committed every day in New York; and American civil liberty campaigners known as the 'Wilmington Ten' have been sentenced to a total of 282 years in prison on trumped-up charges. It is also asserted that the working conditions of Hispano-Americans, brought illegally into the United States, are 'hardly different from those of coloured slaves in the last century'.

As *The Times* summed it up:

All this and more – the stream is unceasing – is part of the Soviet response to President Carter's statements on human rights to the review of the Helsinki agreement . . . and to what the Russians claim is a deliberate campaign in the West to divert attention from domestic troubles by denigrating and attacking the Soviet Union.

But perhaps the most cogent observation, from the point of view of our present study, and with which we might well conclude this chapter, is *The Times* statement that

Far more is involved than just a war of words. The Soviet Union has found that it cannot avoid being sucked into the international debate on human rights . . . It goes on complaining that the West is interfering in its internal affairs, but in the end it finds it has to take up the challenge in its own newspapers. This can hardly fail to have certain political effects. The effect the authorities hope it will have is to persuade their people that human rights are grossly violated in the West, that the 'right to work' is almost wholly ignored, that dissidents are treated no better than in the East, and that bourgeois democracy itself is a sham . . . usually the more people discuss human rights the more they want them, and in any case comparisons do not always have a one-way effect.

5 Self-Determination in the Third World

When I use a word, it means just what I choose it to mean – neither more nor less.

– *Through the Looking Glass*,
Lewis Carroll (1871)

So far, we have been dealing mainly with persons who are individuals. In this chapter we run into difficulties, because we are dealing with persons who are entities, 'peoples'. Yet it is with 'peoples' that the whole United Nations Charter is concerned – from its very first affirmation: 'We, the Peoples'.

At this stage, we shall not attempt to define what a 'people' is; but in the course of describing how the human rights system attempts to protect or uphold the collective rights of 'peoples', the essence and the scope of the term may become clearer, and also its limitations. It is really surprising in how many different legal instruments and declarations the term appears. Yet, as will be seen as our analysis proceeds, the attempt to confer on collective entities the same rights that can be applied to physical individuals leads us at times into an intellectual labyrinth.

The idea of equal rights and self-determination of peoples has come to be regarded as one of the most dynamic concepts in international life today. Its influence on both the political and the legal plane and also on economic affairs runs through the whole UN system. It is being accepted more and more strongly as a legal norm by legal authorities, with the result that it has now become embodied in international law.[1] Yet some serious doubts still remain as to its strict legality; and these will be faithfully probed in this chapter.

In its 'Declaration on Principles of International Law concerning Friendly Relations and Co-operation among States', for example, the General Assembly declared its conviction on 24 October 1970 in these preambular terms:

Convinced that the principle of equal rights and self-determination of peoples constitutes a significant contribution to contemporary international law, and that its effective application is of paramount importance for the promotion of friendly relations among States, based on respect for the principle of sovereign equality.

On the judicial level, the International Court of Justice, in two recent advisory opinions dealing with the legal consequence for states of the continued presence of South Africa in Namibia (1971), and with the Western Sahara case (1975), upheld the positive character of the principle of equal rights and self-determination of peoples. Referring to the development of international law concerning non-self-governing territories, the Court stated in 1971 that 'a further important stage in this development was the Declaration on the Granting of Independence to Colonial Countries and Peoples . . . which embraces all peoples and territories which "have not yet attained independence"'. This important Declaration will engage our attention later.

In the long process of affirming in law the principle of equal rights and self-determination of peoples, the legal instrument which marks a turning-point is, of course, the UN Charter itself. That is where the law starts. But this Charter principle is really an extension of the older concept of nationalities, on which international relations were based during the nineteenth century and at the beginning of the twentieth. The political origins of the principle have been, in fact, closely bound up with the national history of most member states of the United Nations and their struggle to attain or defend their own freedom and independence. The French Revolution of 1789 and the 'October Revolution' of 1917 were both outstanding landmarks in the development of this principle, which, by the end of the nineteenth century, had been accepted as one of the basic elements of modern democracy.

After the First World War, the principle acquired a distinct status under the Minority Treaties, as we noticed in Chapter 1, even though it was not formally included in the Covenant of the League of Nations. During the Second World War, it was proclaimed by the Allies in the Atlantic Charter of 14 August 1941. The provisions of the Atlantic Charter were later restated in the 'Declaration by the United Nations', signed at Washington on 1 January 1942. They were also included in the Moscow Declaration of 1943 and in other important instruments leading up to the San Francisco Conference of 1945.

The *principle* of equal rights and self-determination of peoples took formal shape and was embodied as such in the Charter of the United Nations. Since then the relevant provisions of the Charter have been interpreted progressively over the intervening years. And it has been generally recognised today that the concept of self-determination entails specific international legal rights and obligations, so that a *right* of self-determination accordingly exists.

Yet, as Jenks reminds us:

> The right of self-determination is of a wholly different nature from the civil liberties in that it cannot be made effective by legal process, and also from the economic and social rights in that it is not a guiding principle of national policy to be made effective progressively by legislation and administrative action.[2]

So lawyers have put this right in a class apart. As Jenks points out: 'The beneficiaries of the other rights require no special definition, they are men and women or other recognized legal persons.' Jenks therefore concludes: 'The first problem presented by any claim for self-determination is whether the group of persons claiming the right constitute a "people"; for on an extreme interpretation the provision would justify any claim to secession, wherever made.'

It would not be possible to deal in detail with this progressive interpretation in this chapter. But we can note that discussions in the Human Rights Commission and other UN bodies frequently bring out varying approaches as to how 'legal' a collective right can be or not be. As an example of this recurring ambiguity, we find at the 1977 session of the Commission the representative of the Federal Republic of Germany (no doubt with a doubtful eye on East Germany) stating:

> The term self-determination has not been protected against abuse, since this right comprises many questions which had not yet been thoroughly discussed and settled. It is still necessary to define this right with the clarity which is required, if it is to become a reality all over the world.

Less critically, the representative of India believed that the right to self-determination simply 'embodies man's desire to shape his own destiny and his yearning to live in freedom'. Being enshrined in a number of international instruments, including the United

Nations Charter, the *principle* was of equal importance with certain other fundamental principles, such as the principle of sovereign equality of nation-states or the principle of non-intervention in one another's internal affairs. These principles were linked indissolubly, the Indian delegate remarked; but the right to self-determination had a *definite legal character*, as a basic principle of international law. Therefore, its denial constituted a flagrant violation of international law. Furthermore, the right of peoples to self-determination was an indispensable condition for the realisation of the whole gamut of other human rights.

Egypt's spokesman, as might be expected, went further in the same debate and stated that the real enjoyment of all human rights and fundamental freedoms could be attained only when the right of a people to self-determination had been achieved. It was alarming to note that the peoples of Namibia, South Africa, Zimbabwe and Palestine were still kept under colonial and foreign domination. Yet the right to self-determination now constituted a binding norm of contemporary international law. The Pakistan representative took the same line, insisting that 'the right to self-determination today is a peremptory norm of international law'. And it is noteworthy that the Soviet Union representative recalled that his government had initiated the discussion in the United Nations of the right of peoples to self-determination. This right was the very basis of the existence of the Soviet State, this year being the sixtieth anniversary of the October Revolution. For such reasons, the USSR gave full support to the international movement to end the last vestiges of colonial domination. He concluded by stating that the struggle against it was entitled to take the form of armed combat.

We have featured this 1977 debate because it brought out more clearly than any formal legal analysis the real issues facing the Human Rights Commission. Against the rigid, take-it-for-granted views of most Afro-Asian and all the Communist countries that 'right' means a legal right, incapable of exception or contradiction, the British and US positions called for a distinction between 'principle' and 'right'. In any case, they said, a 'right' can be applied in different ways. Sir Keith Unwin, speaking for the United Kingdom on this occasion, observed that in so far as self-determination was a legal and not merely a political concept, it was properly expressed as a *principle* and not as a right. Nevertheless, as a political principle, self-determination must be subject to the obligations of international law, both customary and conventional.

In his view, this principle was not capable of a sufficiently exact definition, in relation to particular circumstances, to amount to a legal right. It was not recognised *as such* by the Charter or by customary or international law. The *principle* of equal rights and self-determination of peoples, according to Sir Keith Unwin, dated back long before the establishment of the United Nations:

It was intended by the framers of the United Nations Charter to be a principle of universal application, and not necessarily limited to independent sovereign states. But if self-determination were to be regarded as a legal right in itself, regardless of circumstances, it could be invoked in circumstances in which it would conflict with other concepts in the Charter; e.g. to authorize secession or to justify a claim to annexation. It must be considered, therefore, as part of the wider principle which recognizes both the sovereign equality of states, as well as the concept of self-determination.

This, of course, was very strong meat for the majority, for the very first Article of both the political and the economic Covenants, which came into force only in 1976, distinctly says: 'All peoples have the right of self-determination'. We shall look more closely at this important Article 1, when tracing some of the applications or implications of that right; but, meantime, it can be recalled that the US spokesman a year earlier had told the Commission:

The right of self-determination is the right of people to decide freely to which government they will pledge their allegiance, what form that government shall take, and who shall lead that government. It appears in every region of the world . . . a nation has the right to renew or revise its political charter as an intrinsic part of the right of self-determination.

It is beyond argument, the US delegate contended in 1976, that decisions imposed by the force of outsiders or a minority faction within a country are incompatible with the exercise of self-determination. 'For the United States the right of self-determination can never be exercised in the absence of consent.'

These comments from the West were, as it has turned out, not unseemly or untimely, for an ugly event had already occupied much of the Security Council and other UN time and energy in 1975-6, which threw the whole decolonisation movement, so to speak, into reverse gears. This was the 'invasion' (peaceful, to begin with, but nonetheless an invasion) of the territory of Spanish (Western) Sahara by Morocco, and the subsequent deal between Morocco and Mauritania to annex the territory and divide it between them. This blatant act of aggression and deliberate colonisation by two Third World decolonised countries, puts the whole decolonisation process – covering over two decades – back in the melting pot.

Before dealing with this reversal of the much-valued decolonisation process, however, it would be useful, first, to look at some definitions; second, to summarise the classic approach to self-determination, as formalised in President Wilson's League of Nations; and, third, to sketch its later progress under the United Nations Charter.

The dilemma posed by vagueness in fixing on acceptable definitions, may well be a false one, because some international authorities – for example, Mr Hector Gros Espiell, as a Special Rapporteur of the Human Rights Commission – have pointed out that since self-determination has been characterised as a *principle* of international law, this 'does not mean that it cannot also be characterized as a *right* of peoples'.[3] The divergence of opinion which existed on this point some years ago has been overcome, in Mr Gros Espiell's view, by the Declaration on the Granting of Independence to Colonial Countries and Peoples adopted in 1960 and by the International Covenants on Human Rights, which have provided the basis for acceptance in international law of the fact that 'self-determination is a right of peoples under colonial and alien domination and a necessary condition and inescapable prerequisite for the existence of all other individual rights and freedoms'.

That a minority or a foreign state cannot invoke the right of self-determination has nevertheless been raised by certain states, who have internal problems with their minorities or external problems with their neighbours. These governments (such as Iraq or the Philippines) have pressed the need to distinguish between 'peoples' and minorities, since only 'peoples' can possess the right of self-determination.

The United Nations has, however, established since 1960 the right of self-determination as a right 'belonging to peoples under colonial and alien domination'. But this right does not apply to peoples already organised in the form of a state, who are not under colonial and alien domination. Hence, it is to be noted that the 1960 Declaration and other United Nations instruments condemn any attempt aimed at the partial or total disruption of the *national unity* and the territorial integrity of a country. If, however, beneath the guise of ostensible 'national unity', colonial and alien domination does in fact exist, the right of the subject people cannot be disregarded without international law being violated. Thus, the UN formulation of self-determination may be put into a simple pragmatic form: it exists, where the *need* for it exists!

Yet there is, surprisingly, no text or recognised definition from which to determine what is a 'people' possessing the right in question. When various United Nations organs have examined the question of a definition for the term 'people', widely varying opinions have been expressed. One body of opinion holds that, in bestowing the title of 'people', no distinction can be made on the grounds that some peoples are under the sovereignty of another country or live in the territory of a sovereign state. In another view, the word 'peoples' should be understood to mean all those who are *able* to exercise their right of self-determination, and who occupy a homogenous territory and whose members are related ethnically or in other ways. The opinion has also been expressed that the right of self-determination should be accorded only to peoples who can lay an informed claim to it.

THE CLASSICAL APPROACH

In Chapter 1, the Wilsonian concept of self-determination, proclaimed in his Fourteen Points, brought us into a diplomatic minefield for protecting the rights of minorities in Europe. But a later authority has asked the pertinent question: 'What had become of the principle of self-determination only one year after the Treaty of Versailles'?[4] And the same writer goes on to insist in an implied answer:

Our starting-point, therefore, is not the statement of a right, but an attempt to discover how national self-determination has operated as an actual historical process. The demonstration of its practical inadequacy naturally leads to a recognition of the need for a fundamental re-examination of the theory.

While we cannot go deeper into the theory at this stage, it has to be admitted that, although Professor Cobban was writing in 1944, his strictures are still appropriate today, after three decades of 'self-determination' following the Second World War. The inadequacy of self-determination is not, alas, always apparent in the enthusiastic speeches made in its favour at UN meetings today. But it is not surprising, as we saw above, that some member states of the UN still refuse to accept self-determination as a 'right'; although it now stands as Article 1 in both the major Covenants. This is partly because few governments have faced up to the meaning of the territorial entity that is being 'self-determined'. Professor Cobban went to the heart of this hesitancy when he pointed out:

> It is one thing to recognize rights, and another to attribute them to a collective body such as a nation. Before allowing that there is a right of national self-determination, we should have to admit that the nation is a self, capable of determining itself, moved by a General Will, that is, and not merely a combination of individuals, moved by the wills and striving to achieve the desires dictated by a section or sections of their people.

No one will deny today, however, that since modern revolutionary theory has evolved out of the French Revolution, where we began our enquiry in Chapter 1, a 'people' has the right to form its own constitution and government and claim that it has a right to decide whether to attach itself to one state or another, or constitute an independent state by itself. Discarding the Divine Right of Kings, the new national and democratic ideas increasingly took shape and form and the people became a *whole*, called the *Nation*, endowed with sovereignty and identified with the modern state. How did this come about?

The break-up of the historic unity of Christendom was succeeded by the rise of the self-centred political state, with its unqualified sovereignty. Military force became the arbiter of its disputes and war became the instrument of its policy. Disunity therefore became the prevailing factor in this inter-state structure, with each state asserting its own will as the *final* law of its being. But alongside this, events and ideas were always working for an assemblage of unity and integration between states. Commerce was developing and new economic and social contacts between the national groupings were constantly being forged.

The Law of Nature was revived and adapted to the thought of the times, and came to be regarded as binding between nations, no less than individuals. Jean Bodin, for instance, in his *De Republica*, published in 1576, had expounded the view, which was becoming accepted among the schoolmen, that however necessary it was for

practical purposes for states to have a central authority – which was
the source of their internal laws – such state authority was, nonetheless, answerable to Divine Law or to the Law of Nature, and to those
necessary 'laws' which naturally arose in the intercourse of states.

This conception of the supremacy of the Divine Law or of the
Law of Nature, however ill-defined, facilitated the growth of the
operation of international law in later centuries. Grotius (1625) left
no doubt about the sovereignty of the moral law in dealings *between*
states. Thus, the hope of a new unity was engendered within the
disintegrating world of medieval Christendom. Henry Maine was
later to observe: 'The greatest function of the Law of Nature was
discharged in giving birth to modern International Law.'

The growth of international arbitration during the nineteenth
century and its partial success in settling disputes between sovereign
states; the attempted codification, in the Geneva and Hague
Conventions, of rules of humanity to be observed in war, and of rules
governing international commercial transactions, together with the
evolution of international functional organisations of all kinds –
these developments gave to international law a substance which
previously it had lacked. They aided the emergence of the
individual as a subject of world law. They were a tangible
expression of the one-ness of mankind and of the role of reason in
international affairs.

The League of Nations not only provided the world, as we saw,
with a comprehensive institution capable of limiting the irrespon-
sible sovereignty of its member states, but it also provided, as a
necessary complement to its political organs, the Permanent Court
of International Justice, which, for the first time, equipped
international law with a forum of judicial determination.

This event – barely a lifetime away – marked great progress in
world institutional unity. But it was actually a sham unity, in that
there was an almost complete failure to surrender state sovereignty
or political authority to these new institutions, and so translate the
precept of unity into the practice of unity. Neither the new League
nor the remodelled international law could hope to succeed under
conditions which left the old sovereign state still the final arbiter of
its own international behaviour and war the coercive instrument of
its will.

It is essential to our present enquiry to ask how far the United
Nations system has moved forward from this classical position.
Because, so long as there is insistence upon absolute state sov-

ereignty in inter-state relations, so will there continue to be a denial of individual responsibility. For without individual responsibility for world peace, no 'law' can fully function. *The right to peace* – not yet included in any official instrument – is the essence of the rule of law in world affairs. (We shall come back to this argument in our final chapter.)

World law cannot function in a system where the state is still personified and clothed with the faculties of a rational and sentient being. To assert that the state *alone* is a person ('persona') defeats the ends of such purported law, for it tries to vest a political notion with the attributes of a living moral person. This imperialist conception of law (as Léon Duguit thought of it), on the one hand, attempted for two centuries or more to make the state the subject of 'rights'. The democratic conception of law, on the other hand, attempts rather to make the state an organ of social duties. Was Article 1 of the two Covenants, therefore, a throwback?

It is that democratic conception that permeates the UN Charter, though the Charter, paradoxically, also perpetuates the illusions of the sovereign state. But perhaps there is a fresh new voice breaking into these ancient precepts? Comparing persons who have been deprived of their rights with victims of an earthquake, Andrew Young, US Ambassador to the United Nations, declared on 10 August 1977: 'In many respects, human rights assistance is like earthquake assistance. When the overwhelming human need cries out, national sovereignty becomes less important than the human need'. Andy Young has made the Carter administration's controversial championing of human rights the dominant note of almost all his statements since he assumed office. Will this effervescent spirit move into other spheres and help galvanise the whole UN system?

DECOLONISATION

Colonialism, alien domination, racial discrimination and apartheid are associated together in many UN decisions as being incompatible with the right of peoples to self-determination. In this context, it is claimed that the primary solution to the problems of human rights lies in accession to independence. Colonialism and other forms of subjugation are not only incompatible with human dignity, but an obstacle to international peace and co-operation. 'Any form of alien oppression is incompatible with the right of peoples to decide their own fate, and irreconcilable with their independence and equality.' This is the consistent stance of the UN. In Resolution 2105 (XX) on the implementation of the 1960 Declaration on the Granting of Independence to Colonial Countries and Peoples, the General Assembly declared itself plainly: 'Fully aware that the continuation of colonial rule and the practice of *apartheid*, as well as all forms of racial discrimination, threaten international peace and security and constitute a crime against humanity . . .'[5]

In proof thereof, more than seventy nations, whose 'peoples' were once under colonial rule, have joined the United Nations as sovereign independent states since 1945. In this transition of millions of people from colonial domination to national freedom, the United Nations has played a truly crucial role. These decolonisation efforts of the world organisation have given impetus over the years to the aspirations and struggles of many formerly dependent peoples. They derive from the Charter, which asserts the principle of 'equal rights and self-determination of peoples', and which sets out the obligations of member states responsible for the administration of dependent territories in three separate chapters: Chapter XI, which deals with dependent territories in general, and Chapters XII and XIII, which provide for the Trusteeship System.

The United Nations took over the supervision of the League of Nations Mandates and assumed the same task for territories detached from enemy States after the Second World War. The Trusteeship Council was established under the Charter to assist the Assembly in the operation of the System. Eventually, eleven 'Trust Territories' were placed under the Trusteeship System through individual agreements. The administering member states agreed to promote the development of the inhabitants towards government – all except South Africa. So 'decolonisation' is by no means a recent story. It made considerable gains under the Trusteeship System. The process was accelerated by the landmark Declaration on the Granting of Independence to Colonial Countries and Peoples, proclaimed by the General Assembly in 1960. A Special Committee of 24 on decolonisation was established in 1961 to examine the progress actually made in realising that Declaration. Despite the vast inroads made against colonialism, however, there are peoples in various parts of the world still living under alien rule. That is the problem today, since illegal minority regimes in southern Africa continue to oppress the peoples of Southern Rhodesia and Namibia.

The 1960 Declaration began:

Mindful of the determination proclaimed by the peoples of the world in the Charter of the United Nations to reaffirm faith in fundamental human rights, in the dignity and worth of the human person, in the equal rights of men and women and of nations large and small and to promote social progress and better standards of life in larger freedom. . . .

It also stated that 'all armed action or repressive measures' against dependent peoples shall cease, so that they might 'peacefully and freely exercise their right to complete independence'. It called for immediate steps to be taken in all territories which had not 'yet attained independence to transfer all powers to the peoples'. And, for nearly two decades, the Committee of 24 has vigorously examined the application of this Declaration, gathered information on obstacles to its application, and made numerous recommendations to speed its implementation. The Committee has also despatched missions to various territories to gain information at first hand, and has established contact with the representatives of national liberation movements, with the result that, within these two last decades, more than 70 million people have emerged from dependent status, and there has been a consequent increase in United Nations membership from 100 to 147 by the end of 1976.

A major achievement towards ending colonialism took place when, following a change in government, Portugal advised the Secretary-General in August 1974 that it was ready to co-operate fully with the United Nations on the decolonisation of its African territories. Angola and Mozambique have since attained independence – though it is typical of the endemic astigmatism of the world's news media that far more attention was devoted to 'guerrilla' activity (local and foreign) than to yet another example of non-violent decolonisation under UN guidelines.

Since the decolonisation aspects of self-determination so obviously include both political and economic aspects, practically the whole UN system is nowadays involved at some point in this field. For example, the Security Council is continuously engaged with sanctions over southern Africa. So it should be borne in mind that the Human Rights Commission itself can deal with only one segment of the total question.

We must therefore turn to consider the dangers of a new type of economic imperialism, and do so under two heads – the Western

Sahara case and the recent transfer of arms to the Third World – before concluding this chapter with a more positive look at how all this relates to the economic and social rights laid down in the 1976 Covenant.

THE SAHARA CASE

The gravest setback that the Human Rights movement has suffered in respect of the 'right' of self-determination cannot be laid at the door of either the 'Western imperialists' or the 'Communist bloc', but on the shoulders of the decolonised world itself. This unconscionable episode in North-West Africa has been aptly condemned by a leading international lawyer as 'the stealing of the Sahara'. Under this heading Professor Thomas M. Franck of New York University has described how:

> Morocco and Mauritania, by their take-over of the Sahara without the consent of its people, have succeeded in frustrating the application of this norm and have taken the international system a blatant step toward a new set of mutually shared expectations about state behavior – incipient new norms – which are much more likely than their predecessor-rules to be conflict-inducing, even if their outlines are as yet dimly perceived.[6]

The seriousness of this warning is evident when one looks further afield and watches the same land-grab mentality at work in Indonesia, in spite of the UN's continuing efforts to sustain the rights of the 'peoples' of East Timor in their bid for independence and self-determination. Unanswered questions are also being asked: 'Will Guatemala overrun Belize [British Honduras]?', and parallel questions about the Falkland Islands, Palestine, Gibraltar and other 'colonial' territories.

The evil precedent of the Sahara is particularly disturbing because of its long and intensive scrutiny on several agendas of the United Nations since 1956 – all in vain. For, as Professor Franck has rightly stressed:

> The failure of the United Nations to ensure a self-determination election or plebiscite in the Sahara before its final decolonization is a break not only with a well-established and salutary general pattern of norms for colonies in general, but also with the policy

consistently advocated specifically for the Sahara in U.N. debates and resolutions during more than a decade.

The history of the manoeuvres of two fledgling states, recently decolonised themselves, to annex and divide their neighbour as common booty was analysed in comprehensive and meticulous detail in an Advisory Opinion of the World Court, given to the General Assembly in 1975. But here we can only summarise the essential issues as they bear on the expressed wishes of its people – or a vocal majority of them –for independence and self-determination under the UN Charter.

Western (formerly Spanish) Sahara has only about 75,000 inhabitants within a narrow coastal strip of 266,000 square kilometres. A UN Visiting Mission to the territory in 1975 reported that

> the indigenous population of the Territory is comprised for the most part of persons of Moorish, or Bedouin, race who are united by a common language, by strong cultural and traditional ties . . . Today, though nomadism is declining, there is still a marked sense of kindred among the members of tribes and their subdivisions which straddle the frontiers of the Territory and its neighbours, and many Saharans have left the Territory either to live permanently among their relatives and kindred in the neighbouring countries, or to settle temporarily for economic reasons (including the drought) or because they are political exiles and refugees. For this reason, and because of the close affinity between the Saharans of the Territory and those, for example, in the Moroccan province of Tarfaya or the border regions of Mauritania, it is extremely difficult to determine who among them is a Saharan indigenous to the Territory.

One of the truly healthy attitudes of most post-colonial African leaders today has been the wide acceptance that boundary changes between the African states – even though most of them had been delimited so arbitrarily by the old colonial powers – should not be made except by common consent. It was, in fact, at the insistence of Third World countries that the 1960 Declaration on the Granting of Independence to Colonial Countries and Peoples proclaimed that *all* peoples have the right to self-determination and that any attempt aimed at the partial or total disruption of the national unity and the territorial integrity of a country would be incompatible with the purposes and principles of the Charter of the United Nations. Professor Franck has correctly pointed out that:

> The Organization of African Unity has re-enforced the rule that territories must exercise their right to self-determination within established colonial boundaries. If a territory wishes to join with one or several neighbouring states, it should have the right to manifest that preference in the process of decolonization, but it must be the free choice of the majority in that particular colony, and a territory with recognized boundaries may neither be absorbed nor dismembered against the will of its inhabitants.

Despite this sensible policy, therefore, and in keeping with the basic Charter principles of non-use of force and 'respect for the principle of equal rights and self-determination of peoples', the covert conspiracy of the Moroccan and Mauritanian Governments, aided at a later stage by the *volte-face* of the new Government of Spain, has written an ominous page in the annals of human freedom.

According to the facts studiously recorded in that long 1975 judgement of the World Court, the question of self-determination for Western Sahara had been actively before the General Assembly since 1965.[7] The Assembly then called on Spain to implement what had become by that date a rule or pattern of decolonisation procedures. Spain refused to act on the ground that the territory was not a colony, but a 'province' of metropolitan Spain. The following year Morocco voted with the majority of the Assembly for self-determination, 'as soon as possible', but felt little doubt that Western Sahara would decide to opt to 'rejoin' Morocco. Mauritania took the same self-expectant line, while asserting its own 'historic title' to at least part of the territory. In 1967, Spain attempted to set up in her 'province' a pretence of 'self-government' – which no more succeeded in convincing the Assembly than South Africa's similar device did in Namibia a decade later.

By 1974 three developments had occurred: (a) the dying dictator Franco had promised that the territory would vote in a referendum for a 'free and authentic expression' of the people's wishes; (b) King Hassan II had asserted Morocco's 'historic claim to recover the usurped territories'; and (c) Algeria had also put in a claim for its own 'historic title' over the same territory. The General Assembly on 13 December 1974 decided by a large majority to invite the

World Court to guide it by means of an Advisory Opinion. Meantime, the Visiting Mission reported unanimously in 1975 that everywhere the Saharans were in favour of independence. They were against integration with *any* neighbouring country. The Mission recommended that the UN should take steps to organise a plebiscite to enable the various population-groups to decide their own future.[8]

The Court was not asked to advise the Assembly on self-determination as such, but solely on the question whether Morocco and Mauritania had any historic *title* to the territory. The Court, with near-unanimity, did not answer this question directly. It rejected Morocco's and Mauritania's claim of *sovereignty* over the territory; yet admitted that, on the facts put before it, both countries had had *some* past 'legal ties' with Western Sahara. Morocco and Mauritania at once (in truth, had already) moved over the Saharan border, claiming, which was not the case, that the Court had virtually decided in their favour!

It is not easy to simplify in a few sentences this elaborate judgement; but its most significant finding – in every way a landmark in international law – the rival claimants totally ignored. Moreover, the Court's basic ruling accorded with many previous UN decisions, namely, that

> at least during the past fifty years, self-determination has become the rule, that independence, free association with another state, or integration into another state, while all legitimate forms of decolonization must come about only as a result of the freely expressed wishes of the territory's peoples acting with full knowledge of the change in their status, their wishes having been expressed through informed and democratic processes, impartially conducted and based on universal adult suffrage.

Most important, with a view to the future development of the right to self-determination, the Court asserted that the *present* inhabitants' rights took precedence over past 'legal ties', whether or not they were established under some earlier system of law. The UN Charter had changed all that!

In his seventy-seven-page concurring opinion, Judge F. de Castro took a positive line (as did most of the other Judges) and insisted that over and above the Court's duty to answer the specific questions asked by the Assembly on title, the Court had 'to do its best to assist the General Assembly *in its task of decolonization*' (our italics). He then went further than the other Judges by applying to the instant case the accepted principle of intertemporal law, contained in the rule *tempus regit factum*; in other words, whatever the past titles might be or not be, the 'new facts will be subject to the rules of law in force at the time when they occur'. Thus, whatever status the territory had *before* colonisation by Spain in 1884,

> after the entry into force of the United Nations Charter, the territory of Western Sahara became a 'non-self-governing territory', and the administering Power therefore has a duty to recognise the principle that the interests of the inhabitants of the territory are paramount, and to develop self-government.

Yet, in spite of the Court's basic finding that the facts did *not* establish 'a tie of sovereignty', the two conspiring UN members proceeded by the use of force, contrary to the Charter, to assert sovereignty over Western Sahara, with at least the connivance of some European, African and Arab members. The subsequent counter-charges and manoeuvres of Spain, Morocco and Mauritania, assisted by France and Algeria in this miserable trade-in of international delinquency, fall outside the scope of this chapter.

But it can briefly be recorded that the growing armed resistance ('freedom-fighters', in the true sense) of the POLISARIO (Saharan Popular Front) and other armed units of the Saharan civil population soon resulted in bloody battles with the invading forces of Morocco – supplied with the latest American jet-fighters – and of Mauritania. While the inevitable refugees fled from napalm genocide and wended their weary way across the northern and southern borders, to be cared for by the International Red Cross and Algeria. It is perhaps invidious to add that, while the alleged 'guerrillas' (i.e. freedom-fighters) were still menacing the Moroccan invasion force at the end of 1977, Moroccan units were sometimes to be seen engaging in other military excursions, all the way to the south of Zaire's border – usually assisted by French planes and military equipment, as well as by US non-lethal material. Where will this stop? Or is the *new* neo-colonialism only just beginning in Africa?[9]

THE NEW NEO-COLONIALISM?

We have devoted considerable space to what Ambassador Shirley

Amerasinghe, President of the 1976 Assembly, has called a 'depressing' trend among Third World states 'to replace the old imperialism by other forms of foreign control, founded on territorial claims', because the manner in which the United Nations deals with this new peril will have consequences not only in the territory itself, but also beyond its borders and beyond the African continent. Policies of annexation and expansion pursued in total disregard of the aspirations of the inhabitants of the territories concerned would create dangerous precedents and have far-reaching implications for United Nations action in the field of decolonisation. The 'right' to self-determination would disappear under the rule of force.

Professor Franck in his brilliant analysis, on which the present chapter has drawn so liberally, has taken the question much further:

> In particular, it is predictable that Israel, a state carved out of the Arab-Ottoman Middle East by agreement between a colonial-mandatory power (Britain) and a U.N. General Assembly, from which most of Africa and Asia were still excluded, will feel the adverse impact of the greater credibility now inevitably accorded claims of historic title . . . to the extent that its future [also] depends upon its place in the international system; the handling of the Saharan issue by the United Nations has inevitably, by implication, undermined Israel's legitimacy. It has shown that many nations, including the United States, are willing to tolerate the use of force to effect a restoration of historic title even in disregard of the wishes of the inhabitants.

This grave warning as to the use of force has particular relevance for the impoverished peoples of the Third World. The gigantic strides now being made in the traffic in modern weapons of war is beginning to strike at the root of the independence of weaker countries. Morocco is only one of the *nouveau riche* countries – with its eye on untapped phosphate, iron ore, and petroleum resources of Western Sahara – whose élite are becoming more and more dependent on outside 'aid' in sophisticated weaponry to support their take-overs. Yet, according to the *New York Times* correspondent in Casablanca:

> The rich of Morocco are becoming more opulent and the poor are finding survival more difficult. Here in the country's economic capital, luxurious villas with swimming pools and tennis courts are going up in a new élite suburb, while an estimated 25 per cent

of the city's population is unemployed and lives in shacks on the edge of the city [28 March 1977].

Aggressive policies and disregard for the principles and rules of international law have serious adverse consequences, such as the decision to squander material and intellectual resources on the sterile production of armaments. The dependency of the Third World on the industrialised countries for their basic needs is now being intensified by the arms race. Total world military expenditures have expanded from $127, 392 million in 1955 (at 1970 prices) to $213,846 million in 1975 – nearly double. And although money spent by the developing countries on foreign arms deals is only some 15 per cent of this spiralling menace of military waste, the Third World armaments expenditure jumped in the same period from $4065 million in 1955 to $26,000 (approximate) million in 1975 – over a sixfold increase.[10]

Third World countries are not only spending on arms funds urgently needed for their own development, but they are encouraged to do so by an ever-growing army of arms-salesmen, both governmental and non-governmental. The International Peace Research Institute in Oslo has pointed out that military techniques are reinforcing dependency. The military training of Third World élites means that they become used to certain military habits and weapons and wish to continue using them. Thus the military become a 'caste' within the country, with their own special value system. Moreover, domestic arms-production, rather than leading to self-reliance and independence, increases dependency on advanced technology and on the need for training and spare parts. To buy arms or even to manufacture them, developing countries are going deeper into debt. The need for capital to pay off (or even to service) the debt interest places an emphasis upon exports which hinders rational development. The export of food, needed for internal use to raise living standards, is a particularly tragic example of the price the Third World is paying for its eight-fold expansion of military expenditure within barely two decades of slow economic growth. Where is 'self-determination' in this race for a dubious and self-defeating military build-up?

Undoubtedly, Human Rights specialists should now be giving high priority to examining the impact of the arms race on human rights. Fortunately, the last session of the Human Rights Commission in Geneva resolved to set on foot a special study on

Development and Human Rights. Similarly, UNESCO's Division on Human Rights and Peace in Paris has initiated parallel studies on the Impact of Armaments on Human Rights, while in New York the UN Preparatory Committee for the Special General Assembly on Disarmament in 1978 has authorised studies on the socio-economic aspects of disarmament. This growing awareness of the peril that the arms race poses to all economic and social development has not come a moment too soon.

A FAIR INTERNATIONAL ECONOMIC ORDER

Attention was drawn in Chapter 2 to the simultaneous adoption by the General Assembly of the Covenant on Civil and Political Rights and the Covenant on Economic, Social and Cultural Rights, as a recognition of their oneness as a single universal code of international conduct. The economic Covenant came into force with 35 ratifications on 3rd January 1976 and the political Covenant with 35 ratifications on 23 March 1976, together with its Protocol, which required 10 ratifications. Current implementation measures and the actual working of these important instruments will be discussed in Chapter 7; but here it might be useful to examine a little further the relationship of the economic Covenant with the resolution of the Special General Assembly in 1975 to create machinery for a new international economic order (NIEO).

Only a concerted effort at both the national and the international level will make it possible to accelerate the economic development of the countries of the Third World. The establishment of the United Nations Conference on Trade and Development (UNCTAD), the Industrial Development Organization (UNIDO) and the Development Programme (UNDP) has been evidence of the growing concern aroused by the worsening situation of the developing countries. Social progress and economic development are recognised as the common goals of the whole international community, which has decided to supplement, by concerted international action through the UN, national efforts to raise the living standards of the world's peoples.

International co-operation embraces, however, not only the problems between the 'haves' and the 'have nots', but also the collective issues which *all* nations must at some time face as a consequence of recent technical and scientific advances. So increasing use has been made of international conferences, convened by the General Assembly, to deal with specific problems of global concern. Among such United Nations conferences in the 1970s were the Conference on the Human Environment (Stockholm, 1972), which agreed on measures to combat pollution and to protect the environment, and resulted in the establishment of the UN Environment Programme (UNEP) based in Nairobi; the Third World Population Conference (Bucharest, 1974), at which a World Population Plan of Action set forth principles and recommendations on population policies; and the World Food Conference (Rome, 1974) which initiated efforts to improve food stocks and establish a World Food Board (WFB) to avert mass starvation.

Thus the right of self-determination in Article 1 of the two major Covenants would appear to have evolved a long way during the 1970s, without losing its force or importance, from national independence to international interdependence. At this date, it must be envisaged in the context of the UN's global programme for a new international economic order.

That being the case, it would be appropriate in concluding this chapter to review in capsule terms some of the wide-ranging debate which took place in Geneva in 1976 on the item 'Realization of the Economic, Social, and Cultural Rights'.[11]

In the opinion of several national delegates, the realisation of socio-economic rights was essential in order to ensure the meaningful enjoyment of civil and political rights. Illiterates could hardly be expected to appreciate the freedom of information, nor could starving, undernourished or unemployed masses exercise their paper political rights. In developing countries, millions of people were still struggling for subsistence amidst difficulties which had in most cases increased over the previous decade.

In industrialised countries, however, the standard of living had continued to rise. The industrialised countries had, therefore, responsibilities and obligations in this regard, yet they seemed to be trying to escape them by underlining the importance of political and civil rights. The governments of developing countries had to give priority to economic and social development for the further strengthening of their own political institutions. Criticism of occasional curtailment of liberties in such countries could be an unfair over-simplification, it was said, since it did not take into account the dimensions of the problems they had to face.

Some representatives contended that economic and social rights could never be fully realised within capitalistic systems, which, in their view, were based on exploitation and characterised by chronic unemployment. Civil and political rights remained theoretical in such conditions. In the opinion of those speakers, only socialist systems were free from exploitation and could ensure full employment and the realisation of human rights without discrimination.

Some other representatives, who recognised the equal value of all human rights, voiced reservations regarding the concept of economic development as a prerequisite for the exercise of civil and political rights. They maintained that fundamental rights – such as the right to life, protection against torture and safeguards against arbitrary arrest – should and could be implemented in *all* countries, regardless of their level of development. Moreover, at least one of the civil and political rights – the right to freedom of opinion and expression – was essential for the realisation of economic, social and cultural rights, as it allowed for a permanent critical check upon the situation in those fields and was also an indispensable stimulus to scientific and technological progress.

Several delegates expressed the view that there was no universally valid model for the realisation of these rights, and that the right of each country to determine its own policies for this purpose in the light of its specific problems should be fully respected. It was recognised, too, by a number of national delegates, that problems relating to the realisation of economic rights had international as well as national dimensions. Underdevelopment, to them, was basically the sequel of colonial domination.

Even after achieving political independence, developing countries often remained subjected to neo-colonialist exploitation of their natural resources. They had been left dependent upon an unjust international economic system, in respect of terms of trade, transfer of technology and foreign investment. Hence, the importance of implementing the Declaration and Programme of Action on the Establishment of a New International Economic Order and the Charter of Economic Rights and Duties of States, adopted by the General Assembly in 1975.

In the opinion of several speakers, finally, the right to development was closely linked with the right to peace. Disarmament should be promoted and an atmosphere of détente maintained so that the vast resources now being devoted to the arms race should be diverted towards social progress. In their view, assistance for the economic and social development of developing countries was a moral and legal obligation of the international community, and in particular of the industrialised countries. This duty was based upon the UN Charter, particularly Articles 55 and 56, and on the Universal Declaration and other United Nations instruments, which emphasised the fundamental principle of *solidarity between nations*. The entry into force of the International Covenant on Economic, Social and Cultural Rights had greatly strengthened the legal basis of the obligation of all states to co-operate in achieving economic and social development, without which self-determination would be an empty shell.

6 Science and Technology

Machines on their concrete bases act like serenely meditating Buddhas, squatting on their timeless loins. They vanish when more beautiful, more perfect ones are born.

– Henry van de Velde

'Today, faith in the magic power of technical organisation is more widely held than ever,' says philosopher Friedrich Georg Juenger, 'but every process of organisation has two sides, and if we want to count its cost, we must first understand its double-edged nature'.[1]

In an unpublished essay entitled 'Human Rights and Scientific and Technological Developments', Lord Ritchie-Calder, formerly Professor of International Relations at the University of Edinburgh, states that

> throughout history, innovation has encroached on human rights. Material changes, which altered the conditions of living for the benefit of the many, have imposed constraints upon others and required concessions from the individual. That was accepted as the price of progress. The question today is whether the price is too high.

It is Lord Ritchie-Calder's view that, although there is a general concern about the effects on the total environment of ill-considered innovations, especially the pollution and destruction of the living-space of mankind, 'there has been a slower recognition of the erosion of human rights by this deluge of new technical devices.' In this chapter we shall examine, therefore, in terms of human rights, some of the encroachments and constraints which have presented both a warning and a challenge to legislators and administrators, whose task it is to advance and protect the public good.

THE RIGHT TO PRIVACY

We begin with the so-called right to privacy, because it is probably the most intangible of human rights and yet the one hemmed in by more legal and scientific restrictions today than any other. In the words of a French judge dealing with a civil case at Grasse, France, in 1971:

> The sphere of anyone's private life is sometimes rather difficult to define, but that sphere certainly embraces everything that concerns his love life, his family life, his resources and the non-public aspects of his professional life and his leisure. Conversely, what is generally outside the sphere of an individual's private life is that part of his life which is necessarily lived in the public eye and his participation in the public life of his city.[2]

In view of the increasing ease with which the privacy of the individual has been violated in recent years with the aid of new devices and techniques, efforts have been made to define privacy. This has been considered necessary for the purposes of protective legislation, although such overall definitions have not as yet been actually enacted into law. Where such attempts at definition have been attempted, two different approaches have become apparent.

One has been to prepare a detailed, comprehensive definition of the right to privacy that would ban specific acts, among them the use of modern techniques of intrusion. Such a study was undertaken in Stockholm in 1967 by the Nordic Conference on the Right to Privacy. The conclusions adopted by that Conference recommended that the right to privacy be recognised as 'a fundamental right of mankind', protecting the individual against intrusion by 'public authorities, the public in general and other individuals'. They defined the right to privacy, in brief, as 'the right to be let alone to live one's own life with the minimum degree of interference', and they listed specific acts which that definition was intended to cover. This is in line with Article 12 of the UN's Universal Declaration.

The other approach has been to define privacy in general terms and to consider as legally punishable actions that are deemed to violate the privacy of the individual. One example of this approach was a Bill laid before the House of Commons in 1967, which was not, however, adopted. It would have defined the 'right to privacy' as 'the right of any person to preserve the seclusion of himself, his family or his property from any other person', and would have given any person who had been subject to any 'serious and unreasonable infringement of his right of privacy' a course of action against the offender.

Perhaps the fundamental problem is that it is becoming more and more difficult for any individual to defend himself against the invisible or concealable invasion of his privacy by 'bugs' or by wire-tapping. Lord Ritchie-Calder reminds us that

Modern listening devices are manifold. They can be un-obtrusively attached to a telephone. Tiny match-head transistors can fit into a cocktail olive, or be concealed in a lamp or the upholstery of a car. They can be adapted to the fillings of a tooth or embodied in a denture. They can masquerade as wrist-watches or fraternity pins. Stethoscopic microphones can be applied to a wall by suction or driven into a party-wall as a spike. Directional microphones can be used to pick up conversations in an open space. The walking 'bug' – someone equipped with concealed microphones and tape-recorders – can sit at the next table, stand beside you in a crowd, and eavesdrop a private conversation.

For the ordinary person, however, such a battery of James Bond devices would be irrelevant. In fact, his everyday world would indeed be deficient without a vast range of beneficial devices in a variety of fields, such as medicine, education, crime prevention and law enforcement. Portable tape-recorders are in common use in business as dictating-machines, as well as being used for recreational purposes. Directional microphones are used in connection with public television broadcasts. Contact microphones have even been used as super-stethoscopes for tracking termites or detecting stress irregularities in metal structures. Closed-circuit TV is being used to relay lectures to classrooms, to survey stores with high shoplifting records, and to guard warehouses at night or help protect tenants in apartment houses.

Some of these new techniques have been found of great use in medicine. 'Optical fibre' makes it possible to transmit images along curved paths in surgery. Intensive-care nursing techniques are dependent on electronic systems or remote surveillance and the recording of vital processes. Closed-circuit TV is an important tool in certain radiological techniques. When applied in the health and medical fields, of course, such devices have as their objective the good of the individual and any invasion of his privacy is an incidental by-product.

It is unfortunately true that, on the one hand, persons engaged in criminal activities nowadays have at their disposal the products of modern science and technology, including the media of rapid communication, which enable them to carry out their schemes more swiftly and over larger areas. But, on the other hand, law-enforcement agencies also avail themselves of modern techniques to fight crime. The use of surveillance devices in the interests of national security has become a monstrous and expensive element in war preparation. So perhaps a balance is being struck between the good and the bad?

Nevertheless, despite the beneficial uses – real or imagined – of modern methods of surveillance, such methods obviously can be used in ways which threaten the privacy of the individual. Many surveillance devices are relatively low in price, and simple to install or operate. Their power of perception vastly supplements that of the human ear or eye. There is a great temptation to find new uses for such devices, to the detriment of personal privacy. Not only governmental authorities but also private bodies are availing themselves of the new surveillance technology to an increasing extent. An article on 'Privacy in the Year 2000' might well apply to events long before that date:

> Technology may become a commonplace in the hands of private parties – employers interested in the off-hours activities of employees, competitors interested in one another's integrity and trade secrets, estranged spouses interested in perfecting grounds for divorce, insurance companies interested in the subsequent health of personal injury claimants they have paid, and the idly curious who are just interested.[3]

In 1970, UNESCO held a meeting of experts on the Right to Privacy, whose report included the following views:

> The factor which is typical of all the modern recording devices is that of their illicitness. Whether they are a telescope lens, wire-tapping and telephone espionage, polaroid glasses and perhaps, before long, mini-equipment which may make possible the surveillance or even the control of the behaviour of an individual at any time, without his knowledge . . . Hence, the utilization of these different devices by the public authorities raises many legal problems.

But the danger does not come only from state bodies, the UNESCO report continues. The general use of recording devices opens up possibilities of private espionage 'by means which have nothing in common with the rudimentary techniques once used by jealous husbands, gossips, and inquisitive concierges'. In some cases, one member of the family may be spying on another member of the same family, seeking grounds for divorce, for instance. Lastly, in the commercial, technical and financial fields, competing companies can spy on one another, and not only on one another; private espionage can be used also within the company itself.

In France recently a company director who used an intercom as a bugging device to eavesdrop on private conversations of his employees in the plant canteen, was fined 5000 francs for invasion of privacy.

In the USA a Federal Study Commission has called for a new law requiring government agencies to get a court order or follow other 'legal processes' before seeking an individual's records from another federal agency or such private sources as banks, insurance firms and telephone companies. Moreover, the Commission also told Congress that private employers should be forbidden to use polygraph, or 'lie-detector', tests in collecting information about an individual. And it said, further, that private funds should be withheld from schools that violate student privacy rights.

THE RIGHT TO KNOW

Enough has been said to show what the problems are. It remains to sketch, even partially, how this multiple challenge to human rights is being met, however inadequately. In the first place, we find the United Nations system at work at ground level, and we might remind ourselves of these 'basics': the Universal Declaration provides in Article 12

> No one shall be subjected to arbitrary interference with his privacy, family, home or correspondence, nor to attacks upon his honour and reputation. Everyone has the right to the protection of the law against such interference or attacks.

The International Covenant on Civil and Political Rights contains provisions in Article 17 identical with this text, except that it speaks of arbitrary 'or unlawful' interference and of 'unlawful' attacks. Both of these provisions are drafted so as to cover interference and attacks by individuals, as well as by governmental authorities. Article 12 of the Universal Declaration is, however, subject to the provisions of Article 29, which reads, in part:

In the exercise of his rights and freedoms, everyone shall be subject only to such limitations as are determined by law solely for the purpose of securing due recognition and respect for the rights and freedoms of others and of meeting the just requirements of morality, public order and the general welfare in a democratic society.

The European Convention on Human Rights of 1950 takes matters further and states (Article 8) that everyone has the right to respect for his private and family life, home and correspondence. It specifies that there shall be no interference by a public authority with the exercise of this right, except in accordance with the law and as necessary in a democratic society in the interests of national security, for the protection of health or morals, or for the protection of the rights and freedoms of others.

Moreover, the Consultative Assembly of Europe adopted in 1970 a Declaration on Mass Communication Media and Human Rights, which contains guidance concerning respect for privacy. One of its relevant passages reads:

It is the duty of the press and other mass media to discharge their functions with a sense of responsibility towards the community and towards the individual citizens. For this purpose, it is desirable to institute . . . a professional code of ethics for journalists; this should cover *inter alia* such matters as accurate and well balanced reporting, rectification of inaccurate information, clear distinction between reported information and comments, avoidance of calumny, respect for privacy, and respect for the right to a fair trial as guaranteed by Article 6 of the European Convention on Human Rights.

At the national level, various aspects of privacy have enjoyed the protection of the law for some time, without a separate right to privacy appearing on the statute books. Broadly speaking, these aspects are connected with other rights affected by invasions of privacy. But such existing laws have not contemplated dealing with threats posed by modern surveillance devices. Traditional methods protecting, to some extent, the privacy of the individual include constitutional or legislative provisions safeguarding the inviolability of the home, prohibitions against arbitrary searches and seizures, safeguarding the secrecy of correspondence, guaranteeing the accused certain rights in penal matters, and providing against attacks upon honour or reputation. In practice, these measures for protecting privacy vary considerably. Some of them provide protection against intrusions by governmental authorities, others against intrusions by private individuals or groups. In some countries remedies are also available against individual governmental agents acting in an unlawful manner.

It will obviously not be possible here to launch into the wide controversial field of 'freedom of information'; but it should be noted, in passing, that the Council of Europe Declaration referred to above does urge that national press councils be empowered to investigate and 'to censure unprofessional conduct with a view to the exercising of self-control by the press itself'.

Arthur W. J. Lewis, MP, Chairman of the Parliamentary All-Party Committee for Freedom of Information, looks forward to the fulfilment of the (present) Labour Government's own promise to abolish the Official Secrets Act of 1911. He calls for a Freedom of Information Act 'to restore Magna Carta to the People of Britain and their Right to Know the Truth'! This Act would allow, among other freedoms (put in summary form):

(a) *The press*: to cover more governmental and political questions than is possible today;

(b) *The medical profession*: to have access to Department of Health and Social Security records;

(c) *Industry*: to be told the reasons for the Government's industrial policies.[4]

A Privacy Act on the lines of the United States Privacy Act 1957 has been demanded by Mrs Pat Hewitt, General-Secretary of the National Council for Civil Liberties. The Council has been campaigning for nine years for such a law in Britain. She states: 'We want the individual to be able to see files which are kept on him, to be able to correct them if they are wrong, and to be able to control the use to which they are put.' (United States law entitles citizens to find out what information the Government has stored about them and to correct mistakes.)

On this question of whether or not the privacy of the individual would be better protected by the enactment of a statutory 'right to privacy', opinions are divided. One reason for this is the difficulty of drafting a usable *legal* definition of privacy. The 1972 report of the Younger Committee in the United Kingdom pronounced itself *against* the creation of a general right of privacy, largely because of 'the risks involved in propounding a general law, the scope of whose impact upon other important rights seems uncertain'.

The Penal Law Council of Denmark, for instance, takes a similar view and pointed out in 1971 that, in addition to special legal provisions, a 'general unwritten rule on the protection of the right to privacy and the integrity of the personality was assumed to apply in Danish law'.

The Conclusions of the 1967 Nordic Conference on the Right to Privacy, referred to above, do contain a definition of the right to privacy, supplemented by an indicative list of acts violative of the individual's privacy which, for 'practical purposes', includes:

(a) search of the person or entry on and search of premises or other property;
(b) medical examinations, psychological and physical tests;
(c) untrue or embarrassing statements about a person;
(d) interception of correspondence, wire- or telephone-tapping;
(e) use of electronic surveillance or other bugging devices;
(f) recording, photographing or filming;
(g) importuning by the press or other mass media;
(h) public disclosure of private facts;
(i) disclosure of information by professional advisers or public authorities bound to secrecy;
(j) harassing a person (e.g. watching him or subjecting him to nuisance telephone calls).

A study prepared by the International Commission of Jurists at the request of UNESCO and published in 1972, concludes, however, that the need will increasingly be felt in the future for 'an express and formally recognized legal right to privacy'. While a general legal right to privacy 'is bound to come into conflict with other legal rights, and in particular the rights of freedom of expression and freedom of the press', it is argued that 'this is not a reason for refusing to recognize the need for such a right'. Rather, solutions must be found within each country 'in accord with the weight that its society gives to these conflicting interests'.

A number of governments have authorised in-depth studies or hearings on the protection of privacy. These inquiries have varied in scope and emphasis, but generally speaking have been directed towards the preparation of legislation to protect the rights of the individual against intrusion by governmental or private sources.

The complications – and dangers! – of modern life call for these safeguards. For example, blood tests are used to discover substances in a person's blood stream such as poisons, narcotics and alcohol. Because of the social danger posed by drunken drivers, many countries have approved the *compulsory* withdrawal of a certain amount of blood by a syringe to be analysed for its alcohol content. Justice Clark of the United States Supreme Court upheld the taking of blood samples from an unconscious suspect in automobile accident cases, by emphasising society's overriding interests thus:

> As against the right of an individual that his person be held inviolable . . . must be set the interests of society in the scientific determination of intoxication, one of the great causes of the mortal hazards of the road. And the more so since the test may likewise establish innocence, thus affording protection against the treachery of judgment based on one or more of the senses. Furthermore, since our criminal law is to no small extent justified by the assumption of deterrence, the individual's right to immunity from such invasion of the body as is involved in a properly safeguarded blood test is far outweighed by the value of its deterrent effect due to the public.[5]

The use of lie-detector tests is opposed in many quarters, however, not only because of the intrusive nature of the questions that may be asked and persistent doubts concerning the inherent scientific reliability of the measurements involved, but also because of the involuntary nature of the non-verbal reply and the possibility of misinterpreting the tests results. Many courts do not admit the results of 'lie-detector' tests as evidence in penal matters.

As described in *Privacy and Freedom* by Alan F. Westin, certain chemicals exist that affect consciousness and volition in ways that might be used to lead a person to reveal information he would not otherwise disclose. The so-called 'truth drugs', such as scopolamines, sodium pentathol and sodium amytal, are relaxant agents that release inhibiting controls.[6] Yet narco-analysis has been found to have therapeutic uses too. 'Truth drugs' have also been used in police work, for example, as an aid to recalling an event or conversation which the subject cannot remember in his normal, conscious state.

An extensive technical literature now exists on the subjects dealt with in this chapter. In recent years increasing attention has been paid by both scholarly and popular writers to the impact of such methods upon the privacy of the individual and other human rights, seeking an answer to the basic question: 'Is it compatible with the privacy of the individual, to use methods such as those discussed above in order to extract information from a person without his consent or even knowledge?'

Finally, it can be noted that psychological and physical invasions of privacy have been the subject of considerable study in recent years. Government-sponsored inquiries include the above-mentioned Younger Report and a number of Congressional Hearings, as well as a study by the Office of Science and Technology in the United States. The Council of Europe's Committee of Experts on Human Rights deals frequently with the subject. A little-known – or appreciated – service rendered by the UN Commission on Human Rights has been the collation and analysis of these numerous studies, on which many of the topics surveyed in this chapter have relied.

The subject has recently been considered at a number of international gatherings, among them many United Nations seminars on the protection of human rights in criminal law and procedure: at UNESCO's 1970 Meeting of Experts on the Right to Privacy; at the Third International Colloquy About the European Convention on Human Rights; at the Ninth Congress of the International Association of Democratic Lawyers; at the *Colloque sur les méthodes scientifiques de recherche de la vérité*, held in Abidjan, Ivory Coast, in January 1972; and so on. No right has been *less* private than this one, though it is not yet on the Statute Book in Britain!

THE RIGHT TO DIE

'It is hard to realize that at the beginning of this century man had still not learned how to propel himself in a controlled way over long distances against the pull of earth's gravitation; nor how to protect his body against bacterial infection by the use of antibiotics,' says Professor Olumbe Bassir, University of Ibadan, Nigeria; and, he reminds us: 'The break-through of immunization, immunology, aircraft, rocket propellants and control engineering are events of the last few decades.'

It is hardly surprising that human inventiveness in what may roughly be called the bio-medical field has got out of control. Not long ago, for instance, drug and chemical industry officials in the United States told the Government that they could not accept its new rules on creating *new forms of life* in their laboratories, unless they could keep their research secret long enough to patent it! Victor Cohn writes that officers of seventeen firms, including Dow Chemical, Du Pont and Merck & Upjohn, and three trade associations urged the Commerce Department, as a first step, to agree on rules by which companies might safely participate in biology's newest revolution. According to its Chairman, Dr Betsy Ancker-Johnson, then Assistant-Secretary of Commerce for Science and Technology, this step is 'analogous in importance' to the post-Second World War effort to let US industry into the atomic energy business. (*Herald Tribune*, 22 November 1976.)

There is, fortunately, no creation-of-life business *yet*. But it is conceivable that the development of atomic energy and the creation of new forms of life will rank as the most important discoveries of this century. Already, this expected biological revolution sees scientists combining in the near future the genetic material from different life-forms like bacteria, viruses, plants and even animals, to create new living molecules. Such a revolution could lead to new drugs and plants, but many scientists believe it could also create terrible new forms of destruction, unless the research is closely watched.

The impact on human rights – adverse or beneficial – of these revolutionary drugs and novel medical techniques can hardly be exaggerated. On the request of the UN General Assembly, the Human Rights Commission has, during the last five years, set on foot a series of little-known expert studies covering a wide field of relevant scientific and technological advances for the information of governments and the guidance of UN organs and agencies specialising in these activities.[7]

At the other end of the scale – literally and figuratively – we find science and technology in conflict with a right that is not yet in the Declaration or Covenants: the Right to Die. We might recall the lines of A. H. Clough in 'The Latest Decalogue':

Thou shal'st not kill, but need'st not strive
Officiously to keep alive.

The case that opened up world debate, and a still undecided legal issue, occurred in November 1975 when a New Jersey judge ruled that doctors might not detach a life-sustaining respirator from a twenty-one-year-old girl named Karen Anne Quinlan, who had been in a coma for seven months. The suit had been brought by the parents, asking for the right to end the artificial support of the life of their daughter, who has been kept alive by a respirator since she suffered massive brain damage. The Roman Catholic parents wanted their daughter to be permitted to 'return to the gentle hands of the Lord'. But five parties, including the State of New Jersey, argued that disconnecting the life-giving respirator would amount to homicide.

Seven doctors testified that Miss Quinlan had virtually no chance of recovering from the brain damage, caused by a mixture of drugs and drink. In a five-day trial the judge indicated that Miss Quinlan was alive and quoted previous court rulings in saying: 'There is no constitutional right to die', adding that, when a patient cannot choose for himself, 'there is a presumption that one chooses to go on living'.

The reasoning of the judge, which has been both contested and supported by varied opinions given in other cases, is worthy of careful note. He rejected the view that the parents had the right to exercise a religious belief that extraordinary medical measures are not required to sustain terminal patients. He said that removing the respirator did not interfere with religious beliefs because 'it is not a dogma of the church'. But he asserted that the question of life and death is something that must be decided by competent medical men. 'There is a duty to continue the life-assisting apparatus if, within the treating physician's opinion, it should be done . . . It is a medical decision whether or not Karen should be removed from the respirator,' concluded the Judge. 'Just as that decision is a medical one, the continued care and treatment of Karen is a medical one.' She still lives.

It is not intended here to follow up some of the ramifications of that legal judgement and its passage through the appeal courts, which *did* allow her parents to 'pull the plug'; but it certainly opened up a Pandora's Box of complicated issues surrounding the Right to Death. Within a year, for instance, the State of California legislature had passed a 'Right to Death' Bill to permit dying people to instruct doctors not to keep them alive by 'extraordinary means'. It would allow people to sign a 'living will', while they were in full command of their faculties, giving doctors the authority to stop so-called life-support systems if the patient is unquestionably dying. Opponents of the measure claim that it might be a first step along the road to euthanasia. But its supporters insist that it is nothing of the sort. Doctors would have to continue keeping their patients alive, as they do now, unless the patient of his own free will had signed the 'living will'.

It is not irrelevant to mention that, speaking in London in November 1975, the former editor of *Punch*, Malcolm Muggeridge, stated: 'I am unalterably and totally opposed to *euthanasia*', but, nevertheless, he said, would want 'to be allowed to die in peace'. So the seventy-two-year-old editor signed a legal form offered by the Human Rights Society – founded to oppose euthanasia – that is designed to help solve the doctors' dilemma over incurable patients.

From Scotland, Professor Bryan Jennett at the Institute of Neurological Sciences, Glasgow, has supported such views as those of the Bishop of Durban, who, when addressing the British Medical Association in 1972, said: 'We should not maintain a semblance of life in people who can never become more than living vegetables.' Professor Jennett comments:

> These statements clearly refer to patients who are not sentient, rather than to those who are dying in pain, or are simply very old . . . Concern about the quality of life in those whom modern medicine rescues from death is now increasing, and the fact or the duration of survival are no longer accepted as adequate measures of the success of medical intervention . . . 'Many brain damaged patients [he continues] are the victims of head injury, and their average age is about 30 years; when they are 'successfully' rescued they may face many years in a severely crippled state, sometimes without ever regaining consciousness. Even those who become fully conscious often suffer a combination of mental impairment and physical handicap which can make the overall disability quite devastating [*The Times*, 21 February 1977].

In these circumstances, it is not surprising that Andrew J. Martin, Legal Correspondent of the *General Practitioner* should write thus to *The Times* on 21 December 1976:

> The problems involved in providing a statutory right to die are formidable, and there is a strong possibility of abuse. The aged and infirm, and the mentally ill, and for that matter the young, are often incapable of making an informed decision of any sort. When the decision is the most important of their life, and possibly their last, one should be very hesitant before carrying out their so-called wishes. It is as wrong to put them in this position as it is to expect doctors to carry out the execution.

Subject to one further observation – before we conclude this lugubrious section of our chapter – our closest thought might be given to some constructive advice in Mr Martin's letter, namely, that:

> The laws of murder and manslaughter are still operative in this field, but it is interesting to note that there have been no recent prosecutions of doctors for these offences, though it would be unrealistic to assume that euthanasia is not tacitly practised. The advantage of not formalizing the position is that it allows maximum flexibility, and avoids the abuses that many fear might follow the introduction of a statutory right to die . . . My own opinion, which I suspect is fairly widely shared, is that things are probably best left as they are.

The final observation that cannot be ignored in dealing seriously with the alleged Right to Death, concerns the related question, which was expressed in a recent report of an expert group to the Commission on Human Rights in these terms:

> The dignity of the human person relates to the time when death may be said to have occurred. It was pointed out that there are different levels of death: cell death, tissue death, organ death and total death. These were not inseparable, but, in terms of the dignity, the integrity and the wholeness of the individual, a great distinction was to be made. A great many of a person's cells were lost every day: blood cells died by the million, cells came off from the tissues of the mouth and intestines and die. These did not constitute total death . . . With the great developments in artificial organs that are coming, it would perhaps be possible before many years to implant an artificial kidney or an artificial heart or an artificial pancreas, and the individual would continue to function. Such an individual need not lose a sense of self, consciousness, integrity or dignity. This was why brain death is now considered to be equivalent to the real death of the human individuality that possesses that dignity.[8]

GENETIC ENGINEERING

The above-mentioned international group of experts convened by the UN Secretary-General met in Geneva in September 1975 to discuss the topic, under the heading 'The Balance which should be

Established between Scientific and Technological Progress and the Intellectual, Spiritual, Cultural and Moral Advancement of Humanity'. They examined certain scientific and technological advances which were said to pose risks to individual human rights, the welfare of society or the global condition of mankind. Among these were (a) the use of artificial organs, (b) genetic manipulation of microbes and (c) potential modifications of the human 'genome' – the human makeup.[9]

What was the background of this important study, prepared for the guidance of the Human Rights Commission? The revolution in modern biology may be dated from 1944, it stated, when deoxyribonucleic acid (DNA) was shown to be the carrier of the genetic message of inheritable characteristics. Other experiments confirmed these findings and, by mid-century, it was generally accepted that the nucleic acid DNA was the final source of instructions for building a new organism. In 1953, the structure of the DNA molecule was discovered. It is composed of two threads loosely entwined around each other in a double helix like a spiral staircase. The strands are held apart (or linked together) at thousands of points, like steps in the stairs, so the scientists maintain. These stair-steps comprise the information in the genetic code. When a cell divides, the molecule untwists and unzips down the middle. Each half then finds additional materials in the chemical 'soup' of the cell nucleus to form another like the original.

Although scientific understanding of the cell has undergone this revolution in the past thirty years, we have yet to witness *applications* of molecular biology of comparable importance. This has in no way eroded the belief that these discoveries will, eventually, be instrumental in obtaining far-reaching advances in medical technology. A current focus, in fact, for many scientists and law-makers is on a form of genetic engineering called Recombinant DNA, a process developed only a few years ago which now enables scientists to transplant segments of DNA from one form of life – such as bacteria – to other forms, such as viruses or animals. It thereby becomes possible to modify the hereditary characteristics of the organism.

The development of this technique has been viewed by some as a formidable stride in scientific endeavour, and one which may be expected in future to result in numerous beneficial applications. There has been, however, vigorous discussion of the dangers that might accompany the new power to manipulate DNA and, consequently, heredity. The damage that might result if harmful molecules escaped from the laboratory has already occasioned a research 'moratorium', unique in the history of science. In July 1974, when this moratorium had been called by scientists at Stanford University in America genetic engineering studies were being made in approximately eighty laboratories in the USA, the USSR, the UK and other parts of Europe.

In February 1975 an international group of scientists met at Asilomar, California, and voted to lift the moratorium, provided that certain general safety principles were met; but it also decided that, pending the enactment in each country of specific guidelines incorporating these principles, the moratorium stays. In the light of this, the UN Group of Experts were fully justified in framing their own study in ethical terms. Here, at least, is one vital area of human rights that could hardly be 'politicized' – though some news columnists have linked the subject with prospects of future terrorists acquiring genetic 'tools' for anti-human activities!

The *Economist* (8 November 1975) has, however, underlined a domestic aspect in an article 'Playing with Genes':

> The debate is not about extreme fears that some mad dictator might use the techniques of genetic engineering to create a super-race of Frankensteins; ordinary techniques of selective genetic breeding could have allowed mad dictators to breed a super-race centuries ago, but man has used them instead merely to breed pedigree dogs and cows. There are dangers that parents could be moving into an age when they will be able to choose for their children the shape, size and certain other attributes they want, but, even before genetic engineering makes this possible, a cheaper alternative already exists: the equally horrid technique of genetic counselling (e.g. aborting foetuses, unless they will grow up to have blue eyes and blond hair). It is not being used, but such things will become progressively easier.

Some eighty-six universities in the United States are doing DNA research, according to the *New York Times* of 12 March 1977, and so are a number of private companies. Biologists are constantly pursuing practical applications for drugs and vaccines. Synthetic insulin and a vaccine for swine and cattle diseases are two immediate possibilities as a result of these techniques. And it is claimed that Recombinant DNA technology could lead to an increase in the world's food supply by enabling plant genes to manufacture their own nitrogen fertiliser from the air.

Gene 'therapy' on human beings may be only five to ten years away, according to some estimates; and it has been asserted that genetic engineering might wipe out diseases such as sickle-cell anaemia. 'Within the scientific community,' the *New York Times* points out,

> genetic engineering has produced the widest philosophical debate since the splitting of the atom. Is it a promising research tool? Is it an unacceptable dangerous intrusion into the genetic heritage of life? Until recently, the debate was left to the scientists. Now the legislatures of California and New York are considering Bills to control the research, as are several members of Congress. On a scientific issue with such enormous implications, who should decide?

On this topic of adequate controls, at present in a nebulous stage, the moratorium self-imposed by scientists in 1974 brought the ethical and social aspects of Recombinant DNA under public scrutiny. The debate has since been focused almost totally on the possible hazards of the *escape* of new forms of micro-organisms. One urgent source of concern has been the prospect of introducing potential cancer-causing DNA into common bacteria. While it is recognised how speculative this hazard is, the general territory is so little explored that no-one can argue against the need for cautious laboratory procedures.

Recognition of the need to examine the issues involved resulted in the convening of the international conference at Asilomar, California, referred to above, in February 1975. The findings of the Conference may be briefly summarised as follows:

Most work in this field should proceed, but with appropriate safeguards. There were certain experiments, however, which should not be carried out under existing conditions of containment. 'Containment' connotes precautionary steps which may be taken to confine the environmental spread of hybrid DNA molecules. Three types of containment were advocated: (i) *Physical containment*: this is achieved by laboratory discipline (i.e. no eating in the laboratory, wearing white coats and gloves, destruction of experimental materials) and laboratory design (negative-pressure rooms, shower facilities, etc.); (ii) *Biological containment*: the development of fail-safe vectors so that host bacteria could not persist outside the artificial conditions in the laboratory; and (iii) *Training of personnel* in safety precautions.

Following the Conference, action has been taken in various countries to implement its conclusions. Only a passing reference to these can be mentioned here. In the United States, for instance, a committee of the National Institutes of Health has prepared draft guidelines for consideration by the scientific community. However, these guidelines were judged by many scientists to be too lax, so the committee's problem is one of attempting to strike a delicate balance. In the United Kingdom a Government working-party has recommended the establishment of a Genetic Manipulation Advisory Group to screen experiments and to advise on safety precautions, the chief proposal of the working party being that 'disabled' organisms should be created for such experiments and be made widely available. In the Netherlands, a Committee co-sponsored by the Royal Academy of Sciences and Arts and the Health Council has been established in connection with research on DNA Recombinants. In New Zealand most microbiologists and molecular biologists accept as guidelines the consensus of opinion given by the Asilomar Conference in February 1975. And so on, around the globe.

Finally, the World Health Organization has been concerned with the question of genetic manipulation for some time. In June 1976, its Advisory Committee on Medical Research considered the problem of safety in the handling of micro-organisms and cells employed in research, of which Recombinant DNA constitutes a sub-section. But, more important for the future, perhaps, the group of international experts referred to above recommended to the Human Rights Commission that consideration be given to drafting a new Declaration on Human Rights and Scientific and Technological Developments. Among the topics recommended for inclusion in such a future Declaration was the genetic manipulation of microbes, together with the types of controls and monitoring needed universally.

THE ETHICS OF TRANSPLANTS

Successful surgical transplantation of certain organs from one human being to another has become possible in recent years, but transplantation of organs from one human being to another raises a number of legal, ethical and social issues. A statement furnished to the UN by the International Commission of Jurists at the Montreal Assembly for Human Rights in 1968, which discussed new dangers caused by scientific developments, called for an examination of 'the profound implications of artificial transplants'.

As a case in point, a law was rushed through the French parliament in the last week of the autumn session in 1976, making it lawful for organs to be transplanted from a dead person, unless the person has expressly opposed it during his or her life time. French law previously made prohibition the rule, and authorisation the exception. Mme Simone Weil, the Minister of Health, declared that about twenty medical teams in France carried out kidney transplants, and about 800 people now lived with a grafted kidney; also about 50 people were living with a heart transplant and 20 with a liver transplant. One Frenchman with a transplanted heart, she said, had just celebrated the eighth anniversary of his operation. Much progress had been made in this field; but the law had not followed at the same pace.

If the health of living donors in transplant operations is not to be unduly endangered, however, the range of natural organs which can be taken *from* them is obviously limited. 'The employment of living donors,' the report of the Danish Ministry of Justice Committee concerning Legislation on Transplantation, states, 'is possible only in respect of tissue or organs that can be excised without considerable *risk* to the life or health of the donor.' Defining the organs which can be transplanted from a living donor, the report of the Danish Ministry of Justice Committee states: 'Without long-term risk, all that can be taken from living people is certain tissues such as skin, bone marrow and pieces of bone, and of vital organs a single kidney.'

All writers dealing with transplants point out that each operation represents a certain physical risk for living donors. Thus, Dr John Holden says, 'one must bear in mind the physical . . . risk to the . . . donor of an organ in transplantation.' Speaking about nephrectomy operations, Dr E. Pillen says: 'We . . . risk the health of a well person in the future and the later prognosis is still unknown.' And, Drs A. de Coninck, P. Dor and J. R. Fagnart indicate that 'the immediate risk to the donor and the permanent partial disability resulting from the removal of the organ must be taken into account'.[10]

Gerald Leach in a challenging book draws attention to the fact that living donors also face some psychological risk:

> Start with the true 'volunteer' nature of his sacrifice. A family will
> often select a donor from among themselves, even before a live
> transplant has been suggested. Such heavy pressures may be put
> upon that donor that he is made to feel he has murdered his sick
> relative if he refuses. In other cases a donor may 'volunteer' out of
> a sense of duty . . . In yet other cases donors have been left feeling
> that they killed their relative when they have given a kidney, but
> the transplant failed.[11]

A most unusual case reported recently in the *New York Times* tells
of a Brooklyn construction worker who got a kidney transplant by
way of Moscow. The kidney was flown there after being removed
from a young victim of a Moscow automobile accident. Since the
United States has many more car-accidents than the Soviet Union,
it might indeed seem odd that any American should have to look to
the Russians for a used kidney!
A leading article on 4 May 1977 commented:

> There are now at least 6,000 sufferers from kidney disease in this
> country who could benefit from transplants. A lucky few will get
> kidneys from living donors – probably close relatives: but most
> must wait for the kidney of someone who has lately died. Last
> year, about 4,000 such transplants were performed in the United
> States, but some people perished for want of one.

A dozen US states have passed laws that define death, as stated
earlier, in terms of brain death. Physicians are permitted to
pronounce a patient dead when electrical activity in the brain has
ended and when other tests indicate that no return to life is possible
even though artificial mechanisms such as respirators will keep the
heart beating and the blood circulating. During this period of
artificial 'life', the patient's organs deteriorate. When death finally
is acknowledged, they may no longer be suitable for transplant.
The *New York Times* goes further and points out:

> The need for usable organs also runs into the rights of the dying
> person and his relatives. Most physicians are naturally un-
> comfortable about asking grieving kin for permission to make the
> organs of their relatives available – and most of those asked are
> likely to be appalled at the suggestion . . . A legal framework –
> the Uniform Anatomical Gift Acts – already exists for people

who wish to donate their organs for transplant when they die.

The attitudes of governments vary greatly on transplants. We have space to refer only to two. The Government of Romania, for example, has told the Human Rights Commission:

Organ transplantation cannot be permitted except in special medico-surgical centres offering the possibility of examination and treatment of the highest technical order and efficiency and after consultation with a Committee of unquestionable competence capable of establishing an unbiased balance between the hazards for the donor and the success of the transplant. . . . Transplantation should represent the last chance of survival for the recipient, after the exhaustion of other possible therapeutic means.

The Government of Sweden has expressed a more philosophical view:

A balance must always be struck between the advantages of a transplant operation for the recipient and the hazards involved for a living donor. According to a draft law on transplant operations, which is at present being studied in the Ministry of Health and Social Affairs, no surgical operation should be carried out on a living donor if there is a risk of the operation causing serious injury to the donor.

Because of these ethical and physiological uncertainties, transplantation from the dead has certain advantages in comparison with that from living donors. Dr Lillehei, Professor of Heart Surgery at Cornell University, USA, has maintained that organs taken from a single dead person can in theory save the lives of seventeen people.

But how does the question of consent come into this? An analysis of the legislation of approximately thirty countries shows that consent may be expressed during a person's lifetime in a written document or may be expressed orally before death occurs. The most elaborate provisions concerning the form of consent are found in the Uniform Anatomical Gift Act of the United States, referred to above, which has been adopted in all the States.[12]

The British Medical Association has recommended:

The deceased person should preferably have given recorded positive consent in his or her lifetime. Failing this, the donor should be known not to have expressed opposition and in every case the positive consent of the next of kin should be sought . . . Inquiry must also be made as to likely objection by any other relative, as this constitutes a bar . . . 'Any other relative' should be interpreted in the widest sense, though it should be sufficient to make such inquiry of the nearest available relative . . .[13]

At present, the choice of beneficiaries in heart transplants and other life-extending procedures is normally made by doctors and the hospital administrations in whose care patients find themselves. The responsibility for the decision is usually accepted by the head of the service, with or without the assistance of a small committee. To spread responsibility, some hospitals have lay and medical committees through which the claims of potential patients are filtered.

Apparently, the only surgical unit in the world where heart transplantation is a regular routine operation is that at Stanford University, California, where a team has carried out more than a hundred operations, with a survival rate of half at one year and a quarter at five years. These reasonably good results are partly attributable, it is said, to the team's accumulation of practical experience and partly to the legal attitude to transplantation in California. The Stanford surgeons believe it essential to remove the donor heart while it is still beating, and there is no legal objection to their doing so in cases of certified brain death.[14]

In this short outline, only some of the major problems arising from transplant surgery and procedures have been pinpointed; but perhaps enough has been indicated here to emphasise that the undoubted advantages of science and technology in the sixties and seventies have brought their special problems into the broad field of human rights, and that many answers are awaited.

That some issues are by no means excised by the surgeon's knife is illustrated from a recent report from Taiwan where (according to a report by *The Times*) a team of American and Chinese doctors has developed a simple treatment for people with kidney failure; namely, a chemical solution which they drink in large quantities. The doctors claim that this treatment will help liberate thousands of patients from dependence on costly kidney machines and allow them to lead more normal lives. The new method requires the patient to drink a glass of a special solution based on sodium sulphate at five-minute intervals for a long period each morning – as many as thirty-six glasses for the most serious cases! The idea is that the solution flushes out toxic substances which the faulty kidneys cannot handle. One American doctor forecasts that kidney machines will eventually be superseded. However, these future speculations carry us a long way from orthodox human rights.

CRIMES BY COMPUTER

In the United States there is a growing concern by the Government with a new kind of criminal – the specialist who can use a computer to help him steal, defraud, embezzle, sabotage and even blackmail. The Secret Service has accordingly tightened security on its file, partly because it does not want any potential assassins who may infiltrate the file to know that they are being watched. Moreover, it is reported that the National Institutes of Health are putting new locks on psychiatric files in case blackmail might be behind an intruder's attempts to steal the records of members of Congress or the Cabinet hospitalised with mental problems!

Consulting firms are advising Federal agencies on how to avoid computer fraud. The Army teaches its logistics officers about computer fraud and the FBI runs courses where frauds are simulated on a computer and agents-in-training told to break them. Not to be outdone, the Department of Defense Computer Institute employs in its security and privacy department officers who investigate breaches of computer security, since it is well known that crime by computer is on the rise, inside and outside the Federal agencies.

From Scandinavia more reassuring news has come about what are called 'data banks'. The Swedish Data Inspection Board, set up in 1973 to license and supervise data banks containing personal information, stated in 1975 that they had received about 16,000 applications covering between 20,000 and 25,000 personal registers. There had been 'just a few cases of real abuse' said the General Director of the Board, and the Board had refused only a few applications. Problems were normally resolved by discussion, but if a conflict remained, the privacy factor had priority.

The Swedish experience is relevant to the United Kingdom scene, according to *The Times* of 24 February 1976, since similar legislation will follow publication of the Government's White Paper on Computers and Privacy. The White Paper contained four commitments: first, there was an unqualified promise of legislation;

second, there was the commitment to set up a Data Protection Authority, which would be independent of everyone, including the Government; third, the Authority would oversee all computer systems holding personal information; finally, there would be a statutory code, with which all the systems would need to comply.

Certainly, the business world is alive to these swift advances. 'In the last 20 years, the productivity of the computer has increased over 1000 per cent,' states a recent IBM press announcement. It continues:

> With this kind of technological advance, the possibility of storing more and more information at a central point is growing at a phenomenal rate. But so is the possibility of gaining access to the stored information. And that raises serious questions regarding personal privacy.

This is, in fact, an understatement. For some time there has been a growing effort in many European countries to preserve the individual's privacy in the face of expanding requirements for information by government, business and other organisations. In some countries, as we have seen, special legislation has been enacted to protect the individual's privacy; and this is likely to grow. In searching for appropriate legislative guidelines, private and governmental groups have explored many avenues. IBM, as a business organisation, sums up four basic principles as follows:

(1) Individuals should have access to information about themselves in record-keeping systems;
(2) There should also be a way for individuals to correct or amend inaccurate records;
(3) Information on individuals should not be disclosed for other than authorized purposes;
(4) The custodian of data files containing sensitive information should take all precautions that the data are reliable and not misused.

IBM seems to have followed the lead set in the guidelines that the Group of Experts referred to above prepared in 1975 for the Human Rights Commission; namely, that there must be a proper balance between limiting access to information for the protection of individual privacy, on the one hand, and allowing freedom of information, on the other.

The basic right that we are dealing with here, we should remind ourselves, is tersely expressed in Article 19 of the Universal Declaration:

> Everyone has the right to freedom of opinion and expression; this right includes freedom to hold opinions without interference and to seek, receive and impart information and ideas through any media and regardless of frontiers.

The application of this and its related rights to an age of computers and electronic devices is no simple task. It was not even conceived in the early days of the United Nations, which was – and still is – regarded by many people as purely a political organisation to keep peace between troublesome governments.

Now, preparations for the Science and Technology for Development Conference to be held in Vienna in 1979 call for an immense planetary effort directed particularly towards the Third World. Computer communications are coming to be widely used in the economic field. Industrial enterprises are using digital computers to collect data from remote manufacturing plants, warehouses and sales offices and send them directly for immediate processing. In the social field, attempts have been made to establish computerised information systems accessible via terminals. Just one example: a country-wide information system, pooling data of the welfare, juvenile and adult probation and health agencies and of the local medical centre, was recently tied by telephone lines to a computer located at the civic centre. A beginning has also been made in introducing computer-assisted instruction via terminals into elementary schools, as well as universities. Where can this process stop? Or should it?[15]

The final Proclamation at the Teheran Conference on Human Rights in 1968 stated that 'while recent scientific discoveries and technological advances have opened vast prospects for economic, social and cultural progress, such developments may nevertheless endanger the rights and freedoms of individuals'. There was, however, no question of condemning technological progress in the name of some inflexible interpretation of the rights of man.

'On the contrary,' stated the late Pierre Juvigny, Conseiller d'Etat and French member of the Human Rights Commission,

> it was recognised that the new techniques could be powerful instruments in the service of those rights, especially as tools of economic and social development policy. Nevertheless, their

abuse could lead to serious and long-lasting violations of human rights, particularly of the civil and political rights sometimes referred to as traditional freedoms . . . Since 1968, the United Nations has been analysing this whole problem area in the light of the quickening pace of discoveries, their practical applications and the restrictions already imposed on their abuse, from the human rights standpoint, by legislation, jurisprudence and professional ethics.[16]

ANOTHER DECLARATION?

In the course of this chapter some examples have been given of how certain countries and some national scientific bodies have sought to come to grips with the problem of 'control' in the areas we have briefly surveyed. As one of the Human Rights Commission's reports summed up this wide field in 1976:

Methods which have been adopted or proposed for the protection on the national level of human rights against threats posed by recent scientific and technological developments include respect for the privacy of individuals in the light of advances in recording techniques; protection of the human personality and its physical and intellectual integrity in the light of advances in biology, medicine and biochemistry; experiments on human subjects; uses of electronics which may affect the rights of the person and the limits which should be placed on such uses in a democratic society; the right to just and favourable conditions of work and to just and favourable remuneration; the right to form and join trade unions; the right to rest and leisure; the right to food; the right to clothing and to housing; and the right to education and culture.[17]

Methods so far in evidence on the national level have included legislation, regulations, the licensing of devices, official guidelines, codes of ethics and science policies, as well as training programmes, inspection services, the testing of new equipment and housing planning. There have also been a number of judicial decisions on the protection of human rights against the threats posed by scientific developments. There is, however, widespread belief that the explosion of scientific knowledge and of its technological application which has taken place in the three decades of the UN's lifetime has not been accompanied by an urgent, profound and continuous consideration of their implications for human rights. This has become the more urgent since new scientific discoveries pass more rapidly than ever into practical application, and their implications for human rights are often unforeseen.

For this reason, as Ambassador Pierre Juvigny pointed out, the continuing researches and expert studies carried out by the Commission, and the Secretariat specialist staff servicing it, are producing essential guidelines for governments and scientific bodies alike, and these will be of immense value and importance for the future welfare of mankind.

'Areas in which informed *political* decisions on scientific and technical issues are required include technology assessment,' argues one of the Commission's experts. These decisions must cover the new technologies and their likely side-effects; the risk involved in technical processess and its acceptability, bearing in mind social and economic factors; and the early identification of large-scale effects that could arise from technological progress in general. In practice, decisions on matters of this kind are normally taken by Ministers on the advice of technical experts. While the background to the decisions is technical, the decisions themselves are basically political. Hence, the widest possible participation of the public in understanding the issues involved has become necessary and urgent. Judgments of this kind need to be made also in relation to the transfer of technology to new countries.

The acuteness of the issues raised today is due to the growing scale and complexity of communication networks, modern machinery, energy distribution, drug usage, and the increased consequences of failures or secondary effects, leading to disasters such as the failure of the first subsonic jets, the thalidomide tragedy, the Torrey Canyon shipwreck, and so on.

The UN's Expert Group, whose proposals have been embodied in this chapter, recommended that international machinery should be entrusted with technological assessment for mankind *as a whole*. This would include the assessment of the long-range effects of innovations and would aim at determining whether the time was right for such innovations. Both national and international machinery for technological assessment should recognise that it was *a basic human right* to have a voice in such decisions, and that these decisions must be made on the basis of the opinion of bodies of experts and laymen who represent the interests of the people.

Research into genetic engineering techniques was likened by Sir John Kendrew, FRS, in his presidential address to the British Association for the Advancement of Science's meeting in 1974 to the situation in nuclear physics thirty-five years ago, when it was common knowledge among physicists that the discovery of nuclear fission might make it possible to develop a new source of power. There was an urgent need for a permanent international monitoring agency with specialists from the appropriate fields of medicine and biology, who could assess the benefits and dangers of certain types of work. They would draw up safety regulations and specify the conditions of security for public health under which research could be carried out.

Surely the time has come, in addition to setting up international standards for specific human rights in relation to technological developments, for a new Declaration on Human Rights and Scientific and Technological Developments? There are many texts which could be taken into account in drafting such a Declaration. Now is the time for governments to act and to *use* the Commission's expertise for this further achievement.

7 Ways and Means

I must create a System, or be enslav'd by another Man's.

– William Blake (1830)

The point has been made several times in the preceding chapters that, although many approaches exist to human rights protection, official and unofficial, the *essential* framework within which the total movement proceeds is that of the United Nations system. The irony of this situation is that the UN family of organisations – especially the Human Rights Commission – is under constant attack by time-serving politicians and those sensation-seeking columnists who know little about how the system works and care less.

In this chapter, therefore, we shall be looking a little more closely at how it does work – and also at how it might work better. We shall also look further afield and summarise action under the European Convention and some recent proposals for new procedures. But the most important thing (repeating a theme in an earlier chapter) is to recognise that, but for the existence of the overall UN apparatus – Declaration, Covenants and Conventions, Commissions and Sub-Commissions, Working Groups, and so on – the *practice* of human rights on a world scale would become meaningless.

The close relationship between the voluntary societies and the official UN bodies, as stressed in Chapter 3, crops up at unexpected moments. Take a sample episode that occurred at a Working Group meeting of the Sub-Commission on Minorities in August 1977. This body is the five-member Expert Working Group on Slavery that received information from the Anti-Slavery Society of London concerning alleged 'household slavery', involving two United Nations officials stationed in New York. The members of this Group are not government appointees, but independent persons selected because of their special knowledge. They sit in *public* session, and their reports go to the higher bodies, and thus on to the General Assembly itself. So world-wide publicity is assured.

This Working Group discussed the information presented to it, though names of the parties were not given. The spokesman of the

Anti-Slavery Society, Colonel Patrick Montgomery, who was present, gave evidence that women employees of the officials designated were required to work long hours without vacation, were prevented from going out or even answering the telephone, and were subject to threats of deportation.

Members were divided on several points as to what *action* to take, if any. But the Chairman – Benjamin C. G. Whitaker, United Kingdom expert – said he hoped a summary of the discussion would be made available for Secretary-General Kurt Waldheim's attention, via the press reports. This is what in fact happened. The following day, *The Times* and other leading newspapers presented the allegations to the public. Public opinion is becoming one of the most powerful weapons in the fight for individual rights, thanks to the press in this particular case.

Here was a case where a voluntary society, through channels provided by the UN system, could reach a wide public and so stimulate protective action by the appropriate legal machinery – in this case, a suit in the US Courts, based on the international law of Human Rights as contained in the 1956 Supplementary Convention on the Abolition of Slavery, the Slave Trade, and Institutions and Practices Similar to Slavery, which had, in fact, been violated.

This cross-section of the quiet diplomacy of human rights as practised not by political leaders, but through the UN, bears out the statement made by Theodoor van Boven, the new Director of the Division of Human Rights, when in the same month in Geneva he opened the prestigious meeting of the recently appointed Human Rights Committee. Dr van Boven said that he attached 'particular importance' to the interest of *all* sectors of the international and national community in human rights work. The United Nations and, in particular, its human rights organs should not function in isolation, but should be in close rapport with the public at large.

With the adoption of the two International Covenants and other relevant instruments, he continued, 'a solid legal foundation' of human rights law had now been laid down for application at all levels of society: local, national and international. The new Human Rights Committee in its supervisory capacity was entrusted with the important responsibility of affirming, developing and strengthening the basic standards of human rights law as contained in the International Covenant on Civil and Political Rights and its Protocol.

THE NEW COMMITTEE

We can best begin our survey of 'ways and means' with the work of this new Committee of eighteen experts which began its career early in 1977; so it was still, as Dr van Boven said, 'in a pioneering stage'. The eighteen member Human Rights Committee is the most recent functional body to form part of the human rights 'system'. It is an independent body, however, and does not form part of the United Nations, though it is serviced by the UN Secretariat – an encouraging example of the flexibility of the UN system in meeting new situations. It was set up under the International Covenant on Civil and Political Rights after the Covenant entered into force on 23 March 1976. Its main job is to examine reports by states on their implementation of the Covenant. Under the optional provisions of that Covenant it may consider communications from a state that is party to the Covenant which considers that another state party is not fulfilling its Covenant obligations. Its work is rather technical and it is too early yet to assess its value to the system.

Forty-four countries have ratified the Covenant, and sixteen have ratified the Optional Protocol, which has also come into force. The provisions concerning complaints by one state of violations by another have been so far accepted by six states, and will become effective when ten states in all have accepted the procedures. As a general rule, meetings of the Committee will be public, but private meetings will be held when the Committee is considering communications from individuals.

The Committee will study the reports submitted by each state party within one year of the entry into force of the Covenant for the state concerned. These reports will deal with measures adopted to give effect to the rights recognised in the Covenant and on the progress made in the enjoyment of those rights. After studying these reports, the Committee is authorised to send such general comments as it considers appropriate to the states who are party to the Covenant.These, in turn, may submit their observations on any comments made. The Committee will then transmit its comments to the Economic and Social Council. On the basis of these reports, a permanent dialogue is expected to develop between the expert and impartial representatives of the international community, who were chosen to sit on this Committee, and the states parties.

One aspect of this dialogue is expected to be the overcoming of the obstacles which may arise in implementing the Covenant. It should be noted that among the Communist countries who have ratified or adhered to the Covenant are Bulgaria, Byelorussia, Czechoslovakia, East Germany, Hungary, Mongolia, Poland, Romania, the Ukraine, the USSR and Yugoslavia.

Individual 'Communications' (that is to say, complaints) will obviously assume a considerable place in the Committee's pro- gramme as time goes on. The Committee will receive and discuss communications from individuals who claim to be victims of a violation of a right set forth in the Covenant by states who have accepted the Optional Protocol. The states who have done so are: Barbados, Canada, Colombia, Costa Rica, Denmark, Ecuador, Finland, Jamaica, Madagascar, Mauritius, Norway, Surinam, Sweden, Uruguay and Zaire. The Committee cannot receive a complaint against a state not a party to the Optional Protocol, nor can it consider communications which are anonymous or which are an abuse of the right of submission. Moreover, all available domestic remedies must have been exhausted, provided that the application for domestic redress is not too prolonged.

The Rights protected by the Covenants cover so wide a field that the Committee will be bound to come frequently to public notice. To select a few: the political Covenant protects the right to life (Article 6); prohibits torture or cruel, inhuman or degrading treatment or punishment (Article 7); prohibits slavery and forced labour (Article 8); prohibits arbitrary arrest or detention (Article 9); asserts the right to liberty of movement and the freedom to leave any country (Article 12); sets limitations on the expulsion of aliens (Article 13); prohibits retroactive criminal legislation (Article 15); and prohibits arbitrary or unlawful interference with privacy, family, home or correspondence and unlawful attacks on honour and reputation (Article 17). To these earlier provisions we can add the rest of the articles as set out in Appendix I. Finally, the Covenant includes an article dealing with the subject of minorities, not treated in the Universal Declaration; Article 27 of the Covenant provides that persons belonging to ethnic, religious or linguistic minorities shall not be denied the right, in community with the other members of their group, to enjoy their own culture, to profess and practise their own religion or to use their own language.

An interesting debate took place at the second meeting of the Human Rights Committee in August 1977 on the best technique for handling individual complaints. It led to the formation of several rules dealing with the difficult question of their 'admissibility', and the following guidelines were approved:

(a) that the communication is not anonymous and emanates from an individual within the jurisdiction of a state party;

(b) that it is not an abuse of the right to submit a communication;

(c) that it falls within the scope of the provisions of the Covenant;

(d) that the same matter is not being examined under some other procedure of international investigation;

(e) that the individual has exhausted all available *domestic* remedies.

Although the complaint should be submitted by the individual himself (or his legal representative), the Committee may accept one submitted on behalf of an alleged victim when he is unable to submit it himself. This, of course, is often likely to happen if the victim is under illegal detention. Indeed, it is expected that in many cases the mere fact that this weighty UN Committee of Experts has the case in hand, will itself cut short the complainant's illegal detention.

Quite another, and no less important, function of the Committee is to study, as stated above, the reports submitted by each state party to the political Covenant dealing with measures adopted to give effect to the rights recognised in the Covenant, and also on the progress made nationally in the enjoyment of those rights. Difficulties, if any, affecting the implementation of the Covenant will be openly discussed in this Committee. On the basis of these reports and the Committee's study of them, a permanent dialogue between impartial representatives of the international community and the states parties is expected to develop over the years ahead, with the object of overcoming any obstacles that may arise.

The Committee submits to the General Assembly an annual report of these activities. Thus, a new procedure is evolving today within the UN system. Although limited at present to only a few states, it promises to grow into one of the main world-based organs of international justice and individual rights protection as more states adopt the Covenant and its Protocol.

It should be recalled how very recently any official procedure has been devised for governments to *listen collectively* to complaints from individuals! So we might consider, for a moment or two, a parallel procedure to that of the new Committee. In 1970 the Economic and Social Council laid down in Resolution 1503 a procedure for dealing with allegations of violations of human rights and fundamental freedoms. Under this earlier procedure, there are three stages. First, the Sub-Commission on Prevention of Discrimination and Protection of Minorities is authorised to appoint a Working Party

> to consider all communications, including replies of governments thereon . . . with a view to bringing to the attention of the Sub-Commission those communications, together with the replies of governments, if any, which appear to reveal a consistent pattern of gross and reliably-attested violations of human rights and fundamental freedoms.

A large number of complaints have reached this Working Group, whose sessions are naturally held in private.

Second, the Sub-Commission considers the communications brought before it by the Working Group, and any replies of governments and any other relevant information, 'with a view to determining whether to refer to the Commision on Human Rights particular situations which appear to reveal *a consistent pattern of gross* and reliably-attested violations of human rights requiring consideration by the Commission' (our italics).

Third, the Commission, after examining any situation referred to it, is asked to determine: (a) 'whether it requires a thorough study by the Commission and recommendations thereon to the Council', or (b) 'whether it may be a subject of an investigation by an *ad hoc* committee to be appointed by the Commission'. But this latter step can only be taken 'with the express consent of the State concerned and conducted in constant co-operation with that State and under conditions determined by agreement with it'. Admissible communications may originate from individuals or groups who are victims of violations, persons having direct knowledge of violations, or non-governmental organisations (acting in good faith and not politically motivated) having direct knowledge of such violations.

This earlier procedure came into operation for the first time in 1972, when the Working Group singled out complaints relating to three countries: Greece, Iran and Portugal. The communication concerning Greece (to mention one of these) consisted of a complete dossier filed by Professor Frank Newman of the University of California, as Counsel for the International Commission of Jurists, the International League for the Rights of Man, the Fédération Internationale des Droits de l'Homme, the International Association of Democratic Lawyers, Amnesty International and seven Greek exiles who had personally suffered violations of their human rights. One of them was Lady Amelia Fleming. This dossier included a large number of personal affidavits by individuals who had been subjected to arbitrary arrest and detention, torture or cruel or inhuman treatment, and by persons who had been denied fair trials and their right to freedom of opinion, peaceful assembly and association, or deprived of their nationality, and who had also been prevented from expressing their will in genuine elections or had in other respects been subjected to violation of their human rights. In an earlier chapter we dealt with the trials that were soon to follow, when the Greek junta was deposed in 1974.

With all its delays and the obstruction of certain governments, this earlier procedure constituted a landmark in the history of the implementation of human rights. For the first time, within the framework of the United Nations, there was a procedure under which private individuals and non-governmental organisations, as well as governments, could and still can raise complaints about violations of human rights within a state and have those complaints investigated outside it by an impartial international body.

Now, both procedures exist side by side. Human Rights specialists see no inconsistency in the simultaneous existence of the two types of procedure. There may soon be more. The Resolution 1503 procedure is universal in its application, whereas the procedure for the political Covenant will apply only in respect of those states which have made declarations under Article 41 (relating to complaints by other states) or which have signed the Optional Protocol (relating to complaints by individuals). There we must leave this somewhat technical, but very relevant exposition of human rights protection.

THE EUROPEAN CONNECTION

Whereas the enforcement machinery in the field of human rights set up under the UN system has been adopted only recently, as noted above, certain European states have succeeded on a regional basis in erecting a more effective and sometimes speedier mechanism. The original member states of the Council of Europe adopted at

Rome in 1950 a Convention for the Protection of Human Rights and Fundamental Freedoms. Its Preamble exemplifies the advantages it enjoys by stating that the members are 'like-minded and have a common heritage of political traditions, ideals, freedom and the rule of law'. In fact, the relative success of the European system has raised the question many times as to whether *regional* systems could not be more widely initiated. In addition to the South American system (noticed already) there have been calls for a Human Rights organisation in the Caribbean, in Asia, in Africa, and so on. Such a development need not detract from the UN's universal function, but would supplement it.

By 1977, eighteen European states had ratified the Convention. This Convention limits the rights to be protected to a number of elementary rights and freedoms, but does not contain any social or economic rights, such as those covered by the Universal Declaration and the Covenants that we have been studying. A Protocol to the Rome Convention, however, deals with the right of education, the right to own property, and the right to participate in free elections. The limitations of this Convention and the earlier reluctance of member states to expand it by a Protocol, as well as its omission of general economic and social rights, we must pass over here. They are dealt with at length in *Human Rights in Europe*, by Dr A. H. Robertson, formerly Human Rights Director of the Council of Europe.[1]

Yet this Convention is perhaps most noteworthy in that it provides for measures of *compliance* with its provisions, namely, through the European Commission of Human Rights and the European Court of Human Rights. The Commission itself consists of members of different nationalities equal to that of the eighteen contracting states. The members are elected by the Committee of Ministers for a period of six years, but sit on the Commission in their individual capacity. The jurisdiction of the Commission is obligatory when one of the contracting states submits an alleged breach of the provisions of the Convention by another contracting state. If the Commission accepts a complaint as admissible, it carries out a thorough examination. If a friendly settlement is arrived at, the Commission draws up a statement of the facts and the solution reached. Failing such a friendly settlement, the Commission submits its opinion to the Council of Ministers, which determines by a two-thirds majority whether a violation of the Convention has taken place, and if so, what remedial measures should be taken.

States are bound to act on the decision thus reached.

In addition, the Commission is authorised to receive petitions from any persons, non-governmental organisations or groups of individuals claiming to be the victim of a violation by one of the contracting states of the rights in the Convention, provided that the contracting state against which the complaint has been lodged has recognised the competence of the Commission to receive petitions. Petitions are handled in the same way as applications from the states. The Commission has received some 7000 petitions to date, but more than 98 per cent of these have been declared inadmissible.[2]

The European Court of Human Rights, which handled the controversial Ireland v. United Kingdom case (see Chapter 3), consists of eighteen judges of different nationalities, one for each member state of the Council of Europe. These judges are elected by the Consultative Assembly for a period of nine years from a list of persons nominated by the Council of Europe. Only contracting states and the Commission itself have the right to submit cases to the Court concerning the interpretation and application of the Convention. The Court began to function in 1960. A contracting state may declare that it recognises as compulsory and without special agreement the jurisdiction of the Court in all such matters.[3]

A case is brought before the Court if the Contracting state is subject to the compulsory jurisdiction of the Court, or with its consent. The Court can deal with a case only after the Commission has acknowledged the failure of efforts for a friendly settlement. It should be noted that *an individual* has no recourse to this Court and he is not a party to the proceedings before the Court, even though he has been the applicant before the Commission. The judgement of the Court is final and is transmitted to the Committee of Ministers which is to supervise its execution. The contracting states have all agreed by the Convention to abide by the decision of the Court in any case where they are a party.

It will perhaps serve to illustrate the considerable variety of cases that in the last few years have come within the scope of the European Convention, if we conclude this outline by sketching two quite different procedures: one that is currently before the Court and another, few years ago, that involved questions of high politics and left the sufferers without any immediate measure of redress.

The first relates to a case of corporal punishment against the Manx Government that came before the European Human Rights

Court in Strasbourg in the autumn of 1977. It had been presented five years earlier by the National Council for Civil Liberties on behalf of a youth, then aged fifteen, who received three strokes of the birch after pleading guilty to assaulting and causing bodily harm to a prefect who had reported some boys for taking beer into their school. He appealed against sentence, but his local appeal was dismissed and the birching was carried out. The young man, now twenty-one, had tried to withdraw the appeal to Strasbourg; but the case was proceeded with because, in the opinion of the Human Rights Commission, it was still a 'case of general concern'.

The other example is of quite a different order. It occurred when the Greek colonels seized power in Athens on 21 April 1967. There was no question that the Government was in open breach of its obligations when it suppressed the rights and liberties of the Greek people. As a party to the European Convention on Human Rights, the military junta thus struck at the heart of the European system. The evidence the European Commission gathered in the course of more than two years of investigation roundly indicted the regime for its denial of human rights. The Commission called for an undertaking by the Greek Government to restore democratic freedom, to exercise control over the methods used by the security police, to close certain prisons and to punish those found guilty of torture and maltreatment of prisoners and political opponents.

There is a close parallel here with the UN Human Rights Commission's confrontation with Pinochet's Chile since 1973. The European Commission's proper demand for the restoration of civil and political liberties, including the right to parliamentary democracy, not only questioned the legitimacy of the regime, but also challenged its right to exist! The junta's justification for seizing power was that it had 'saved' the country from an imminent Communist take-over; the suspension of civil and political rights was a necessary 'emergency' measure to ensure internal order. When the Commission concluded that there was not sufficient ground for the claim that a Communist take-over was imminent, it again denied the legitimacy of the regime itself and questioned its right to political existence. As with the Chile revolution, it was a *political* solution that was sought and one denied by the junta.

The matter was taken further when, in September 1967, Denmark, Norway, Sweden and The Netherlands accused the Papadopoulos regime of violating Greece's obligations under the European Convention, and they jointly asserted that the

Government's derogation from its obligations was not justified by the facts. The Commission declared the application admissible and received during the next eighteen months written and oral submissions from some hundred witnesses, within Greece and abroad. All attempts to reach a friendly settlement with the Greek Government came to nothing; so the European Commission on Human Rights transmitted its report to the Committee of Ministers for final action, maintaining its competence to examine the acts of *governments* in political situations of an extraordinary character, such as following a revolution and even the violent overthrow of a regime.

Since, however, the Commission's further investigations and appeals turned out to be negative, and since the Colonels' vicious dictatorship eventually collapsed – as such anti-human regimes may be expected to do when exposed to the united will of civilised men – we need not pursue here the Commission's further labours; but some cogent observations by a well-known writer in the field of human rights might well close this section:

> Whether the indictment of junta-ruled Greece constitutes the hope of the future or is no more than a fleeting promise, which quickly fades into disillusion, this was perhaps the first time that governments combined in an attempt to compel another government to abandon its repressive use of power at home and invoked the ultimate sanction at their command. In a sense, and within the limited area of jurisdiction, the Council of Europe made the recognition and observance of human rights the criterion and judgment of a government's worth.[4]

A HIGH COMMISSIONER?

There are thirty-eight Ombudsmen in the world today, working at state level to investigate the complaints of individuals against their own government or administration, called Parliamentary Commissioner in Britain and 'Médiateur' in France.[5] But there is as yet no High Commissioner working at the global level to investigate the complaints of those individuals who have been turned down or ignored by their own governments or have no other means of redress. Ever since 1963, however, proposals have been explored under the UN's ample mandate for the institution of a High

Commissioner or 'Attorney-General' for Human Rights to fill in the gaps, as it were, of the present limited international system of human rights protection, outlined earlier in this chapter. Undoubtedly, this is one of the biggest and most overdue reforms in that system. So it is important to study both the advantages and the limitations of such an office, which might be compared in status with that of an Assistant or even Deputy Secretary-General, appointed to deal especially with human rights.

Not surprisingly, non-governmental organisations have been pressing this sort of proposal for years; but, not unnaturally, some governments within the UN still regard the proposal as anathema and rigidly oppose it – it would open up too many skeletons in too many cupboards to earth-wide scrutiny!

Actually, the idea goes back to 1947, when the late Professor Cassin, Director of the Institute of Human Rights at Strasbourg, advocated the creation of an Attorney-General at the time the Universal Declaration was being drafted. But the possibility that an international official could present and defend *individual* grievances against governments was then considered an idealist's dream. Nevertheless, the UN was at that same time grappling with the massive refugee problems left over from the Second World War; and in 1949 the General Assembly decided to establish a High Commissioner for Refugees.[6]

It was a non-governmental organisation, however, the Consultative Council of Jewish Organisations, backed by the Government of Uruguay, which presented to the Human Rights Commission in 1950 a memorandum entitled 'A U.N. Attorney-General or High Commissioner for Human Rights'. As from that date, for a quarter of a century the proposal has been on the official *tapis* – to be revived, as we have seen, in 1963. It was, in fact, put on the agenda of the 1977 General Assembly, which passed the question to the 1978 session of the Commission on Human Rights for detailed consideration.

What would be the functions of such an official, if appointed? In the several debates that have taken place in UN organs, a High Commissioner's functions have not been clearly defined, except perhaps in a negative sense. The Soviet Union, no doubt casting a jaundiced eye back on the old colonial system, once proudly asserted that 'the Russian people had never been under the thumb of a High Commissioner'. Supporting governments' proposals have always been modest. Costa Rica, for example, first put the question to the General Assembly in 1965, proposing that the holder of the post should undertake four main tasks:

(1) assist in securing wider observance of the Universal Declaration;

(2) advise the Commission on Human Rights and other UN bodies on periodical reports coming from Governments;

(3) report annually to the General Assembly; and also in case of urgency

(4) render assistance and services to any government so requesting.

It will be seen from this brief summary of functions, presented to ECOSOC and the General Assembly at one time or another, that such an appointment, if and when it came about, could hardly be deemed epoch-making. But the degree of resistance coming from governments, both West and East, would make any more ambitious plan less likely of adoption at this stage. Some supporting non-governmental organisations have rather envisaged the High Commissioner in the shape of an orthodox UK or US Attorney-General – a Lord High Inquisitor? – bent on prosecuting offending governments who violate human rights laws and defending individual victims of oppressive dictatorships. It is important, however, to surmount the first hurdle first, and get the office established.

In addition to the pioneer initiative of the Consultative Council of Jewish Organisations a quarter of a century ago, the mounting support for action at the General Assembly level has caused many non-governmental organisations, such as the International Commission of Jurists and the International Confederation of Free Trade Unions, to come together and focus their efforts on the Thirtieth Anniversary of the Universal Declaration. For example, 'Campaign Human Rights 78', under the direction of Rita Maran of London, its Co-ordinator, and sponsored by Lord Noel-Baker, the Quakers, the Fellowship of Reconciliation and other organisations committed to non-violence, seeks to co-ordinate like-minded groups in Europe and South America. It calls for the following objectives:

(1) the setting up of the Office of United Nations High Commissioner for Human Rights, and

(2) a Special Session of the General Assembly to deal exclusively with questions of human rights.

The Campaign stresses that

the HCHR would be like an Ombudsman, initiating studies into situations involving human rights, publicising his findings, and persuading states to review their laws and standards. While Governments would not be obligated to accept these findings or make changes, public opinion pressure would make compliance more likely.

It is sometimes feared that such an office would interfere with national sovereign rights, as guaranteed in Article 2(7) of the UN Charter; *i.e.*: 'Nothing contained in the present Charter shall authorize the United Nations to intervene in matters which are essentially within the domestic jurisdiction of any state . . .' The Communist countries have repeatedly fallen back on this clause, though they are by no means alone in so doing. This point has already been taken up in our first chapter, where it was argued that the prominent place given to human rights in the Charter has driven an even bigger hole through Article 2(7). In any case, a High Commissioner (like the Secretary-General) could only respond to *individual* complaints – as U Thant once put it – 'from a personal and humanitarian standpoint'.

There is no possibility here of going into the elaborate discussion that has been proceeding for over a decade and which has been so well delineated in Dr Roger Clark's book, especially on the delicate problem of receiving complaints from individuals. But several general lines of possible action may be suggested before we close this topic:

1 a High Commissioner would be only one further element in the structure of human rights development; he would supplement, not replace existing methods of redress;

2 in his personal contacts with Governments, he might often be able to encourage them to *ratify* long-outstanding conventions;

3 like the UN Secretary-General, he would be able to play a quiet behind-the-scenes role of considerable value to governments in difficulty, both in terms of finding the facts and offering them his 'good offices';

4 especially in emergency situations – e.g. a detainee awaiting execution – responsible non-governmental organisations (NGOs) might make direct appeals to his office;

5 In fact, NGOs, with their special access to sources of information across the world, would often be able to 'brief' him,

where governments might be more reticent.

From the bare sketch of the possibilities outlined above, it is clear that, if and when the General Assembly does establish a High Commissioner for Human Rights (as it was strongly pressed to do at its 1977 session), the fourth decade of the Universal Declaration will see an expansion of the Rule of Law among sovereign states and a further consolidation of the Rights of Man.

A BRITISH BILL OF RIGHTS?

Coming, finally, to Britain, 'it is nearly three centuries since the last Bill of Rights was passed in this country', says Sir Leslie Scarman; and he continues:

> The enactment of a modern one, which would take account of the social, political, legal, and cultural changes in our environment since 1689, has many attractions. But it also raises a number of problems of content, of form, of enforcement, and of the manner and degree of the constitutional protection to be given it.[7]

Unlike some countries (Austria, Belgium, France, Italy, for instance), the European Convention does not become, as lawyers say, 'self-executing' in English domestic law. Special legislation would be needed to transform the provisions of the Convention into directly applicable law. This has happened with Common Market law, but not with the European Convention on Human Rights. For this and other reasons a wide public debate has developed in Britain – and not among lawyers only – as to whether Lord Justice Scarman's proposal (raised in the first chapter of this book) should not find its way onto the Statute Book. A number of public enquiries have already been set on foot; but the issue – a revolutionary one in British constitutional practice – is by no means near settlement. Only a brief conspectus of some of the elements involved, bearing on the human rights of British subjects, can be attempted before concluding this chapter.

For example, a leading layman protagonist for enacting the European Convention as part of English law, so that the courts can enforce it directly at the suit of all citizens, sets out the case as follows: 'If conflicting claims to rights are to be resolved in ways that are just, and are seen and felt to be just,' says Tom Sargant, the redoubtable Secretary of Justice, the British branch of the International Commission of Jurists,

> then there must be just laws, and just courts in which they can be asserted, defended, and enforced. An independent judiciary, and a fearless, honest and independent legal profession are essential prerequisites for the Rule of Law – all the more so now that there is an appeal to International Human Rights Law to determine whether domestic laws are just laws . . . and each nation must find the most appropriate means for achieving that end within its territory.[8]

As Lord Gardiner, a former Lord Chancellor, has pointed out on more than one occasion, the European Convention is still not part of our domestic law, though it is more than a quarter of a century since we became bound by it. The anomaly is, suggests Sargant, that our own courts, unlike those of many other European countries, cannot therefore apply the Convention yet, and our citizens cannot go to them to seek redress for its infringement, but must go to Strasbourg instead. 'That alone', Sargant continues, 'is a powerful argument for now enacting it as part of our domestic law.' He adds:

> What is important to remember – as the British Institute of Human Rights has again pointed out quite recently – is that this has nothing to do with a written constitution, the sovereignty of Parliament, or administrative law. We could have a Bill of Rights (as, for example, in the form of the European Convention) without a written constitution. We could have a written constitution without having a Bill of Rights. We could have either, or both, without fettering the sovereignty of Parliament.[9]

There is no doubt that this variety of constitutional choices has slowed down any governmental or Parliamentary decision on so vital a subject – quite apart from the preceding 300 years of non-action. Some constitutional lawyers still believe in 'letting sleeping dogs lie'. But others, shaken by the Strasbourg judgements, know all too well that that faithful English mastiff, the Law, can no longer be left to slumber peacefully in seventeenth-century nostalgia. For Lord Justice Scarman warned us in his 1974 Hamlyn Lecture of new challenges. More recently, he has stated:

> A few years ago there was almost no English legal literature on the subject. The unwritten constitution enshrining the sov-

ereignty of Parliament was the basic assumption of English legal thinking. All is changed: the volume of literature is now impressive. The English, who are in one of their revolutionary phases, are questioning all their institutions and assumptions – including their constitution and the efficacy of their legal system to protect their fundamental rights and freedoms.[10]

'The question is no longer: do we need a Bill of Rights?' asserts the Lord Justice:

> But, what sort of Bill of Rights do we need? Bearing in mind that we as a people prefer our revolutions to be painless, I think the answer must be an ordinary statute based on the European Convention and limited to the regulation of the relations between State and citizen . . . My conclusion is that we need a new Bill of Rights now; and that there is nothing to fear. It would rejuvenate English law.

Under the newsy caption 'One more reason why Britain urgently needs a Bill of Rights', Mr Keith Kyle writes that the Strasbourg case 'has dramatized the existence of the European Convention on Human Rights in a way in which perhaps only the proceedings against the Greek junta had done before'. He draws the conclusion:

> This leaves Britain in a rather curious position. If we fail to get into the Bill of Rights game soon, we may find bits of the European Convention enforced by our courts in their Community capacity, while the ordinary citizen, most of the time, has no such safeguard [*The Times*, 6 September 1976].[11]

Meantime, warnings against expecting too much from a Bill of Rights have been falling thick and fast, delaying still further any positive action by the authorities. Are we not taking on too much by thinking that where the Continent leads, Britain can safely follow? Another former Lord Chancellor, Lord Hailsham, delivering the annual Richard Sullivan lecture, thought that it would hardly be worth the trouble of having a British Bill of Rights, except as part of a basic constitutional change. Lord Hailsham expressed his lukewarm support for a British Bill, but he insisted:

> A Bill of Rights is no panacea. It will not wash woollens. It will not meet the growing pressure for local assemblies in Scotland, Wales and Northern Ireland. It will offer no protection against our present system of voting, if protection is required.

In his view:

It will offer only a limited safeguard against the misuse of
Parliament's unlimited power of legislation by a temporary junta
of jacks in office. It will do nothing to supply the want of an
acceptable and effective second chamber. It may do little or
nothing to prevent oppression by large corporations or unions.

'By itself,' Lord Hailsham concludes:

It is only marginally worth the trouble and the labour. As part,
however, of a radical overhaul of our constitutional arrangements, a Bill of Rights entrenching the European Convention on
Human Rights, is a modest but desirable addition to the
armament of liberty against populist or bureaucratic intrusion
and oppression [*The Times*, 26 May 1977].

In other words, if there *were* to be a Bill of Rights for the United
Kingdom, Lord Hailsham was in favour of incorporating the
European Convention on Human Rights, rather than drawing up a
'custom-built' Bill.

Among the various committees and groups now working on the
topic, the House of Lords has set up an all-party committee under
the chairmanship of Lord Allen of Abbeydale, to examine whether
a Bill on human rights is desirable. Another is the Standing
Advisory Commission on Human Rights, set up to advise the
Northern Ireland Secretary. Under the chairmanship of an English
trade-union leader, Cyril Plant, the Commission would seem to be
tending to the conclusion that Northern Ireland certainly needs a
Bill of Rights. The somewhat circular case is that historical factors
necessitate *special* protection; that there is an instrument to hand in
the shape of the European Convention; but that this cannot be
brought to bear on one part only of the United Kingdom; so that it
must, therefore, be applied to the whole country!

There are admittedly considerable difficulties about the whole
proposal. British judges have no experience in interpreting rules as
vaguely drawn as the Convention is, and the TUC is uneasy at the
picture of still wider judicial discretion. So are certain Cabinet
Ministers. Moreover, the United Kingdom forces of order in
Northern Ireland wonder what limits the Convention would put on
their own powers, especially over holding suspects.

The fairness of judges, in being given yet greater power to
interpret social legislation, was strongly attacked at a recent

National Council for Civil Liberties Conference called to debate whether Britain should introduce a Bill of Rights. 'Our judiciary has a long and continuing record of fighting progress and of opposing Parliament's reforms,' said Mr Stephen Sedley, a Labour barrister, arguing against a Bill: 'Once the courts are presented with a choice of interpretations, the field is open to the judges to decide according to their own predilections and prejudices, and every practising lawyer knows what they are.' Mr Sedley said that the list of examples was endless: the Rent Acts, slum-clearance legislation, factory safety legislation – all had a long history of judicial obstruction, 'causing Parliament to legislate to repair the damage done by lawyers and judges. How much more obstruction could they create with the backing of a Bill of Rights, that set them in judgment on Parliament?'

The danger of British judges becoming linked with politics if a Bill of Rights were introduced was discussed also at a seminar at the 1975 annual conference of the Law Society. Lord Justice Scarman, whose Hamlyn Lecture a year earlier had been instrumental in reviving the call for a Bill, presided over a panel consisting of Mr James Fawcett, who was President of the European Commission of Human Rights, and Professor Harry Street, Professor of English Law at Manchester University.

Professor Street asserted that there were many areas in which the citizen was being unfairly treated by the executive. The balance between the state and the individual was not a fair one. But would the judges correct this imbalance under a Bill of Rights? 'When I think', he said,

> of the opportunities judges have had in the past to protect the citizens by fashioning the common law contrary to the wishes of the executive, how sure can we be that the courts will welcome the onerous task of finding an Act of Parliament void because it was inconsistent with the Bill of Rights?

This was strong language. If the judges were to assume that power, would it not make them into a different kind of animal, more political; more like the judges of the United States Supreme Court? Was that desirable?

Lord Justice Scarman naturally disagreed that judges might become political if a Bill of Rights were introduced. 'The courts are already in the arena of politics,' he said: 'Yet, instead of being the bold matador looking the bull in the face, they are running away.

But they are still in the arena.' Dr Fawcett also took the view that a
Bill of Rights would not make British judges political. The
Crossman diaries case was one example of a court being asked, in
effect, to make a political decision. What was there to fear?

The politicisation of English judges is, however, too involved a
subject on which to end this chapter. It is sufficient that the debate
goes on. There is, however, still a big gap between feasibility and
desirability. For instance, at a recent symposium arranged by the
British Institute of Human Rights to look at the problems which
would attend the establishment of guarantees for human rights in
the United Kingdom, it was finally agreed that a Bill of Rights
would be *feasible* – 'if thought desirable'.

It is in those last three words that the essence of the problem still
remains unresolved. In winding up a 1976 debate in the House of
Lords on the Second Reading of a Bill providing that the European
Convention should have the force of law, the Minister of State for
the Home Office said:

> The Government's acceptance of the Convention as binding in
> international law in no way required them to incorporate that
> provision into the domestic legal system. All that was required
> was that the United Kingdom law and the way it was adminis-
> tered should conform to the Convention and not be inconsistent
> with it. The Government . . . were some way yet from being
> ready to form an informed and balanced judgment. In the
> Government's view the need was for wide public discussion so
> that they could begin to form such a judgment.

8 Sovereignty of Man

We can no longer separate the traditional issues of war and peace from the new global questions of justice, equity and human rights.
  – President Carter (Indiana, 22 May 1977)

Recalling that no 'doctrine' of Human Rights has yet been created, so as to sustain a comprehensive political or ethical order (like Democracy or Communism, or Totalitarianism) we can best begin this final chapter by looking afresh at some of the fundamentals that have come to the surface in the foregoing survey and ask: What are the long-term objectives towards which – however long it may take – the modern movement is striving?

To this question Dr Hersch Lauterpacht has offered a practical answer:

An international legal system which aims at effectively safeguarding human freedom in all its aspects is no longer an abstraction . . . International law, which has excelled in punctilious insistence on the respect owed by one sovereign State to another, henceforth acknowledges the sovereignty of Man. For fundamental human rights are rights superior to the law of the sovereign State.[1]

This passage might well become an opening call for the supreme battle of the twenty-first century. For the twentieth century is clearly still dominated by the sovereign State. National sovereignty permeates countless resolutions and declarations that flow nowadays from the world forum. The reasons for this tidal wave of national egotism are many and cannot be itemised here: but two major reasons for the emphasis – some would say obsession – on national sovereignty are, first, the rediscovery by the Communist countries that it will strengthen their world role; and, second, the newly found independence of the Third World, shaking off the age-long fetters of colonisation.

The debate on 'national sovereignty' (barely touched on in this section) is bound to widen and deepen during the 1980s. The following view, for instance, dominated an NGO Conference on Indian Treaty Rights held in Geneva in September 1977:

> The issues being raised by Indian peoples are different from the challenging and legitimate civil rights questions. The Sioux are raising the question of *sovereignty*, throwing into perspective the very validity of United States political control of the Continent. In asserting sovereignty, the Sioux join other colonies [*sic*.] and former colonies all over the world who have been subjected to European and United States colonialism, in declaring integrity as a separate Nation.

It should be noticed, however, that the UN Charter speaks of 'sovereign equality', rather than sovereignty in any absolute sense. The fact remains, nevertheless, that all the members states of the UN never hesitate to assert their 'sovereign rights' in their relations with other states on all possible occasions. Unfortunately, it is not generally appreciated that this obsession with the sovereign rights of the 150 separate sovereign states who compose the UN is an almost certain guarantee of inter-state war – whether small but containable 'brush' wars, or a nuclear-weapon global conflict which, however it began or ended, would render questions like 'human rights' irrelevant for all time.

State sovereignty and world peace – as Thomas Hobbes postulated and John Locke refined – are incompatible with human survival. Yet our nation-states today are asking for both at the same time. They cannot, logically, have both; so they compromise as crisis follows crisis. This is the daily dilemma facing the United Nations. Speeches by national spokesmen upon the General Assembly rostrum give fluent verbal utterance to the priority of peace; but their Foreign Offices or State Departments back home ignore the contradiction and carry on as if it did not exist.

Peace societies – especially the World Federalists – have for many years focused their policies and educational programmes on resolving the dilemma. Surely mankind cannot be destined to remain impaled on the horns of such a dilemma until catastrophe falls? Where then can we look for some talisman to escape from it?

It is at this point that human rights would seem to have become the forgotten key to human survival. If Lauterpacht is right, the sovereign state is already yielding to the Sovereignty of Man. The present book has sought, therefore, to describe *how* that process has been developing. Again, in Lauterpacht's words:

In so far as the denial of the fundamental rights of man has been associated with the nation-State asserting the claim to ultimate reality and utterly subordinating the individual to a mystic and absolute personality of its own, the recognition of these rights is a brake upon exclusive and aggressive nationalism, which is the obstacle, both conscious and involuntary, to the idea of a world community under the rule of law.

Addressing the School of Political Science at Athens on 17 December 1964, Dr C. Wilfred Jenks left no doubt as to his own views:

Sovereignty holds no promise of peace; it affords no prospect of defence; it provides no assurance of justice; it gives no guarantee of freedom; it offers no hope of prosperity; it furnishes no prescription for welfare; it disrupts the discipline without which scientific and technological change becomes the Frankenstein of our society. It is a mockery, not a fulfilment, of the deepest aspirations of humanity.[2]

Yet as Jenks warned in his *Common Law of Mankind* these changes might take several generations. But they are happening. No-one knows what directions human rights will take in the 1980s; but, from now on, human rights and world peace are inseparable links in what Arthur O. Lovejoy, the Harvard philosopher, has so well encapsulated in the title of his important work *The Great Chain of Being*.[3]

It would offer a strong temptation for us to trace some of the means by which the claims of state sovereignty can be diverted to serve the rights of man; but it has been the chief aim of the present book to focus on operative programmes concerned with the pragmatic protection of human rights, rather than to explore their philosophical foundations or possible future constitutional structures.[4]

This final chapter will therefore concentrate on elucidating what human rights specialists regard as the most comprehensive research undertaking yet proposed by the Human Rights Commission, and which was sanctioned by the United Nations General Assembly at its 1977 session. The main elements of the New Resolution, adopted by the Commission on 21 February 1977, are summarised in the following pages, though we will be chiefly concerned here with four specific topics on which the Resolution calls for detailed studies, namely:

1 the realisation of economic, social and cultural rights;
2 the international dimensions of the right to development;
3 measures leading to general and complete disarmament;
4 the right to peace.

A NEW HUMAN ORDER?

In the formal language of the Resolution: 'The question of the realization of the economic, social and cultural rights contained in the Universal Declaration of Human Rights and in the International Covenant on Economic, Social and Cultural Rights', now calls for, in the Commission's words, 'a study of the special problems relating to human rights in developing countries'.

Earlier chapters have already outlined both the importance of what has been termed the New International Economic Order and its relationship to human rights, hence we need only underline at this point the fact that the Western powers no longer dominate the Commission (or any other UN organ for that matter), so that existing obstacles to the 'full realization of economic, social and cultural rights' will be steadily reduced. Moreover, 'the increasing disparity of living conditions and income levels between the developed and the developing countries', which the Resolution deplores, will yield to 'the duty of the international community to contribute to putting an end to this disparity'.

All these objectives are summed up in the Resolution itself as guidelines for the next two years of the Commission's action, in an overall request to the UN Secretary-General to undertake a study on the following subject:

The international dimensions of the right to development as a human right in relation with other human rights based on international co-operation, including the right to peace, taking into account the requirements of the New International Economic Order and the fundamental human needs.

It is, indeed, one of the signs today that, amidst the conflicting forces of world struggle—encouraging and often clamouring—for drastic economic and social change, the movement of thought and even the practice by some governments is towards 'fundamental human needs'. In the present divergent policies over trade and resources, investment and the transfer of technology, *basic human needs* are assuming an ever larger place as an incentive and objective of international social policy.

The refugee, for example, has always represented the sad symbol of the right-less person. In a recent letter to President Carter, the United Nations former High Commissioner for Refugees, Sadruddin Aga Khan, raised this new approach to this perennial problem that we are emphasising in this chapter. He recalled that there were millions of refugees in all continents and that this surely revealed the most tangible manifestation of violation of human rights. 'I strongly believe,' the High Commissioner wrote,

> that parallel to the strenuous efforts now being made by governments to develop a New Economic Order, there is urgent need to promote a *New Human Order*, ensuring that the principles underlying the Universal Declaration of Human Rights are more widely practised.

THE RIGHT TO DEVELOPMENT

The new dimensions of human rights are marked, as we have seen, by an increasingly organised public opinion that is constantly pushing governments forward along freedom's road. A recent NGO declaration of policy headed: 'Human Rights, Touchstone of Development', states that, since 'Human Rights encompass all aspects of human life, including work, employment, standard of living and education, as well as freedom of thought, speech, association and movement', all the major non-governmental organisations in consultative status with the UN urged the Economic and Social Council in July 1976, when preparing a revision of the International Development Strategy,' to take into specific account the application of the standards laid down in the International Human Rights Covenants, so clarifying Human Rights as being a fundamental objective of Development and the guideline for its implementation'.[5]

It has been suggested (and sometimes even practised) that where a government or an international agency, such as the World Bank or the UN Development Programme, decides to grant aid – economic or financial – to a 'poor' country or to a needy country seeking such aid, the first responsibility of the donor should be to ascertain the situation of human rights observance in that country. And to grant, to proportion, or to withhold its aid accordingly. Obviously, this procedure, deliberately linking external assistance programmes to domestic conditions within the legal jurisdiction of the country concerned, will promote endless frictions and objections. We cannot, however, examine these implications here; but 'weighted' aid is clearly objectionable as a form of foreign intervention. It is also contrary to the principles of law we studied in our first chapter. Whatever its motivation, it may well be counter-productive in the long run.

The Right to Development, by definition, cannot be a bargain between the righteous and the unrighteous. If it has a legal meaning – and no doubt the expert studies that the Resolution contemplates will produce a reasonable definition in due time – it must surely mean that it is an *individual* right, like all the defined rights are, even if it is set within a collective context. It therefore belongs alongside the so-called right of self-determination and other collective rights. Bearing in mind, too, the uncertainties raised in Chapter 5, we must expect that some authorities and, no doubt, some governments will refuse to be bound by it as a *right*, but will accept the term somewhat loosely as a 'principle of development' – which, in fact, possibly all governments have done already.

Yet, either the principle or the right of development must seek, in the long run, the satisfaction of what the World Employment Programme of the ILO in 1976 has called the 'fundamental human needs'. Such a phrase must be included somewhere in a definition, since it covers all the orthodox human rights – personal freedom, education, employment, health care, and everything else listed in the Declarations and Conventions.

What the Resolution is asking, therefore, is that, by both international agreement and national action, every individual should in due time enjoy the same standards set down in the two major Covenants, and the others as well where applicable. The right to development thus becomes a sort of master key, excluding no-one from the benefits offered in the Declaration of Human Rights. And, since the peoples of the developing nations are the ones presently deprived of so many of these rights, the right to development will apply particularly to them.

THE ARMS MENACE

But the Resolution gives us due warning in one of its preambular paragraphs that there exist a number of dangerous trip-wires on the road to development. The most pernicious of these, with which we can deal here, is the prostitution of the world's limited resources to an expanding arms trade in the means of death. The Secretary-General opened the 736 session of the Conference of the Committee on Disarmament (CCD) in Geneva with an obvious understatement: 'Despite the conclusion of a number of limited arms control agreements in the last decade, there has been no significant breakthrough to stop the ever-accelerating growth of the world's arsenals of weapons, whether nuclear or conventional.' The result, he said, was an accumulation of arms far beyond legitimate 'defence' needs. This not only endangered world security, but absorbed about $350,000 million a year at a time when the struggle to alleviate the hunger, poverty and disease which afflicted hundreds of millions of people suffered from a lack of resources.

As far as the facts and figures are concerned, the UN's collective record has been one of dismal failure in this respect The arms race, frantically pursued by its members, though deplored by all national speech-makers in the 1950s, has become a monstrous scandal as we near the 1980s. The causes and consequences of this spiralling threat to all life on this planet, this outrage to normal human intelligence, cannot be pursued here; but it must be recognised today as the biggest of all collective violations of the Right to Development, committed by the same developed nations who are being called upon to establish that new right!

Yet it happens, fortunately, that this insane arms race is meeting two significant challenges: one moral, the other organisational. The 1977 Helsinki recall conference at Belgrade sadly failed to be a genuine test of whether the statesmen who delivered themselves of such high-toned oratorial commitments at Helsinki I, really meant what they said. For if it *is* true that it is human rights that count most, there is something unspeakably immoral in a strategic war-game that has reduced millions of human beings to mere cyphers on military targets, with an overkill of mathematical co-efficients. Organisationally, the United Nations system offered a supreme opportunity by its Special Session on Disarmament (SSD) in the summer of 1978 for competing member states to make a genuine beginning to replace the moribund right of the sword by the modern right of development. The struggle continues.

RIGHT TO PEACE

For the first time, as far as this author is aware, the Right to Peace has been seriously put forward, and without diplomatic opposition, on the recommendation of one of the most prestigious of international bodies, namely the UN Commission on Human Rights, in the Resolution first formulated on 14 February 1977. No one has yet defined the right to peace, but the Commission has called for a study of it for formal presentation at its annual session in 1979.

Of one thing we can be certain, and that is what the right to peace is *not*. It is not an interval between wars, as is popularly understood, while new wars are being prepared. It is not the 'peace' unilaterally proclaimed by sovereign states intent on leaving their erstwhile enemies under threat of further hostility. It is not a compromise between rivals who cannot get what they want by war. Peace is the most abused and maligned of words.[6] It is certainly not the spurious doctrine of 'deterrence', which drives on the arms race to further excesses and perils.

However it may one day be defined, it has to comprise many varied elements, which have already engaged the attention of the whole UN family. It is impossible to list thirty years of attempts and efforts recorded in the UN's wide repertoire. For example, the Thirty-First Session of the General Assembly in 1976 adopted by 94 to 2, with 35 abstentions, a recommendation for the 'conclusion of a world treaty on the non-use of force in international relations'. The Assembly noted

> with satisfaction that the principle of the non-use of force or the threat of force has been incorporated into a number of bi-lateral and multilateral international instruments, treaties, agreements and declarations, including resolutions adopted by the United Nations

and it invited Member States 'to examine further the draft World Treaty on the Non-Use of Force in International Relations, as well as other proposals and statements made during the consideration of . . . a world treaty on the non-use of force in international relations'.

Naturally, non-governmental bodies, especially the international peace societies, have for years been presenting in their various capacities proposals and plans aimed at transforming the United Nations from a forum of sovereign states to a defender of individual rights. As one instance of this, the Commission on Human Rights in March 1971 took the initial steps towards considering whether *conscientious objection to military service* should be officially declared a human right.

Accordingly, the Secretary-General sent a letter to the member states requesting information on such questions as:

> whether there is any national legislation, other measures or practice relating to conscientious objection to military service and alternative service; the grounds upon which conscientious objection to military service may be claimed; the authorities competent to determine exemptions from military service on grounds of conscientious objection, and the procedures applicable [and so on].

In its response, one NGO, the World Conference on Religion and Peace, stated:

> We consider that the exercise of conscientious judgment is inherent in the dignity of human beings and that, accordingly, each person should be assured the right, on grounds of conscience or profound conviction, to refuse military service, or any other direct or indirect participation in wars or armed conflicts.

At the 1978 session of the Human Rights Commission the International Student Movement for the UN (ISMUN) and other youth and religious NGOs have presented a detailed case for an eventual Convention on the Rights of Conscience to reject war service.

These few examples, chosen almost at hazard, point to the vast terrain that is accessible to searchers for the right to peace. No-one can imagine today that the catalogue of human rights has been exhausted by the instruments now in force. The right to tolerance in religious belief, with its long history, is one of the 'new' rights on its way to the statute book of the international community via the agendas of the 1978 and 1979 sessions.

Finally, reference was made earlier in this chapter to the vexed problem of national sovereignty and the belief of World Federalists that its supersession is crucial for the establishment of world peace.

Alas! the institution of an eventual world government, as a *sine qua non* of peace, carries with it implications and complexities far beyond the scope of this book. Like the present author, Dr Evan Luard envisages the functional agencies, which have assumed an ever-larger role in the UN system, as the potential departments of an eventual world order, without which peace will always remain transient or illusory.

Yet Dr Luard states:

Clearly, international government is something different in kind from government within nations. Though there exists in the international community a relatively elaborate administrative structure, a wide variety of political institutions, and many public services, international bodies do not possess the ultimate sanction of authority, the power to impose decisions, which, in the final resort, national governments can exert, and which many would regard as the hallmark of government.[7]

CONCLUSION

Whether or not national states will yield enough of their external sovereignty in our lifetime to make international government possible, or even visible, as a future world order, one basic fact emerges from our study. It is that the individual, not the sovereign state, is the end purpose of the new legal order that has been erected in our generation under the title of Human Rights.

Of course, this is not really a new phenomenon. 'The world society which existed in the minds of the Stoics, of Cicero and St Augustine', states Professor P. E. Corbett,

was a society of men considered as all sons of one God, brothers one of another, owing mutual duties which acknowledged no political frontiers. This idea became mixed in the political theory and jurisprudence of the Renaissance, when writers appeared to be thinking now of a society of individuals transcending State boundaries, now of a society of States. Gradually the concepts of the personality and sovereignty of the State gained pre-eminence.[8]

In that sense, twentieth-century man is regaining his lost son-ship. Or as Socrates well put it, his natural world citizenship: 'When you are asked for your country, never reply: "I am an Athenian" or "I am a Corinthian"; but say: "I am a Citizen of the World".'

Today that operational world citizenship is far more in evidence than in the fifth century BC. In a recent UN study entitled 'The Individual's Duties to the Community and the Limitations on Human Rights and Freedoms under Article 29 of the Universal Declaration', Mrs Erica-Irene Daes reminds us that:

> The authors of the Charter of the United Nations assumed the existence of a world community. But the Charter includes two concepts which are in conflict with each other. According to one of these concepts, the component units are States; while the other concept focuses on individual human beings. In the organizational structure of the United Nations, the former concept is the most prominent one . . . The latter concept expresses itself in other institutions, designed to relieve individual suffering, to promote human rights and fundamental freedoms for individuals everywhere, to create conditions of stability, well-being and progress, and to provide for services now regarded as necessary for the full development of the individual's personality in a democratic community.[9]

Perhaps the whole story of the human rights movement in the modern world has never been more succinctly expressed than in those final words, where the full development of the individual's personality is recognised as the end and purpose of a democratic community which it is the objective of the United Nations to transform, step by step, into an ordered peace.

Appendix I
The International Bill of Rights

A. UNIVERSAL DECLARATION OF HUMAN RIGHTS

**Adopted and proclaimed by General Assembly
resolution 217 A (III) of 10 December 1948**

PREAMBLE

Whereas recognition of the inherent dignity and of the equal and inalienable rights of all members of the human family is the foundation of freedom, justice and peace in the world,

Whereas disregard and contempt for human rights have resulted in barbarous acts which have outraged the conscience of mankind, and the advent of a world in which human beings shall enjoy freedom of speech and belief and freedom from fear and want has been proclaimed as the highest aspiration of the common people,

Whereas it is essential, if man is not to be compelled to have recourse, as a last resort, to rebellion against tyranny and oppression, that human rights should be protected by the rule of law,

Whereas it is essential to promote the development of friendly relations between nations,

Whereas the peoples of the United Nations have in the Charter reaffirmed their faith in fundamental human rights, in the dignity and worth of the human person and in the equal rights of men and women and have determined to promote social progress and better standards of life in larger freedom,

Whereas Member States have pledged themselves to achieve, in co-operation with the United Nations, the promotion of universal respect for and observance of human rights and fundamental freedoms,

Whereas a common understanding of these rights and freedoms is of the greatest importance for the full realization of this pledge,

Now, therefore,

The General Assembly

Proclaims this Universal Declaration of Human Rights as a common standard of achievement for all peoples and all nations, to the end that every individual and every organ of society, keeping this Declaration constantly in mind, shall strive by teaching and education to promote respect for these rights and freedoms and by progressive measures, national and international to secure their universal and effective recognition and observance, both among the peoples of Member States themselves and among the peoples of territories under their jurisdiction.

Article 1

All human beings are born free and equal in dignity and rights. They are endowed with reason and conscience and should act towards one another in a spirit of brotherhood.

Article 2

Everyone is entitled to all the rights and freedoms set forth in this Declaration, without distinction of any kind, such as race, colour, sex, language, religion, political or other opinion, national or social origin, property, birth or other status.

Furthermore, no distinction shall be made on the basis of the political, jurisdictional or international status of the country or territory to which a person belongs, whether it be independent, trust, non-self-governing or under any other limitation of sovereignty.

Article 3

Everyone has the right to life, liberty and the security of person.

Article 4

No one shall be held in slavery or servitude; slavery and the slave trade shall be prohibited in all their forms.

Article 5

No one shall be subjected to torture or to cruel, inhuman or degrading treatment or punishment.

Article 6

Everyone has the right to recognition everywhere as a person before the law.

Article 7

All are equal before the law and are entitled without any discrimination to equal protection of the law. All are entitled to equal protection against any discrimination in violation of this Declaration and against any incitement to such discrimination.

Article 8

Everyone has the right to an effective remedy by the competent national tribunals for acts violating the fundamental rights granted him by the constitution or by law.

Article 9

No one shall be subjected to arbitrary arrest, detention or exile.

Article 10

Everyone is entitled in full equality to a fair and public hearing by an independent and impartial tribunal, in the determination of his rights and obligations and of any criminal charge against him.

Article 11

1. Everyone charged with a penal offence has the right to be presumed innocent until proved guilty according to law in a public trial at which he has had all the guarantees necessary for his defence.
2. No one shall be held guilty of any penal offence on account of any act or omission which did not constitute a penal offence, under national or international law, at the time when it was commited. Nor shall a heavier penalty be imposed than the one that was applicable at the time the penal offence was committed.

Article 12

No one shall be subjected to arbitrary interference with his privacy, family, home or correspondence, nor to attacks upon his honour and reputation. Everyone has the right to the protection of the law against such interference or attacks.

Article 13

1. Everyone has the right to freedom of movement and residence within the borders of each State.
2. Everyone has the right to leave any country including his own, and to return to his country.

Article 14

1. Everyone has the right to seek and to enjoy in other countries asylum from persecution.
2. This right may not be invoked in the case of prosecutions genuinely arising from non-political crimes or from acts contrary to the purposes and principles of the United Nations.

Article 15

1. Everyone has the right to a nationality.
2. No one shall be arbitrarily deprived of his nationality nor denied the right to change his nationality.

Article 16

1. Men and women of full age, without any limitation due to race, nationality or religion, have the right to marry and to found a family. They are entitled to equal rights as to marriage, during marriage and at its dissolution.
2. Marriage shall be entered into only with the free and full consent of the intending spouses.
3. The family is the natural and fundamental group unit of society and is entitled to protection by society and the State.

Article 17

1. Everyone has the right to own property alone as well as in association with others.
2. No one shall be arbitrarily deprived of his property.

Article 18

Everyone has the right to freedom of thought, conscience and religion; this right includes freedom to change his religion or belief, and freedom, either alone or in community with others and in public or private, to manifest his religion or belief in teaching, practice, worship and observance.

Article 19

Everyone has the right to freedom of opinion and expression; this right includes freedom to hold opinions without interference and to seek, receive and impart information and ideas through any media and regardless of frontiers.

Article 20

1. Everyone has the right to freedom of peaceful assembly and association.
2. No one may be compelled to belong to an association.

Article 21

1. Everyone has the right to take part in the government of his country, directly or through freely chosen representatives.
2. Everyone has the right of equal access to public service in his country.
3. The will of the people shall be the basis of the authority of government; this will shall be expressed in periodic and genuine elections which shall be by universal and equal suffrage and shall be held by secret vote or by equivalent free voting procedures.

Article 22

Everyone, as a member of society, has the right to social security and is entitled to realization, through national effort and international co-operation and in accordance with the organization and resources of each State, of the economic, social and cultural rights indispensable for his dignity and the free development of his personality.

Article 23

1. Everyone has the right to work, to free choice of employment,

to just and favourable conditions of work and to protection against unemployment.

2. Everyone, without any discrimination, has the right to equal pay for equal work.

3. Everyone who works has the right to just and favourable remuneration ensuring for himself and his family an existence worthy of human dignity, and supplemented, if necessary, by other means of social protection.

4. Everyone has the right to form and to join trade unions for the protection of his interests.

Article 24

Everyone has the right to rest and leisure, including reasonable limitation of working hours and periodic holidays with pay.

Article 25

1. Everyone has the right to a standard of living adequate for the health and well-being of himself and of his family, including food, clothing, housing and medical care and necessary social services, and the right to security in the event of unemployment, sickness disability, widowhood, old age or other lack of livelihood in circumstances beyond his control.

2. Motherhood and childhood are entitled to special care and assistance. All children, whether born in or out of wedlock, shall enjoy the same social protection.

Article 26

1. Everyone has the right to education. Education shall be free, at least in the elementary and fundamental stages. Elementary education shall be compulsory. Technical and professional education shall be made generally available and higher education shall be equally accessible to all on the basis of merit.

2. Education shall be directed to the full development of the human personality and to the strengthening of respect for human rights and fundamental freedoms. It shall promote understanding, tolerance and friendship among all nations, racial or religious groups, and shall further the activities of the United Nations for the maintenance of peace.

3. Parents have a prior right to choose the kind of education that shall be given to their children.

Article 27

1. Everyone has the right freely to participate in the cultural life of the community, to enjoy the arts and to share in scientific advancement and its benefits.

2. Everyone has the right to the protection of the moral and material interests resulting from any scientific, literary or artistic production of which he is the author.

Article 28

Everyone is entitled to a social and international order in which the rights and freedoms set forth in this Declaration can be fully realized.

Article 29

1. Everyone has duties to the community in which alone the free and full development of his personality is possible.

2. In the exercise of his rights and freedoms, everyone shall be subject only to such limitations as are determined by law solely for the purpose of securing due recognition and respect for the rights and freedoms of others and of meeting the just requirements of morality, public order and the general welfare in a democratic society.

3. These rights and freedoms may in no case be exercised contrary to the purposes and principles of the United Nations.

Article 30

Nothing in this Declaration may be interpreted as implying for any State, group or person any right to engage in any activity or to perform any act aimed at the destruction of any of the rights and freedoms set forth herein.

B. INTERNATIONAL COVENANT ON ECONOMIC, SOCIAL AND CULTURAL RIGHTS

**Adopted and opened for signature, ratification and accession
by General Assembly Resolution 2200 A (XXI) of 16 December 1966**

Entry into force: 3 January 1976
(see article 27).

PREAMBLE

The States Parties to the present Covenant,

Considering that, in accordance with the principles proclaimed in the Charter of the United Nations, recognition of the inherent dignity and of the equal and inalienable rights of all members of the human family is the foundation of freedom, justice and peace in the world,

Recognizing that these rights derive from the inherent dignity of the human person,

Recognizing that, in accordance with the Universal Declaration of Human Rights, the ideal of free human beings enjoying freedom from fear and want can only be achieved if conditions are created whereby everyone may enjoy his economic, social and cultural rights, as well as his civil and political rights,

Considering the obligation of States under the Charter of the United Nations to promote universal respect for, and observance of, human rights and freedoms,

Realizing that the individual, having duties to other individuals and to the community to which he belongs, is under a responsibility, to strive for the promotion and observance of the rights recognized in the present Covenant,

Agree upon the following articles:

PART I

Article 1

1. All peoples have the right of self-determination. By virtue of that right they freely determine their political status and freely pursue their economic, social and cultural development.

2. All peoples may, for their own ends, freely dispose of their natural wealth and resources without prejudice to any obligations

arising out of international economic co-operation, based upon the principle of mutual benefit, and international law. In no case may a people be deprived of its own means of subsistence.

3. The States Parties to the present Covenant, including those having responsibility for the administration of Non-Self-Governing and Trust Territories, shall promote the realization of the right of self-determination, and shall respect that right, in conformity with the provisions of the Charter of the United Nations.

PART II

Article 2

1. Each State Party to the present Covenant undertakes to take steps, individually and through international assistance and co-operation, especially economic and technical, to the maximum of its available resources, with a view to achieving progressively the full realization of the rights recognized in the present Covenant by all appropriate means, including particularly the adoption of legislative measures.

2. The States Parties to the present Covenant undertake to guarantee that the rights enunciated in the present Covenant will be exercised without discrimination of any kind as to race, colour, sex, language, religion, political or other opinion, national or social origin, property, birth or other status.

3. Developing countries, with due regard to human rights and their national economy, may determine to what extent they would guarantee the economic rights recognized in the present Covenant to non-nationals.

Article 3

The States Parties to the present Covenant undertake to ensure the equal right of men and women to the enjoyment of all economic, social and cultural rights set forth in the present Covenant.

Article 4

The States Parties to the present Covenant recognize that, in the enjoyment of those rights provided by the State in conformity with the present Covenant, the State may subject such rights only to such limitations as are determined by law only in so far as this may be compatible with the nature of these rights and solely for the purpose of promoting the general welfare in a democratic society

Article 5

1. Nothing in the present Covenant may be interpreted as implying for any State, group or person any right to engage in any activity or to perform any act aimed at the destruction of any of the rights or freedoms recognized herein, or at their limitation to a greater extent than is provided for in the present Covenant.

2. No restriction upon or derogation from any of the fundamental human rights recognized or existing in any country in virtue of law, conventions, regulations or custom shall be admitted on the pretext that the present Covenant does not recognize such rights or that it recognizes them to a lesser extent.

PART III

Article 6

1. The States Parties to the present Covenant recognize the right to work, which includes the right of everyone to the opportunity to gain his living by work which he freely chooses or accepts, and will take appropriate steps to safeguard this right.

2. The steps to be taken by a State Party to the present Covenant to achieve the full realization of this right shall include technical and vocational guidance and training programmes, policies and techniques to achieve steady economic, social and cultural development and full and productive employment under conditions safeguarding fundamental political and economic freedoms to the individual.

Article 7

The States Parties to the present Covenant recognize the right of everyone to the enjoyment of just and favourable conditions of work which ensure, in particular:

(*a*) Remuneration which provides all workers, as a minimum, with:

    (i) Fair wages and equal remuneration for work of equal value without distinction of any kind, in particular women being guaranteed conditions of work not inferior to those enjoyed by men, with equal pay for equal work;

(ii) A decent living for themselves and their families in accordance with the provisions of the present Covenant;

(*b*) Safe and healthy working conditions;

(*c*) Equal opportunity for everyone to be promoted in his employment to an appropriate higher level, subject to no considerations other than those of seniority and competence;

(*d*) Rest, leisure and reasonable limitation of working hours and periodic holidays with pay, as well as remuneration for public holidays.

Article 8

1. The States Parties to the present Covenant undertake to ensure:

(*a*) The right of everyone to form trade unions and join the trade union of his choice, subject only to the rules of the organization concerned, for the promotion and protection of his economic and social interests. No restrictions may be placed on the exercise of this right other than those prescribed by law and which are necessary in a democratic society in the interests of national security or public order or for the protection of the rights and freedoms of others;

(*b*) The right of trade unions to establish national federations or confederations and the right of the latter to form or join international trade-union organizations;

(*c*) The right of trade unions to function freely subject to no limitations other than those prescribed by law and which are necessary in a democratic society in the interests of national security or public order or for the protection of the rights and freedoms of others;

(*d*) The right to strike, provided that it is exercised in conformity with the laws of the particular country.

2. This article shall not prevent the imposition of lawful restrictions on the exercise of these rights by members of the armed forces or of the police or of the administration of the State.

3. Nothing in this article shall authorize States Parties to the International Labour Organisation Convention of 1948 concerning Freedom of Association and Protection of the Right to Organize to take legislative measures which would prejudice, or apply the law in such a manner as would prejudice, the guarantees provided for in that Convention.

Article 9

The States Parties to the present Covenant recognize the right of everyone to social security, including social insurance.

Article 10

The States Parties to the present Covenant recognize that:

1. The widest possible protection and assistance should be accorded to the family, which is the natural and fundamental group unit of society, particularly for its establishment and while it is responsible for the care and education of dependent children. Marriage must be entered into with the free consent of the intending spouses.

2. Special protection should be accorded to mothers during a reasonable period before and after childbirth. During such period working mothers should be accorded paid leave or leave with adequate social security benefits.

3. Special measures of protection and assistance should be taken on behalf of all children and young persons without any discrimination for reasons of parentage or other conditions. Children and young persons should be protected from economic and social exploitation. Their employment in work harmful to their morals or health or dangerous to life or likely to hamper their normal development should be punishable by law. States should also set age limits below which the paid employment of child labour should be prohibited and punishable by law.

Article 11

1. The States Parties to the present Covenant recognize the right of everyone to an adequate standard of living for himself and his family, including adequate food, clothing and housing, and to the continuous improvement of living conditions. The States Parties will take appropriate steps to ensure the realization of this right, recognizing to this effect the essential importance of international co-operation based on free consent.

2. The States Parties of the present Covenant, recognizing the fundamental right of everyone to be free from hunger, shall take, individually and through international co-operation, the measures, including specific programmes, which are needed:

(a) To improve methods of production, conservation and distribution of food by making full use of technical and scientific knowledge, by disseminating knowledge of the principles of nutrition and by developing or reforming agrarian systems in such a way as to achieve the most efficient development and utilization of natural resources;

(*b*) Taking into account the problems of both food-importing and food-exporting countries, to ensure an equitable distribution of world food supplies in relation to need.

Article 12

1. The States Parties to the present Covenant recognize the right of everyone to the enjoyment of the highest attainable standard of physical and mental health.

2. The steps to be taken by the States Parties to the present Covenant to achieve the full realization of this right shall include those necessary for:

(*a*) The provision for the reduction of the stillbirth-rate and of infant mortality and for the healthy development of the child;

(*b*) The improvement of all aspects of environmental and industrial hygiene;

(*c*) The prevention, treatment and control of epidemic, endemic, occupational and other diseases;

(*d*) The creation of conditions which would assure to all medical service and medical attention in the event of sickness.

Article 13

1. The States Parties to the present Covenant recognize the right of everyone to education. They agree that education shall be directed to the full development of the human personality and the sense of its dignity, and shall strengthen the respect for human rights and fundamental freedoms. They further agree that education shall enable all persons to participate effectively in a free society, promote understanding, tolerance and friendship among all nations and all racial, ethnic or religious groups, and further the activities of the United Nations for the maintenance of peace.

2. The States Parties to the present Covenant recognize that, with a view to achieving the full realization of this right:

(*a*) Primary education shall be compulsory and available free to all;

(*b*) Secondary education in its different forms, including technical and vocational secondary education, shall be made generally available and accessible to all by every appropriate means, and in particular by the progressive introduction of free education;

(c) Higher education shall be made equally accessible to all, on the basis of capacity, by every appropriate means, and in particular by the progressive introduction of free education;

(d) Fundamental education shall be encouraged or intensified as far as possible for those persons who have not received or completed the whole period of their primary education.

(e) The development of a system of schools at all levels shall be actively pursued, an adequate fellowship system shall be established, and the material conditions of teaching staff shall be continuously improved.

3. The State Parties to the present Covenant undertake to have respect for the liberty of parents and, when applicable, legal guardians to choose for their children schools, other than those established by the public authorities, which conform to such minimum educational standards as may be laid down or approved by the State and to ensure the religious and moral education of their children in conformity with their own convictions.

4. No part of this article shall be construed so as to interfere with the liberty of individuals and bodies to establish and direct educational institutions, subject always to the observance of the principles set forth in paragraph 1 of this article and to the requirement that the education given in such institutions shall conform to such minimum standards as may be laid down by the State.

Article 14

Each State Party to the present Covenant which, at the time of becoming a Party, has not been able to secure in its metropolitan territory or other territories under its jurisdiction compulsory primary education, free of charge, undertakes, within two years, to work out and adopt a detailed plan of action for the progressive implementation, within a reasonable number of years, to be fixed in the plan, of the principle of compulsory education free of charge for all.

Article 15

1. The State Parties to the present Covenant recognize the right of everyone:

(*a*) To take part in cultural life;

(*b*) To enjoy the benefits of scientific progress and its applications;

(*c*) To benefit from the protection of the moral and material interests resulting from any scientific, literary or artistic production of which he is the author.

2. The steps to be taken by the States Parties to the present Covenant to achieve the full realization of this right shall include those necessary for the conservation, the development and the diffusion of science and culture.

3. The States Parties to the present Covenant undertake to respect the freedom indispensable for scientific research and creative activity.

4. The States Parties to the present Covenant recognize the benefits to be derived from the encouragement and development of international contacts and co-operation in the scientific and cultural fields.

PART IV

Article 16

1. The States Parties to the present Covenant undertake to submit in conformity with this part of the Covenant reports on the measures which they have adopted and the progress made in achieving the observance of the rights recognized herein.

2. (*a*) All reports shall be submitted to the Secretary-General of the United Nations, who shall transmit copies to the Economic and Social Council for consideration in accordance with the provisions of the present Covenant;

(*b*) The Secretary-General of the United Nations shall also transmit to the specialized agencies copies of the reports, or any relevant parts therefrom, from States Parties to the present Covenant which are also members of these specialized agencies in so far as these reports, or parts therefrom, relate to any matters which fall within the responsibilities of the said agencies in accordance with their constitutional instruments.

Article 17

1. The States Parties to the present Covenant shall furnish their reports in stages, in accordance with a programme to be established by the Economic and Social Council within one year of the entry into force of the present Covenant after consultation with the States Parties and the specialized agencies concerned.

2. Reports may indicate factors and difficulties affecting the degree of fulfilment of obligations under the present Covenant.

3. Where relevant information has previously been furnished to the United Nations or to any specialized agency by any State Party to the present Covenant, it will not be necessary to reproduce that information, but a precise reference to the information so furnished will suffice.

Article 18

Pursuant to its responsibilities under the Charter of the United Nations in the field of human rights and fundamental freedoms, the Economic and Social Council may make arrangements with the specialized agencies in respect of their reporting to it on the progress made in achieving the observance of the provisions of the present Covenant falling within the scope of their activities. These reports may include particulars of decisions and recommendations on such implementation adopted by their competent organs.

Article 19

The Economic and Social Council may transmit to the Commission on Human Rights for study and general recommendation or, as appropriate, for information the reports concerning human rights submitted by States in accordance with articles 16 and 17, and those concerning human rights submitted by the specialized agencies in accordance with article 18.

Article 20

The States Parties to the present Covenant and the specialized agencies concerned may submit comments to the Economic and Social Council on any general recommendation under article 19 or reference to such general recommendation in any report of the Commission on Human Rights or any documentation referred to therein.

Article 21

The Economic and Social Council may submit from time to time to the General Assembly reports with recommendations of a general nature and a summary of the information received from the States Parties to the present Covenant and the specialized agencies on the measures taken and the progress made in achieving general observance of the rights recognized in the present Covenant.

Article 22

The Economic and Social Council may bring to the attention of other organs of the United Nations, their subsidiary organs and specialized agencies concerned with furnishing technical assistance any matters arising out of the reports referred to in this part of the present Covenant which may assist such bodies in deciding, each within its field of competence, on the advisability of international measures likely to contribute to the effective progressive implementation of the present Covenant.

Article 23

The States Parties to the present Covenant agree that international action for the achievement of the rights recognized in the present Covenant includes such methods as the conclusion of conventions, the adoption of recommendations, the furnishing of technical assistance and the holding of regional meetings and technical meetings for the purpose of consultation and study organized in conjunction with the Governments concerned.

Article 24

Nothing in the present Covenant shall be interpreted as impairing the provisions of the Charter of the United Nations and of the constitutions of the specialized agencies which define the respective responsibilities of the various organs of the United Nations and of the specialized agencies in regard to the matters dealt with in the present Covenant.

Article 25

Nothing in the present Covenant shall be interpreted as impair-

254 The New Politics of Human Rights

ing the inherent right of all peoples to enjoy and utilize fully and freely their natural wealth and resources.

PART V

Article 26

1. The present Covenant is open for signature by any State Member of the United Nations or member of any of its specialized agencies, by any State Party to the Statute of the International Court of Justice, and by any other State which has been invited by the General Assembly of the United Nations to become a party to the present Covenant.

2. The present Covenant is subject to ratification. Instruments of ratification shall be deposited with the Secretary-General of the United Nations.

3. The present Covenant shall be open to accession by any State referred to in paragraph 1 of this article.

4. Accession shall be effected by the deposit of an instrument of accession with the Secretary-General of the United Nations.

5. The Secretary-General of the United Nations shall inform all States which have signed the present Covenant or acceded to it of the deposit of each instrument of ratification or accession.

Article 27

1. The present Covenant shall enter into force three months after the date of the deposit with the Secretary-General of the United Nations of the thirty-fifth instrument of ratification or instrument of accession.

2. For each State ratifying the present Covenant or acceding to it after the deposit of the thirty-fifth instrument of ratification or instrument of accession, the present Covenant shall enter into force three months after the date of the deposit of its own instrument of ratification or instrument of accession.

Article 28

The provisions of the present Covenant shall extend to all parts of federal States without any limitations or exceptions.

Article 29

1. Any State Party to the present Covenant may propose an amendment and file it with the Secretary-General of the United Nations. The Secretary-General shall thereupon communicate any proposed amendments to the States Parties to the present Covenant with a request that they notify him whether they favour a conference of States Parties for the purpose of considering and voting upon the proposals. In the event that at least one third of the State Parties favours such a conference, the Secretary-General shall convene the conference under the auspices of the United Nations. Any amendment adopted by a majority of the States Parties present and voting at the conference shall be submitted to the General Assembly of the United Nations for approval.

2. Amendments shall come into force when they have been approved by the General Assembly of the United Nations and accepted by a two-thirds majority of the States Parties to the present Covenant in accordance with their respective constitutional processes.

3. When amendments come into force they shall be binding on those States Parties which have accepted them, other States Parties still being bound by the provisions of the present Covenant and any earlier amendment which they have accepted.

Article 30

Irrespective of the notifications made under article 26, paragraph 5, the Secretary-General of the United Nations shall inform all States referred to in paragraph 1 of the same article of the following particulars:

(*a*) Signatures, ratifications and accessions under article 26;

(*b*) The date of the entry into force of the present Covenant under article 27 and the date of the entry into force of any amendments under article 29.

Article 31

1. The present Covenant, of which the Chinese, English, French, Russian and Spanish texts are equally authentic, shall be deposited in the archives of the United Nations.

2. The Secretary-General of the United Nations shall transmit certified copies of the present Covenant to all States referred to in article 26.

C. INTERNATIONAL COVENANT ON CIVIL AND POLITICAL RIGHTS

Adopted and opened for signature, ratification and accession by General Assembly Resolution 2200 A (XXI) of 16 December 1966

Entry into force: 26 March 1976
(see article 49).

PREAMBLE

The States Parties to the present Covenant,

Considering that, in accordance with the principles proclaimed in the Charter of the United Nations recognition of the inherent dignity and of the equal and inalienable rights of all members of the human family is the foundation of freedom, justice and peace in the world,

Recognizing that these rights derive from the inherent dignity of the human person,

Recognizing that, in accordance with the Universal Declaration of Human Rights, the ideal of free human beings enjoying civil and political freedom and freedom from fear and want can only be achieved if conditions are created whereby everyone may enjoy his civil and political rights, as well as his economic, social and cultural rights,

Considering the obligation of States under the Charter of the United Nations to promote universal respect for, and observance of, human rights and freedoms,

Realizing that the individual, having duties to other individuals and to the community to which he belongs, is under a responsibility to strive for the promotion and observance of the rights recognized in the present Covenant,

Agree upon the following articles:

PART I

Article 1

1. All peoples have the right of self-determination. By virtue of that right they freely determine their political status and freely pursue their economic, social and cultural development.

2. All peoples may, for their own ends, freely dispose of their natural wealth and resources without prejudice to any obligations arising out of international economic co-operation, based upon the principle of mutual benefit, and international law. In no case may a people be deprived of its own means of subsistence.

3. The States Parties to the present Covenant, including those having responsibility for the administration of Non-Self-Governing and Trust Territoris, shall promote the realization of the right of self-determination, and shall respect that right, in comformity with the provisions of the Charter of the United Nations.

PART II

Article 2

1. Each State Party to the present Covenant undertakes to respect and to ensure to all individuals within its territory and subject to its jurisdiction the rights recognized in the present Covenant, without distinction of any kind, such as race, colour, sex, language, religion, political or other opinion, national or social origin, property, birth or other status.

2. Where not already provided for by existing legislative or other measures, each State Party to the present Covenant undertakes to take the necessary steps, in accordance with its constitutional processes and with the provisions of the present Covenant, to adopt such legislative or other measures as may be necessary to give effect to the rights recognized in the present Covenant.

3. Each State Party to the present Covenant undertakes:

(*a*) To ensure that any person whose rights or freedoms as herein recognized are violated shall have an effective remedy, notwithstanding that the violation has been committed by persons acting in an official capacity;

(*b*) To ensure that any person claiming such a remedy shall have his right thereto determined by competent judicial, administrative or legislative authorities, or by any other competent authority provided for by the legal system of the State, and to develop the possibilities of judicial remedy;

(*c*) To ensure that the competent authorities shall enforce such remedies when granted.

Article 3

The States Parties to the resent Covenant undertake to ensure the equal right of men and women to the enjoyment of all civil and political rights set forth in the present Covenant.

Article 4

1. In time of public emergency which threatens the life of the nation and the existence of which is officially proclaimed, the States Parties to the present Covenant may take measures derogating from their obligations under the present Covenant to the extent strictly required by the exigencies of the situation, provided that such measures are not inconsistent with their other obligations under international law and do not involve discrimination solely on the ground of race, colour, sex, language, religion or social origin.

2. No derogation from article 6, 7, 8 (paragraphs 1 and 2), 11, 15, 16 and 18 may be made under this provision.

3. Any State Party to the present Covenant availing itself of the right of derogation shall immediately inform the other States Parties to the present Covenant, through the intermediary of the Secretary-General of the United Nations, of the provisions from which it has derogated and of the reasons by which it was actuated. A further communication shall be made, through the same intermediary, on the date on which it terminates such derogation.

Article 5

1. Nothing in the present Covenant may be interpreted as implying for any State, group or person any right to engage in any activity or perform any act aimed at the destruction of any of the rights and freedoms recognized herein or at their limitation to a greater extent than is provided for in the present Covenant.

2. There shall be no restriction upon or derogation from any of the fundamental human rights recognized or existing in any State Party to the present Covenant pursuant to law, conventions, regulations or custom on the pretext that the present Covenant does not recognize such rights or that it recognizes them to a lesser extent.

PART III

Article 6

1. Every human being has the inherent right to life. This right shall be protected by law. No one shall be arbitrarily deprived of his life.

2. In countries which have not abolished the death penalty, sentence of death may be imposed only for the most serious crimes in accordance with the law in force at the time of the commission of the crime and not contrary to the provisions of the present Covenant and to the Convention on the Prevention and Punishment of the Crime of Genocide. This penalty can only be carried out pursuant to a final judgement rendered by a competent court.

3. When deprivation of life consititutes the crime of genocide, it is understood that nothing in this article shall authorize any State Party to the present Covenant to derogate in any way from any obligation assumed under the provisions of the Convention on the Prevention and Punishment of the Crime of Genocide.

4. Anyone sentenced to death shall have the right to seek pardon or commutation of the sentence. Amnesty, pardon or commutation of the sentence of death may be granted in all cases.

5. Sentence of death shall not be imposed for crimes committed by persons below eighteen years of age and shall not be carried out on pregnant women.

6. Nothing in this article shall be invoked to delay or to prevent the abolition of capital punishment by any State Party to the present Covenant.

Article 7

No one shall be subjected to torture or to cruel, inhuman or degrading treatment or punishment. In particular, no one shall be subjected without his free consent to medical or scientific experimentation.

Article 8

1. No one shall be held in slavery; slavery and the slave-trade in all their forms shall be prohibited.

2. No one shall be held in servitude.

3. (*a*) No one shall be required to perform forced or compulsory labour;

(*b*) Paragraph 3 (*a*) shall not be held to preclude, in countries where imprisonment with hard labour may be imposed as a punishment for a crime, the performance of hard labour in pursuance of a sentence to such punishment by a competent court;

(*c*) For the purpose of this paragraph the term "forced or compulsory labour" shall not include:

(i) Any work or service, not referred to in sub-paragraph (*b*), normally required of a person who is under detention in consequence of a lawful order of a court, or of a person during conditional release from such detention;

(ii) Any service of a military character and, in countries where conscientious objection is recognized, any national service required by law of conscientious objectors;

(iii) Any service exacted in cases of emergency or calamity threatening the life or well-being of the community;

(iv) Any work or service which forms part of normal civil obligations.

Article 9

1. Everyone has the right to liberty and security of person. No one shall be subjected to arbitrary arrest or detention. No one shall be deprived of his liberty except on such grounds and in accordance with such procedure as are established by law.

2. Anyone who is arrested shall be informed, at the time of arrest, of the reasons for his arrest and shall be promptly informed of any charges against him.

3. Anyone arrested or detained on a criminal charge shall be brought promptly before a judge or other officer authorized by law to exercise judicial power and shall be entitled to trial within a reasonable time or to release. It shall not be the general rule that persons awaiting trial shall be detained in custody, but release may be subject to guarantees to appear for trial, at any other stage of the judicial proceedings, and, should occasion arise, for execution of the judgement.

4. Anyone who is deprived of his liberty by arrest or detention shall be entitled to take proceedings before a court, in order that that court may decide without delay on the lawfulness of his detention and order his release if the detention is not lawful.

5. Anyone who has been the victim of unlawful arrest or detention shall have an enforceable right to compensation.

Article 10

1. All persons deprived of their liberty shall be treated with humanity and with respect for the inherent dignity of the human person.

2. (*a*) Accused persons shall, save in exceptional circumstances, be segregated from convicted persons and shall be subject to separate treatment appropriate to their status as unconvicted persons;

(*b*) Accused juvenile persons shall be separated from adults and brought as speedily as possible for adjudication.

3. The penitentiary system shall comprise treatment of prisoners the essential aim of which shall be their reformation and social rehabilitation. Juvenile offenders shall be segregated from adults and be accorded treatment appropriate to their age and legal status.

Article 11

No one shall be imprisoned merely on the ground of inability to fulfil a contractual obligation.

Article 12

1. Everyone lawfully within the territory of a State shall, within that territory, have the right to liberty of movement and freedom to choose his residence.

2. Everyone shall be free to leave any country, including his own.

3. The above-mentioned rights shall not be subject to any restrictions except those which are provided by law, are necessary to protect national security, public order (*ordre public*), public health or morals or the rights and freedoms of others, and are consistent with the other rights recognized in the present Covenant.

4. No one shall be arbitrarily deprived of the right to enter his own country.

Article 13

An alien lawfully in the territory of a State Party to the present Covenant may be expelled therefrom only in pursuance of a decision reached in accordance with law and shall, except where compelling reasons of national security otherwise require, be allowed to submit the reasons against his expulsion and to have his case reviewed by, and be represented for the purpose before, the competent authority or a person or persons especially designated by the competent authority.

Article 14

1. All persons shall be equal before the courts and tribunals. In the determination of any criminal charge against him, or of his rights and obligations in a suit at law, everyone shall be entitled to a fair and public hearing by a competent, independent and impartial tribunal established by law. The Press and the public may be excluded from all or part of a trial for reasons of morals, public order (*ordre public*) or national security in a democratic society, or when the interest of the private lives of the parties so requires, or to the extent strictly necessary in the opinion of the court in special circumstances where publicity would prejudice the interests of justice; but any judgement rendered in a criminal case or in a suit at law shall be made public except where the interest of juvenile persons otherwise requires or the proceedings concern matrimonial disputes or the guardianship of children.

2. Everyone charged with a criminal offence shall have the right to be presumed innocent until proved guilty according to law.

3. In the determination of any criminal charge against him, everyone shall be entitled to the following minimum guarantees, in full equality:

(*a*) To be informed promptly and in detail in a language which he understands of the nature and cause of the charge against him;

(*b*) To have adequate time and facilities for the preparation of his defence and to communicate with counsel of his own choosing;

(*c*) To be tried without undue delay;

(*d*) To be tried in his presence, and to defend himself in person or through legal assistance of his own choosing; to be informed, if he does not have legal assistance, of this right; and to have legal assistance assigned to him, in any case where the interests of justice so require, and without payment by him in any such case if he does not have sufficient means to pay for it;

(*e*) To examine, or have examined, the witnesses against him and to obtain the attendance and examination of witnesses on his behalf under the same conditions as witnesses against him;

(*f*) To have the free assistance of an interpreter if he cannot understand or speak the language used in court;

(*g*) Not to be compelled to testify against himself or to confess guilt.

4. In the case of juvenile persons, the procedure shall be such as will take account of their age and the desirability of promoting their rehabilitation.

5. Everyone convicted of a crime shall have the right to his conviction and sentence being reviewed by a higher tribunal according to law.

6. When a person has by a final decision been convicted of a criminal offence and when subsequently his conviction has been reversed or he has been pardoned on the ground that a new or newly discovered fact shows conclusively that there has been a miscarriage of justice, the person who has suffered punishment as a result of such conviction shall be compensated according to law, unless it is proved that the non-disclosure of the unknown fact in time is wholly or partly attributable to him.

7. No one shall be liable to be tried or punished again for an offence for which he has already been finally convicted or acquitted in accordance with the law and penal procedure of each country.

Article 15

1. No one shall be held guilty of any criminal offence on account of any act or omission which did not constitute a criminal offence, under national or international law, at the time when it was committed. Nor shall a heavier penalty be imposed than the one that was applicable at the time when the criminal offence was committed. If, subsequent to the commission of the offence, provision is made by law for the imposition of the lighter penalty, the offender shall benefit thereby.

2. Nothing in this article shall prejudice the trial and punishment of any person for any act or omission which, at the time when it was committed, was criminal according to the general principles of law recognized by the community of nations.

Article 16

Everyone shall have the right to recognition everywhere as a person before the law.

Article 17

1. No one shall be subjected to arbitrary or unlawful interference with his privacy, family, home or correspondence, nor to unlawful attacks on his honour and reputation.

2. Everyone has the right to the protection of the law against such interference or attacks.

Article 18

1. Everyone shall have the right to freedom of thought, conscience and religion. This right shall include freedom to have or to adopt a religion or belief of his choice, and freedom, either individually or in community with others and in public or private, to manifest his religion or belief in worship, observance, practice and teaching.

2. No one shall be subject to coercion which would impair his freedom to have or to adopt a religion or belief of his choice.

3. Freedom to manifest one's religion or beliefs may be subject only to such limitations as are prescribed by law and are necessary to protect public safety, order, health, or morals or the fundamental rights and freedoms of others.

4. The States Parties to the present Covenant undertake to have respect for the liberty of parents and, when applicable, legal guardians to ensure the religious and moral education of their children in conformity with their own convictions.

Article 19

1. Everyone shall have the right to hold opinions without interference.

2. Everyone shall have the right to freedom of expression; this right shall include freedom to seek, receive and impart information and ideas of all kinds, regardless of frontiers, either orally, in writing or in print, in the form of art, or through any other media of his choice.

3. The exercise of the rights provided for in paragraph 2 of this article carries with it special duties and responsibilities. It may therefore be subject to certain restrictions, but these shall only be such as are provided by law and are necessary:

   (a) For respect of the rights or reputations of others;

   (b) For the protection of national security or of public order (*ordre public*), or of public health or morals.

Article 20

1. Any propaganda for war shall be prohibited by law.

2. Any advocacy of national, racial or religious hatred that constitutes incitement to discrimination, hostility or violence shall be prohibited by law.

Article 21

The right of peaceful assembly shall be recognized. No restrictions may be placed on the exercise of this right other than those imposed in conformity with the law and which are necessary in a democratic society in the interests of national security or public safety, public order (*ordre public*), the protection of public health or morals or the protection of the rights and freedoms of others.

Article 22

1. Everyone shall have the right to freedom of association with others, including the right to form and join trade unions for the protection of his interests.

2. No restrictions may be placed on the exercise of this right other than those which are prescribed by law and which are necessary in a democratic society in the interests of national security or public safety, public order (*ordre public*), the protection of public health or morals or the protection of the rights and freedoms of others. This article shall not prevent the imposition of lawful restrictions on members of the armed forces and of the police in their exercise of this right.

3. Nothing in this article shall authorize States Parties to the International Labour Organisation Convention of 1948 concerning Freedom of Association and Protection of the Right to Organize to take legislative measures which would prejudice, or to apply the law in such a manner as to prejudice the guarantees provided for in that Convention.

Article 23

1. The family is the natural and fundamental group unit of society and is entitled to protection by society and the State.

2. The right of men and women of marriageable age to marry

and to found a family shall be recognized.

3. No marriage shall be entered into without the free and full consent of the intending spouses.

4. States Parties to the present Covenant shall take appropriate steps to ensure equality of rights and responsibilities of spouses as to marriage, during marriage and at its dissolution. In the case of dissolution, provision shall be made for the necessary protection of any children.

Article 24

1. Every child shall have, without any discrimination as to race, colour, sex, language, religion, national or social origin, property or birth, the right to such measures of protection as are required by his status as a minor, on the part of his family, society and the State.

2. Every child shall be registered immediately after birth and shall have a name.

3. Every child has the right to acquire a nationality.

Article 25

Every citizen shall have the right and the opportunity, without any of the distinctions mentioned in article 2 and without unreasonable restrictions:

(a) To take part in the conduct of public affairs, directly or through freely chosen representatives;

(b) To vote and to be elected at genuine periodic elections which shall be by universal and equal suffrage and shall be held by secret ballot, guaranteeing the free expression of the will of the electors;

(c) To have access, on general terms of equality, to public service in his country.

Article 26

All persons are equal before the law and are entitled without any discrimination to the equal protection of the law. In this respect, the law shall prohibit any discrimination and guarantee to all persons equal and effective protection against discrimination on any ground such as race, colour, sex, language, religion, political or other opinion, national or social origin, property, birth or other status.

Article 27

In those States in which ethnic, religious or linguistic minorities exist, persons belonging to such minorities shall not be denied the right, in community with the other members of their group, to enjoy their own culture, to profess and practice their own religion, or to use their own language.

PART IV

Article 28

1. There shall be established a Human Rights Committee (hereafter referred to in the present Covenant as the Committee). It shall consist of eighteen members and shall carry out the functions hereinafter provided.

2. The Committee shall be composed of nationals of the States Parties to the present Covenant who shall be persons of high moral character and recognized competence in the field of human rights, consideration being given to the usefulness of the participation of some persons having legal experience.

3. The members of the Committee shall be elected and shall serve in their personal capacity.

Article 29

1. The members of the Committee shall be elected by secret ballot from a list of persons possessing the qualifications prescribed in article 28 and nominated for the purpose by the States Parties to the present Covenant.

2. Each State Party to the present Covenant may nominate not more than two persons. These persons shall be nationals of the nominating State.

3. A person shall be eligible for renomination.

Article 30

1. The initial election shall be held no later than six months after the date of the entry into force of the present Covenant.

2. At least four months before the date of each election to the Committee, other than an election to fill a vacancy declared in accordance with article 34, the Secretary-General of the United Nations shall address a written invitation to the States Parties to the

present Covenant to submit their nominations for membership of the Committee within three months.

3. The Secretary-General of the United Nations shall prepare a list in alphabetical order of all the persons thus nominated, with an indication of the States Parties which have nominated them, and shall submit it to the States Parties to the present Covenant no later than one month before the date of each election.

4. Elections of the members of the Committee shall be held at a meeting of the States Parties to the present Covenant convened by the Secretary-General of the United Nations at the Headquarters of the United Nations. At that meeting, for which two thirds of the States Parties to the present Covenant shall constitute a quorum, the persons elected to the Committee shall be those nominees who obtain the largest number of votes and an absolute majority of the votes of the representatives of states Parties present and voting.

Article 31

1. The Committee may not include more than one national of the same State.

2. In the election of the Committee, consideration shall be given to equitable geographical distribution of membership and to the representation of the different forms of civilization and of the principal legal systems.

Article 32

1. The members of the Committee shall be elected for a term of four years. They shall be eligible for re-election if renominated. However, the terms of nine of the members elected at the first election shall expire at the end of two years; immediately after the first election, the names of these nine members shall be chosen by lot by the Chairman of the meeting referred to in article 30, paragraph 4.

2. Elections at the expiry of office shall be held in accordance with the preceding articles of this part of the present Covenant.

Article 33

1. If, in the unanimous opinion of the other members, a member of the Committee has ceased to carry out his functions for any cause other than absence of a temporary character, the Chairman of the

Committee shall notify the Secretary-General of the United Nations, who shall then declare the seat of that member to be vacant.

2. In the event of the death or the resignation of a member of the Committee, the Chairman shall immediately notify the Secretary-General of the United Nations, who shall declare the seat vacant from the date of death or the date on which the resignation takes effect.

Article 34

1. When a vacancy is declared in accordance with article 33 and if the term of office of the member to be replaced does not expire within six months of the declaration of the vacancy, the Secretary-General of the United Nations shall notify each of the States Parties to the present Covenant, which may within two months submit nominations in accordance with article 29 for the purpose of filling the vacancy.

2. The Secretary-General of the United Nations shall prepare a list in alphabetical order of the persons thus nominated and shall submit it to the States Parties to the present Covenant. The election to fill the vacancy shall then take place in accordance with the relevant provisions of this part of the present Covenant.

3. A member of the Committee elected to fill a vacancy declared in accordance with article 33 shall hold office for the remainder of the term of the member who vacated the seat on the Committee under the provisions of that article.

Article 35

The members of the Committee shall, with the approval of the General Assembly of the United Nations, receive emoluments from United Nations resources on such terms and conditions as the General Assembly may decide, having regard to the importance of the Committee's responsibilities.

Article 36

The Secretary-General of the United Nations shall provide the necessary staff and facilities for the effective performance of the functions of the Committee under the present Covenant.

Article 37

1. The Secretary-General of the United Nations shall convene the initial meeting of the Committee at the Headquarters of the United Nations.

2. After its initial meeting, the Committee shall meet at such times as shall be provided in its rules of procedure.

3. The Committee shall normally meet at the Headquarters of the United Nations or at the United Nations Office at Geneva.

Article 38

Every member of the Committee shall, before taking up his duties, make a solemn declaration in open committee that he will perform his functions impartially and conscientiously.

Article 39

1. The Committee shall elect its officers for a term of two years. They may be re-elected.

2. The Committee shall establish its own rules of procedure, but these rules shall provide, *inter alia*, that:

(*a*) Twelve members shall constitute a quorum;

(*b*) Decisions of the Committee shall be made by a majority vote of the members present.

Article 40

1. The States Parties to the present Covenant undertake to submit reports on the measures they have adopted which give effect to the rights recognized herein and on the progress made in the enjoyment of those rights:

(*a*) Within one year of the entry into force of the present Covenant for the State Parties concerned;

(*b*) Thereafter whenever the Committee so requests.

2. All reports shall be submitted to the Secretary-General of the United Nations, who shall transmit them to the Committee for consideration. Reports shall indicate the factors and difficulties, if any, affecting the implementation of the present Covenant.

3. The Secretary-General of the United Nations may, after consultation with the Committee, transmit to the specialized

agencies concerned copies of such parts of the reports as may fall within their field of competence.

4. The Committee shall study the reports submitted by the States Parties to the present Covenant. It shall transmit its reports, and such general comments as it may consider appropriate, to the States Parties. The Committee may also transmit to the Economic and Social Council these comments along with the copies of the reports it has received from States Parties to the present Covenant.

5. The States Parties to the present Covenant may submit to the Committee observations on any comments that may be made in accordance with paragraph 4 of this article.

Article 41

1. A State Party to the present Covenant may at any time declare under this article that it recognizes the competence of the Committee to receive and consider communications to the effect that a State Party claims that another State Party is not fulfilling its obligations under the present Covenant. Communications under this article may be received and considered only if submitted by a State Party which has made a declaration recognizing in regard to itself the competence of the Committee. No communication shall be received by the Committee if it concerns a State Party which has not made such a declaration. Communications received under this article shall be dealt with in accordance with the following procedure:

(a) If a State Party to the present Covenant considers that another State Party is not giving effect to the provisions of the present Covenant, it may, by written communication, bring the matter to the attention of that State Party. Within three months after the receipt of the communication the receiving State shall afford the State which sent the communication an explanation or any other statement in writing clarifying the matter, which should include, to the extent possible and pertinent, reference to domestic procedures and remedies taken, pending, or available in the matter.

(b) If the matter is not adjusted to the satisfaction of both State Parties concerned within six months after the receipt by the receiving State of the initial communication, either State shall have the right to refer the matter to the Committee, by notice given to the Committee and to the other State.

(c) The Committee shall deal with a matter referred to it only after it has ascertained that all available domestic remedies have been invoked and exhausted in the matter, in conformity with the generally recognized principles of international law. This shall not be the rule where the application of the remedies is unreasonably prolonged.

(*d*) The Committee shall hold closed meetings when examining communications under this article.

(*e*) Subject to the provisions of sub-paragraph (*c*), the Committee shall make available its good offices to the State Parties concerned with a view to a friendly solution of the matter on the basis of respect for human rights and fundamental freedoms as recognized in the present Covenant.

(*f*) In any matter referred to it, the Committee may call upon the States Parties concerned, referred to in sub-paragraph (*b*), to supply any relevant information.

(*g*) The States Parties concerned, referred to in sub-paragraph (*b*), shall have the right to be represented when the matter is being considered in the Committee and to make submissions orally and/or in writing.

(*h*) The Committee shall, within twelve months after the date of receipt of notice under sub-paragraph (*b*), submit a report:

   (i) If a solution within the terms of sub-paragraph (*e*) is reached, the Committee shall confine its report to a brief statement of the facts and of the solution reached;

   (ii) If a solution within the terms of sub-paragraph (*e*) is not reached, the Committee shall confine its report to a brief statement of the facts; the written submissions and record of the oral submissions made by the States Parties concerned shall be attached to the report.

In every matter, the report shall be communicated to the States Parties concerned.

2. The provisions of this article shall come into force when ten States Parties to the present Covenant have made declarations under paragraph 1 of this article. Such declarations shall be deposited by the States Parties with the Secretary-General of the United Nations who shall transmit copies thereof to the other States Parties. A declaration may be withdrawn at any time by notification to the Secretary-General. Such a withdrawal shall not prejudice the consideration of any matter which is the subject of a communication already transmitted under this article; no further communication by any State Party shall be received after the

notification of withdrawl of the declaration has been received by the Secretary-General, unless the State Party concerned has made a new declaration.

Article 42

1. (*a*) If a matter referred to the Committee in accordance with article 41 is not resolved to the satisfaction of the States Parties concerned, the Committee may, with the prior consent of the States Parties concerned, appoint an *ad hoc* Conciliation Commission (hereinafter referred to as the Commission). The good offices of the Commission shall be made available to the States Parties concerned with a view to an amicable solution of the matter on the basis of respect for the present Covenant;

(*b*) The Commission shall consist of five persons acceptable to the States Parties concerned. If the States Parties concerned fail to reach agreement within three months on all or part of the composition of the Commission, the members of the Commission concerning whom no agreement has been reached shall be elected by secret ballot by a two-thirds majority vote of the Committee from among its members.

2. The members of the Commission shall serve in their personal capacity. They shall not be nationals of the States Parties concerned, or of a State not party to the present Covenant, or of a State Party which has not made a declaration under article 41.

3. The Commission shall elect its own Chairman and adopt its own rules of procedure.

4. The meetings of the Commission shall normally be held at the Headquarters of the United Nations or at the United Nations Office at Geneva. However, they may be held at such other convenient places as the Commission may determine in consultation with the Secretary-General of the United Nations and the States Parties concerned.

5. The secretariat provided in accordance with article 36 shall also service the commissions appointed under this article.

6. The information received and collated by the Committee shall be made available to the Commission and the Commission may call upon the States Parties concerned to supply any other relevant information.

7. When the Commission has fully considered the matter, but in any event not later than twelve months after having been seized of

the matter, it shall submit to the Chairman of the Committee a report for communication to the States Parties concerned:

(*a*) If the Commission is unable to complete its consideration of the matter within twelve months, it shall confine its report to a brief statement of the status of its consideration of the matter;

(*b*) If an amicable solution to the matter on the basis of respect for human rights as recognized in the present Covenant is reached, the Commission shall confine its report to a brief statement of the facts and of the solution reached;

(*c*) If a solution within the terms of sub-paragraph (*b*) is not reached, the Commission's report shall embody its findings on all questions of fact relevant to the issues between the States Parties concerned, and its views on the possibilities of an amicable solution of the matter. This report shall also contain the written submissions and a record of the oral submissions made by the States Parties concerned;

(*d*) If the Commission's report is submitted under sub-paragraph (*c*), the States Parties concerned shall, within three months of the receipt of the report, notify the Chairman of the Committee whether or not they accept the contents of the report of the Commission.

8. The provisions of this article are without prejudice to the responsibilities of the Committee under article 41.

9. The States Parties concerned shall share equally all the expenses of the members of the Commission in accordance with estimates to be provided by the Secretary-General of the United Nations.

10. The Secretary-General of the United Nations shall be empowered to pay the expenses of the members of the Commission, if necessary, before reimbursement by the States Parties concerned, in accordance with paragraph 9 of this article.

Article 43

The members of the Committee, and of the *ad hoc* conciliation commissions which may be appointed under article 42, shall be entitled to the facilities, privileges and immunities of experts on mission for the United Nations as laid down in the relevant sections of the Convention on the Privileges and Immunities of the United Nations.

Article 44

The provisions for the implementation of the present Covenant shall apply without prejudice to the procedures prescribed in the field of human rights by or under the constituent instruments and the conventions of the United Nations and of the specialized agencies and shall not prevent the States Parties to the present Covenant from having recourse to other procedures for settling a dispute in accordance with general or special international agreements in force between them.

Article 45

The Committee shall submit to the General Assembly of the United Nations, through the Economic and Social Council, an annual report on its activities.

PART V

Article 46

Nothing in the present Convenant shall be interpreted as impairing the provisions of the Charter of the United Nations and of the constitutions of the specialized agencies which define the respective responsibilities of the various organs of the United Nations and of the specialized agencies in regard to the matters dealt within the present Covenant.

Article 47

Nothing in the present Covenant shall be interpreted as impairing the inherent right of all peoples to enjoy and utilize fully and freely their natural wealth and resources.

PART VI

Article 48

1. The present Covenant is open for signature by any State Member of the United Nations or member of any of its specialized agencies, by any State Party to the Statute of the International Court of Justice, and by any other State which has been invited by

the General Assembly of the United Nations to become a party to the present Covenant.

2. The present Covenant is subject to ratification. Instruments of ratification shall be deposited with the Secretary-General of the United Nations.

3. The present Covenant shall be open to accession by any State referred to in paragraph 1 of this article.

4. Accession shall be effected by the deposit of an instrument of accession with the Secretary-General of the United Nations.

5. The Secretary-General of the United Nations shall inform all States which have signed this Covenant or acceded to it of the deposit of each instrument of ratification or accession.

Article 49

1. The present Covenant shall enter into force three months after the date of the deposit with the Secretary-General of the United Nations of the thirty-fifth instrument of ratification or instrument of accession.

2. For each State ratifying the present Convenant or acceding to it after the deposit of the thirty-fifth instrument of ratification or instrument of accession, the present Covenant shall enter into force three months after the date of the deposit of its own instrument of ratification or instrument of accession.

Article 50

The provisions of the present Covenant shall extend to all parts of federal States without any limitations or exceptions.

Article 51

1. Any State Party to the present Covenant may propose an amendment and file it with the Secretary-General of the United Nations. The Secretary-General of the United Nations shall thereupon communicate any proposed amendments to the States Parties to the present Covenant with a request that they notify him whether they favour a conference of States Parties for the purpose of considering and voting upon the proposals. In the event that at least one third of the States Parties favours such a conference, the Secretary-General shall convene the conference under the auspices of the United Nations. Any amendment adopted by a majority of

the States Parties present and voting at the conference shall be submitted to the General Assembly of the United Nations for approval.

2. Amendments shall come into force when they have been approved by the General Assembly of the United Nations and accepted by a two-thirds majority of the States Parties to the present Covenant in accordance with their respective constitutional processes.

3. When amendments come into force, they shall be binding on those States Parties which have accepted them, other States Parties still being bound by the provisions of the present Covenant and any earlier amendment which they have accepted.

Article 52

Irrespective of the notifications made under article 48, paragraph 5, the Secretary-General of the United Nations shall inform all States referred to in paragraph 1 of the same article of the following particulars:

(*a*) Signatures, ratifications and accessions under article 48;

(*b*) The date of the entry into force of the present Covenant under article 49 and the date of the entry into force of any amendments under article 51.

Article 53

1. The present Covenant, of which the Chinese, English, French, Russian and Spanish texts are equally authentic, shall be deposited in the archives of the United Nations.

2. The Secretary-General of the United Nations shall transmit certified copies of the present Covenant to all States referred to in article 48.

D. OPTIONAL PROTOCOL TO THE INTERNATIONAL COVENANT ON CIVIL AND POLITICAL RIGHTS

Adopted and opened for signature, ratification and accession by General Assembly Resolution 2200 A (XXI) of 16 December 1966

Entry into force: 26 March 1976

The States Parties to the present Protocol,

Considering that in order further to achieve the purposes of the Covenant on Civil and Political Rights (hereinafter referred to as the Covenant) and the implementation of its provisions it would be appropriate to enable the Human Rights Committee set up in part IV of the Covenant (hereinafter referred to as the Committee) to receive and consider, as provided in the present Protocol, communications from individuals claiming to be victims of violations of any of the rights set forth in the Covenant.

Have agreed as follows:

Article 1

A State Party to the Covenant that becomes a party to the present Protocol recognizes the competence of the Committee to receive and consider communications from individuals subject to its jurisdiction who claim to be victims of a violation by that State Party of any of the rights set forth in the Covenant. No communication shall be received by the Committee if it concerns a State Party to the Covenant which is not a party to the present Protocol.

Article 2

Subject to the provisions of article 1, individuals who claim that any of their rights enumerated in the Covenant have been violated and who have exhausted all available domestic remedies may submit a written communication to the Committee for consideration.

Article 3

The Committee shall consider inadmissible any communication under the present Protocol which is anonymous, or which it considers to be an abuse of the right of submission of such communications or to be incompatible with the provisions of the Covenant.

Article 4

1. Subject to the provisions of article 3, the Committee shall bring any communications submitted to it under the present Protocol to the attention of the State Party to the present Protocol alleged to be violating any provision of the Covenant.

2. Within six months, the receiving State shall submit to the Committee written explanations or statements clarifying the matter and the remedy, if any, that may have been taken by that State.

Article 5

1. The Committee shall consider communications received under the present Protocol in the light of all written information made available to it by the individual and by the State Pary concerned.

2. The Committee shall not consider any communication from an individual unless it has ascertained that:

(*a*) The same matter is not being examined under another procedure of international investigation or settlement;

(*b*) The individual has exhausted all available domestic remedies.

This shall not be the rule where the application of the remedies is unreasonably prolonged.

3. The Committee shall hold closed meetings when examining communications under the present Protocol.

4. The Committee shall forward its views to the State Party concerned and to the individual.

Article 6

The Committee shall include in its annual report under article 45 of the Covenant a summary of its activities under the present Protocol.

Article 7

Pending the achievement of the objectives of resolution 1514 (XV) adopted by the General Assembly of the United Nations on 14 December 1960 concerning the Declaration on the Granting of

Independence to Colonial Countries and Peoples, the provisions of the present Protocol shall in no way limit the right of petition granted to these peoples by the Charter of the United Nations and other international conventions and instruments under the United Nations and its specialized agencies.

Article 8

1. The present Protocol is open for signature by any State which has signed the Covenant.

2. The present Protocol is subject to ratification by any State which has ratified or acceded to the Covenant. Instruments of ratification shall be deposited with the Secretary-General of the United Nations.

3. The present Protocol shall be open to accession by any State which has ratified or acceded to the Covenant.

4. Accession shall be effected by the deposit of an instrument of accession with the Secretary-General of the United Nations.

5. The Secretary-General of the United Nations shall inform all States which have signed the present Protocol or acceded to it of the deposit of each instrument of ratification or accession.

Article 9

1. Subject to the entry into force of the Covenant, the present Protocol shall enter into force three months after the date of the deposit with the Secretary-General of the United Nations of the tenth instrument of ratification or instrument of accession.

2. For each State ratifying the present Protocol or acceding to it after the deposit of the tenth instrument of ratification or instrument of accession, the present Protocol shall enter into force three months after the date of the deposit of its own instrument of ratification or instrument of accession.

Article 10

The provisions of the present Protocol shall extend to all parts of federal States without any limitations or exceptions.

Article 11

1. Any State Party to the present Protocol may propose an amendment and file it with the Secretary-General of the United

Nations. The Secretary-General shall thereupon communicate any proposed amendments to the States Parties to the present Protocol with a request that they notify him whether they favour a conference of States Parties for the purpose of considering and voting upon the proposal. In the event that at least one third of the States Parties favours such a conference, the Secretary-General shall convene the conference under the auspices of the United Nations. Any amendment adopted by a majority of the States Parties present and voting at the conference shall be submitted to the General Assembly of the United Nations for approval.

2. Amendments shall come into force when they have been approved by the General Assembly of the United Nations and accepted by a two-thirds majority of the States Parties to the present Protocol in accordance with their respective constitutional processes.

3. When amendments come into force, they shall be binding on those States Parties which have accepted them, other States Parties still being bound by the provisions of the present Protocol and any earlier amendment which they have accepted.

Article 12

1. Any State Party may denounce the present Protocol at any time by written notification addressed to the Secretary-General of the United Nations. Denunciation shall take effect three months after the date of receipt of the notification by the Secretary-General.

2. Denunciation shall be without prejudice to the continued application of the provisions of the present Protocol to any communication submitted under article 2 before the effective date of denunciation.

Article 13

Irrespective of the notifications made under article 8, paragraph 5, of the present Protocol, the Secretary-General of the United Nations shall inform all States referred to in article 48, paragraph 1, of the Covenant of the following particulars:

(*a*) Signatures, ratifications and accessions under article 8;

(*b*) The date of the entry into force of the present Protocol under article 9 and the date of the entry into force of any amendments under article 11;

(*c*) Denunciations under article 12.

Article 14

1. The present Protocol, of which the Chinese, English, French, Russian and Spanish texts are equally authentic, shall be deposited in the archives of the United Nations.

2. The Secretary-General of the United Nations shall transmit certified copies of the present Protocol to all States referred to in article 48 of the Covenant.

Appendix II
Basic Human Rights
Instruments in Force*

(Entry into force.)

1. International Covenant on Economic, Social and Cultural Rights — 3 January 1976
2. International Covenant on Civil and Political Rights — 23 March 1976
3. Optional Protocol to the International Covenant on Civil and Political Rights — 23 March 1976
4. Convention on the Prevention and Punishment of the Crime of Genocide — 12 January 1951
5. Convention on the Non-Applicability of Statutory Limitations to War Crimes and Crimes against Humanity — 11 November 1970
6. International Convention on the Elimination of All Forms of Racial Discrimination — 4 January 1969
7. Convention relating to the Status of Refugees — 22 April 1954
8. Protocol relating to the Status of Refugees — 4 October 1967
9. Convention relating to the Status of Stateless Persons — 6 June 1960
10. Convention on the Reduction of Statelessness — 13 December 1975
11. Convention on the Political Rights of Women — 7 July 1954

* For the text of all these instruments see *HUMAN RIGHTS, International Documents*, compiled and edited by J. Avery Joyce and published in three volumes, Sijthoff Company, Alphen aan den Rijn, The Netherlands.

12. Convention on the Nationality of Married Women — 11 August 1958
13. Convention on Consent to Marriage, Minimum Age for Marriage and Registration of Marriages — 9 December 1964
14. Convention on the International Right of Correction — 24 August 1962
15. Protocol amending the Slavery Convention signed at Geneva on 25 September 1926 — 7 December 1953
16. Slavery Convention of 25 September 1926 as amended — 7 July 1955
17. Supplementary Convention on the Abolition of Slavery, the Slave Trade, and Institutions and Practices Similar to Slavery — 30 April 1957
18. Convention for the Suppression of the Traffic in Persons and of the Exploitation of the Prostitution of Others — 25 July 1951
19. International Convention on the Suppression and Punishment of the Crime of *Apartheid* — 18 July 1976

Notes

CHAPTER 1

1 W. E. Woodward, *A New American History* (Faber & Faber, 1938).
2 C. Dawson, *The Gods of Revolution* (Sidgwick & Jackson, 1972).
3 T. Paine, *Rights of Man*, Everyman edition.
4 F. Tavernier, *Vingt siècles d'histoire de France* (IAC, Lyon).
5 *Modern Constitutions since 1787* (Macmillan, 1939).
6 J. V. Fifer, 'Unity by Inclusion', *Geographical Journal*, vol. 142, III, November 1976.
7 J. T. Shotwell, *The United States in History* (Simon & Schuster, 1956).
8 A more thorough and scholarly survey can be found in a paper on 'The Rights of Man since the Reformation' by Professor J. H. Burns in the symposium volume *Introduction to Human Rights*, edited by Francis Vallat (Europa, 1970).
9 C. W. Jenks, *Common Law of Mankind* (Stevens, 1958).
10 J. R. Spears, *The American Slave Trade* (Ballantine, 1960).
11 R. H. Tawney, *Religion and the Rise of Capitalism* (Mentor, 1961).
12 See A. Harding, *A Social History of English Law* (Penguin Books, 1966).
13 J. C. Furnas, *The Road to Harper's Ferry* (Faber, 1956).
14 See, for a clear account of this terrible American dilemma, R. S. Henry, *The Story of the Confederacy* (Grosset & Dunlap, 1936).
15 For the text of the Convention see *Human Rights: A Compilation of International Instruments of the United Nations* (Sales no. E.73.XIV.2)
16 *Guardian Gazette*, September 1976.
17 *The Times*, 19 November 1976.
18 J. P. Humphrey, Foreword to *Humanitarian Intervention and the U.N.*, edited by R. B. Lillich (Virginia Press, 1973).
19 British Institute of International Law, *International Law Series*, no. 5. Some international lawyers argue that a failure of *collective* measures under the Security Council might still leave a limited opportunity for *individual* measures by a single state 'to preserve life'. *Vide* P. Jessup's *Modern Law of Nations*, 1948 (p. 170). But such arguments need not detain us at this point.
20 A thorough analysis will be found in M. Ganji, *International Protection of Human Rights* (1962).
21 H. A. L. Fisher, *A History of Europe*, vol. II (Fontana edition, 1960).
22 See Ganji, *op. cit.*, and Michael Reisman, *Humanitarian Intervention and the U.N.* (Virginia, 1973). Appendix A.
23 J. Stone, *International Guarantees of Minority Rights* (Oxford University Press, 1932).
24 Published in *Humanitarian Intervention and the U.N.*

25 This 'anarchy of sovereign states' is no euphemism. The Brookings Institution issued an intensive study from Washington on 2 January 1977 (based on recently de-classified information) that the United States had deployed its military forces for political impact abroad in at least 215 incidents in the three decades since the end of the Second World War, and that this 'show of force' by ships, aircraft or troops was 'successful' in the view of the policymakers who ordered it!

26 Since we have by no means seen the last of these miserable adventures, which are painted in heroic colours by the invading country, note might be taken of the Security Council's condemnation in April 1977 of aggression against Benin. The UN enquiry team – made up of representatives of Panama, India, and Libya – concluded that the state of Benin had been subjected to aggression by an invading force which came from outside the country with the aim of overthrowing the Government. It also concluded that most of those taking part in the attack were mercenaries 'acting for pecuniary motives'. And it took the view that 'similar action was possible elsewhere against small defenceless countries'.

27 Examining this unilateral intervention in some detail in my *End of an Illusion* (Allen & Unwin, 1968), I there recorded the conclusion:

> Looking back, there can be little doubt that the landing on April 28, 1965 of United States marines and paratroopers was a deliberate violation of the U.N. Charter, as well as of the Charter of the Organization of American States, which laid down in Article 17 that the territory of a State was inviolable and could not be subject, even temporarily, to military occupation.

28 Resolution 1790 (LIV) E/5345.

29 This is a complicated topic. Footnote references alone to the ILA Reports and other recent documentation, covering the main aspects of alien and non-citizen 'rights', occupy four-fifths of p. 434 of the *American Journal of International Law*, vol. 70, no. 3 (July 1976).

30 The legal niceties cannot be pursued here. See C. F. Amerasinghe *State Responsibility for Injuries to Aliens* (Clarendon Press, 1967).

31 A draft of this Declaration appears in a Report by Lady Elles to the Sub-Commission–E/CN. 4/Sub. 2. 369 (1976).

32 The language of this proposed Article 7 is similar to Article 13 of the Covenant on Civil and Political Rights, *already in force*.

33 These excerpts are from the forthcoming *Human Rights and World Order*, by Myers S. McDougal, Harold D. Lasswell, and Lung-chu Cheng, and are reproduced from the American Journal of Institutional Law, vol. 70. no. 3 (July 1976).

34 The Special Rapporteur of the Human Rights Sub-Commission stated in 1974 that he envisaged in a forthcoming official study the following interpretation of the term "minority":

> An ethnic, religious or linguistic minority is a group numerically smaller than the rest of the population of the State to which it belongs and possessing cultural, physical or historical characteristics, a religion or a language different from those of the rest of the population [UN document E/CN. 4/Sub. 2/L. 582].

35 *Op. cit.*
36 F. P. Walters, *A History of the League of Nations* (Oxford University Press, 1952).
37 H. Nicholson, *Peacemaking 1919* (Grosset & Dunlap, 1933).
38 In 1976 the Sub-Commission on the Prevention of Discrimination and the Protection of Minorities (see next chapter) resolved to ask ECOSOC to request an Advisory Opinion of the present World Court on 'the legal nature, scope and impact of Declarations and resolutions of the main organs of the United Nations, in particular the General Assembly, in the field of human rights'.
39 Minority Rights Group (36 Craven Street, London WC 2) *The Kurds*, Report no. 23 (1975).
40 Minority Rights Group (36 Craven Street, London WC2) Report no. 23 (1976).
41 *The New World* (London, 1977).
42 Minority Rights Group, Report no. 25 (1976).
43 A typical press item that appeared in April 1977 reveals all too clearly that the 'Armenian Problem' has not disappeared into history:

> In Beirut . . . members of an 'Armenian Genocide Organization' claimed responsibility for the shooting of a Mr. Carim. Armenian-Turkish enmity stems from the 1915 massacre of 1.5 million Armenians in Turkey and the deportation of another million from eastern Turkey.

44 In giving its Advisory Opinion on Namibia in 1971, the World Court referred to ways in which principles of the Mandate System had developed during the last fifty years, and stated:

> These developments leave little doubt that the ultimate objective of the sacred trust was the self-determination and independence of the peoples concerned. In this domain, as elsewhere, the *corpus iuris gentium* has been considerably enriched, and the Court, if it is faithfully to discharge its functions, may not ignore it.

45 See J. Avery Joyce, *Broken Star: The Story of the League of Nations* (Christopher Davies, 1978).
46 A compact handbook on the history and functions of the ILO has been written by the present author, entitled, *Labour Faces the New Age*, Workers' Education Manuals, ILO (Geneva, 1964 and later revisions).
47 The tripartite nature of the ILO has long been a bone of contention with the United States, who threatened in 1975–7 to withdraw if certain changes were not made. One of its main complaints was that the Soviet Union's employers' and workers' participation was not a genuine one. Yet this complaint ignored the provision in the ILO Constitution's Article 3(5), allowing two non-governmental delegates to be chosen where their 'industrial organisations *existed*'. The French version runs:

> 5. Les Membres s'engagent à désigner les délégués et conseillers techniques non gouvernementaux d'accord avec *les organisations professionnelles les plus représentatives soit des employeurs, soit des travailleurs du pays considéré, sous la réserve que de telles organisations existent* [our italics].

CHAPTER 2

1 M. Moskowitz, *The Politics and Dynamics of Human Rights* (Oceana, 1968).
2 H. Lauterpacht, *International Law and Human Rights* (Stevens, 1950).
3 *Ibid.*
4 UN document A/CN. 4/291/Add. 2 (1976).
5 *Guardian* Gazette London, 20 September 1976.
6 A fuller account of the discussion of the capital punishment issue at the UN can be found in the present author's *The Right to Life* (Gollancz, 1961).
7 The present author has written an illustrated hundred years' history of the movement in his *Red Cross International* (Hodder & Stoughton, 1959).
8 The Red Cross emblem was never intended to have a religious significance. When the Israeli authorities proposed the 'Star of David' to replace the Red Cross on (presumably) Palestine battlefields, the Geneva Humanitarian Law Conference in 1977 wisely turned down the proposal.
9 See F. Kalshowen, *The Law of Warfare* (Sijthoff, 1973).

CHAPTER 3

1 *Ecumenical Press Service*, Geneva, 21 April 1977.
2 *Le Monde*, 5 October 1976.
3 In an interview in the staff magazine, *UN Special* (Geneva, April 1977).
4 Caroline Moorehead in *The Times*, 24 May 1976.
5 This General Assembly on 9 December 1975 in Resolution 3452 (XXX), adopted a Declaration on the Protection of All Persons from being subjected to Torture, setting out definitions, procedures and remedies in twelve Articles.
6 J. Bronowski, *The Face of Violence* (Turnstile Press, 1954).
7 J. Avery Joyce, *The Right to Life* (Gollancz, 1962) Chapter VII.
8 Simone Weil, '*The Iliad*, The Poem of Force', *Politics* (November 1945).

CHAPTER 4

1 UN document ECO SOC/875 (1977).
2 UN document E/CN. 4/1222 (1977).
3 UN document *Centre Against Apartheid*, Report no. 8 (1977).
4 The violent death of Steve Biko has been described on an earlier page.
5 The desperate need for such an international investigation has since been emphasised by the publication of Henry Kyemba's *State of Blood* (Corgi, 1977).
6 UN document A/PV. 2096 (translated from the Spanish).
7 Our notes of interview with Allende.
8 *Sunday Times*, 4 January 1976.
9 Professor Edgardo Enriquer, Allende's Minister of Education (with no political affiliation) and a university rector, described to UNESCO's Executive Board on 16 September 1975 how his place had been taken by an admiral specialising in torpedoes and that retired air-marshals now headed Chilean universities.
10 DINA – Dirección de Intelligencia Nacional (the Chilean 'CIA' *cum* security police), which was allegedly replaced in late 1977 by the National Information Centre, since Pinochet told the visiting US Ambassador that DINA had done its job! The Roman Catholic Church then listed 507 persons, who had

'disappeared' (*Herald Tribune*, 13 August 1977).

11 UN documents E/CN. 4/1188 (1976) and 1221 (1977).

12 The paranoia of General Pinochet towards the UN mission was exhibited in these terms:

> World Marxism, which senses that it has lost this battle, does not hesitate to express condemnations and to send permanent commissions to see if human rights are being observed here . . . I have taken a momentous decision. I have asked that the Commission on Human Rights should not come to Chile. *I know that this will produce many reactions in the Marxist world* and that they will continue to abuse us. We are David and they are Goliath.

13 UN document E/CN. 4/1188 (4 February 1976). Confirmed and amplified by document E/CN. 4/1221 (10 February 1977).

14 It should be noted that, although Pinochet's propaganda features his generosity in freeing Communists, in Allende's administration Communists were always in a minority and frequently his most troublesome allies, along with the MIR, who rejected Allende's bourgeois 'liberalism' outright.

15 UN documents (seven annual reports) A/8089 (1970)–A/31/218 (1976). An article by Haim H. Cohn, Justice of the Supreme Court of Israel, strongly contested the 'fact-finding' value of such UN reports, (see *The Review*, International Commission of Jurists, no. 18 [June 1977].) These reports are accepted by the General Assembly, after open debate, year by year.

16 M. Arakie, *The Broken Sword of Justice* (Quartet Books, 1973).

17 UN document A/8089 (1970).

18 The *Washington Post* Outlook, 22 May 1977.

19 General Assembly Resolution 3005 (XXVII) of 1972.

20 There exists no 'new majority' at the United Nations, as Korey asserts. Countries group themselves according to their interests and the gravity of the decisions to be made. At the contemporary Law of the Sea Conference the USA and USSR are frequently together, but are outvoted by the '77' and the rest of the Third World.

21 *The Times*, 4 June 1977.

22 The over-play of Western concern for Soviet emigrés has brought forward the following cynical comment by Valentin Prussa Kov:

> Presumably the general assumption is that since Sakharov holds to a pro-Western orientation, the Western press must sing his praises and eulogize him and, of course, only agents of Moscow would stoop so low as to criticize him [*The Times*, 9 August 1977].

CHAPTER 5

1 UN document E/CN. 4/Sub. 2/L. 641 (1977).

2 C. W. Jenks, *The World Beyond the Charter* (Allen & Unwin, 1969).

3 UN document E/CN. 4/Sub. 2/377

4 Alfred Cobban, *National Self-Determination* (Chicago, 1944).

5 UN document E/CN. 4/Sub. 2/L. 641 (1976).

6 T. M. Franck, 'The Stealing of the Sahara', *American Journal of International Law*, vol. 70, no. 4 (October 1976).

7 [1975] I.C.J. Rep. 12.

8 UN document A/10023/Add. 5 (1975).

9 Sided by Algeria, the POLISARIO proclaimed the Saharan Republic in May 1977 and has an observer at the United Nations (*Le Monde*, 27 May 1977).

10 *Sources*: Swedish International Peace Research Institute (SIPRI) data, Stockholm, 1976; also 'The Third World: Autonomy or Dependence?', *Le Monde Diplomatique*, February 1977.

11 UN document E/CN. 4/L. 1350/Add. 2.

CHAPTER 6

1 F. G. Juenger, *The Failure of Technology* (Regnery Co., 1949).

2 This citation and much of the material that follows in this section are taken from UN document E/CN. 4/1116 (1973).

3 Harry Kalven in *Daedalus*, summer 1967.

4 A. W. J. Lewis writes on 'Freedom of Information' in *The Contemporary Review*, July 1977. It should be noted, however, that *The Times* reported on 6 August 1977 that

> The Cabinet is having great difficulty in drafting a new Official Information Bill which would replace the clumsy, unusable section two of the Official Secrets Act, 1911 . . . A Cabinet committee, chaired by the Prime Minister, set up to construct a new statute, has met periodically during the past year.

5 Breithaupt *v.* Abram, 352 II. S. 432 (1956).

6 Alan F. Westin, *Privacy and Freedom* (New York: Atheneum, 1967).

7 *See* the UN document 'Human Rights and Scientific and Technological Developments,' E. CN. 4/1199 (2 February 1976) and other documents in the same series, which form the basis of later proposals in this chapter.

8 UN document E/CN. 4/1199 (1976).

9 UN document E/CN. 4/1936 (1976).

10 Cited in UN document E/CN. 4/1172 (1975).

11 Gerald Leach, *The Biocrats* (Penguin Books, 1972).

12 UN document E/CN. 4/1172 (1975).

13 *British Medical Journal*, 18 April 1970.

14 *Journal of the American Medical Association*, 1 November 1976.

15 See UN document E/CN. 4/1142 for many more examples of this process.

16 P. Juvigny, *International Labour Review*, December 1976.

17 See UN document E/CN. 4/1199 (text abbreviated)

CHAPTER 7

1 A. H. Robertson, *Human Rights in Europe* (Manchester University Press, 1977).

2 *Le Monde*, 1 June 1977.

3 The structure of the Council of Europe and its associated bodies is not dealt with in this book; but see *Le Conseil de l'Europe*, Guide édité par les Services de Presse, 67006 Strasbourg-Cédex, France.

4 M. Moskowitz, *International Concern With Human Rights* (Oceana, 1976).

5 D. Widdicombe, *Our Fettered Ombudsman* (Justice, 1977).

6 R. S. Clark, *A U. N. High Commissioner for Human Rights* (The Hague: Nijhoff, 1972).

7 Introduction to a British Institute of Human Rights pamphlet entitled *A British Bill of Rights*, by Michael Zander (1975).

8 *Justice* (International Commission of Jurists' annual report) (London, 1976).

9 *Op. cit.*

10 The Law Society's *Gazette*, 29 September 1976.

11 This means that an English court will enforce a personal right (e.g. the right to a job or a pension) brought in under Common Market law, which it could not do under the European Convention.

CHAPTER 8

1 H. Lauterpacht, *International Law and Human Rights* (Stevens, 1950).

2 *Law in the World Community* (MacKay, 1967).

3 Arthur O. Lovejoy, *The Great Chain of Being* (Harper & Row, 1960).

4 A slight volume bearing on these aspects is the present author's *World Organisation: Federal or Functional* (Watts, 1944). A more thorough analysis will be found in Ronald Dworkin's recent *Taking Rights Seriously* (Duckworth, 1977).

5 UN document E/NGO/46.

6 'Peace is only a name,' said Plato (*Laws*).

7 E. Luard, *International Agencies* (Oceana and Macmillan, 1977).

8 P. E. Corbett, *The Individual and World Society* (Princeton University, 1953).

9 UN document E/CN. 4/2. 642.

Envoi

IMPROVING THE EFFECTIVE ENJOYMENT OF HUMAN RIGHTS

The creation of an international human rights court and new substantive instruments concerning human rights protection, as well as the establishment of a United Nations High Commissioner for human rights and of regional organs to deal with human rights issues, are among the topics discussed in an updated report by the United Nations Secretary-General submitted to the 32nd session of the General Assembly.

The report is an analysis of replies received by the Secretary-General up to 1 August 1977 from 24 governments, 25 non-governmental organizations and specialized UN agencies. It makes no recommendations. The report was prepared in response to a General Assembly resolution on 9 December 1975 which asked the Secretary-General to update a report that he submitted to that session. It is entitled: "Alternative Approaches and Ways and Means within the United Nations System for Improving the Effective Enjoyment of Human Rights and Fundamental Freedoms: Further Report of the Secretary-General".

The Report covers the following points relating to enjoyment of human rights and fundamental freedoms: strengthening the capacity of the existing UN organs, ratification of international covenants, suggestions concerning possible new instruments, systems of periodic reports by governments on human rights, procedures concerning allegations of human rights violations, fact-finding and investigation procedures, questions relating to establishment of an international court on human rights, a UN High Commissioner for Human Rights or similar machinery, regional organs in the field of human rights, studies on human rights and information and education in that field, co-operation with non-governmental organizations and human rights promotion through advisory services, and action by specialized agencies.

International Court on Human Rights

In its reply, the Federal Republic of Germany said there was need for an independent international authority which could pass objective judgements to ensure the protection of human rights in all parts of the world. Such an institution would not necessarily overshadow others already operating in this field, such as under the European Convention on Human Rights. On the other hand, India said that in the present state of international law, establishment of such an international court and similar institutions was not practical.

United Nations Commissioner for Human Rights

At the 30th session of the General Assembly some representatives supported the establishment of a UN High Commissioner for Human Rights, who would approach governments directly, particularly to help on the settlement of disputes and encourage ratification of human rights conventions. Others said such a new institution might lead to open or covert intervention in the domestic affairs of States. One representative suggested the creation of a five-man board of human rights commissioners – one from each region.

In their replies, the Federal Republic of Germany, Netherlands and the United Kingdom said the creation of a High Commissioner's Office should be given further consideration, while India, the Ukrainian SSR and the Soviet Union opposed the idea.

Regional Organs in the Field of Human Rights

In its reply, the United Kingdom particularly stressed the value of developing regional machinery in areas where no such organs exist at present. Chile said that regional systems for human rights protection should be established only in geographical areas where there are none at present, or machinery should be set up for co-ordination between the UN and regional organizations where these exist. In the absence of such regional machinery there is a risk that certain aspects which can be properly appreciated only by persons living in the same region will not be taken into account. Chile claims that such problems occurred to its detriment as regards the human rights situation on its territory. In its view, the United Nations General Assembly at its 31st session wrongly disregarded previous action taken by the competent regional organization, the Organization of American States.

New Substantive Instruments

At the 30th session of the General Assembly, attention was drawn in particular to the need for a declaration and, in due course, a convention on elimination of all forms of religious intolerance, and a convention on the elimination of discrimination against women. In its reply, India placed high value on both these ideas. The Ukrainian SSR drew attention to a Soviet proposal concerning the right to live in conditions of international peace and security, and proposals on legal guarantees and international measures to promote economic, social and cultural rights, on protecting the activities of professional workers' organizations and on the unfavourable consequences of the activities of multinational monopolies for the enjoyment of human rights.

Suggestions from non-governmental organizations included the preparation of a covenant based on the Declaration on the Protection of All Persons from Torture and Other Cruel, Inhuman, Degrading Treatment or Punishment, a body of principles for the protection of all persons subject to any form of detention or imprisonment, and a convention on the suppression of torture and the protection of all prisoners, confirming torture to be a crime under international law and incorporating the principles contained in the declaration against torture. The General Assembly should also continue to co-operate with the World Health Organization (WHO) with a view to approving a code of ethics for medical personnel relevant to the prevention of torture and other cruel, inhuman or degrading treatment or punishment.

Reading List

(Titles in English only)

Arakie, M., *The Broken Sword of Justice* (Quartet, 1973).

Bowett, D. W., *Law of International Institutions* (Stevens, 1955).

Brownlie, I., *Basic Documents in Human Rights* (Oxford University Press, 1971).

Buergenthal, T. & *Basic Documents on International Protection of Human*
Sohn, L. B. *Rights* (Oceana, 1973).

Clark, R. S., *A Commissioner of Human Rights* (The Hague: Nijhoff, 1976).

Eagleton, C., *International Government* (Ronald Press).

Fawcett, J. E. S., *Application of European Convention on Human Rights* (Oxford University Press, 1969).
The Law of Nations (Penguin Books, 1971).

Gardner, R. N., *In Pursuit of World Order* (Praeger, 1966).

Hadwen, J., *How UN Decisions are Made* (Leyden: Sijthoff, 1961).

Harding, A., *Social History of English Law* (Penguin Books, 1966).

ILO, *Labour Faces the New Age* (Geneva: written by author 1964).

Jenks, C. W., *The Common Law of Mankind* (Stevens, 1958).
Law in the World Community (McKay, 1967).
Prospects of International Adjudication (Oceana, 1961).

Jessup, P., *Transnational Law* (Yale University Press, 1956).

Joyce, J. Avery, *Justice at Work* (Chapman & Hall, 1952).
Red Cross International (Hodder & Stoughton, 1959).
The Right to Life (Gollancz, 1962).

Kalshoven, F., *The Law of Warfare* (Leyden: Sijthoff, 1973).

Kelson, Hans, *Law of the United Nations* (Praeger, 1950).

Landy, E. A., *The Effectiveness of International Supervision* (Stevens, 1966).

295

Lauterpacht, H., *International Law and Human Rights* (Stevens, 1950).

Lloyd, D., *The Idea of Law* (Penguin Books, 1973).

Luard, E. (ed.), *International Protection of Human Rights* (Thames & Hudson, 1967).

Moskovitz, M., *Human Rights and World Order* (Oceana, 1968). *International Concern with Human Rights* (Oceana, 1976).

Nicholson, H., *Peacemaking 1919* (Grossett & Dunlap, 1965).

Pictet, J., *Humanitarian Law and the Protection of War Victims* (Leyden: Sijthoff, 1975).

Ramcharan, B., *The International Law Commission* (The Hague: Nijhoff, 1977).

Robertson, A. H., *Human Rights in Europe* (Manchester University Press, 1977).. *Human Rights in the World* (Manchester University Press, 1972). *Privacy and Human Rights* (Manchester University Press, 1973).

Scarman, L., *English Law – The New Dimension* (Stevens, 1974).

Stone, J., *International Guarantee of Minority Rights* (Oxford University Press, 1932).

Street, H., *Freedom, the Individual and the Law* (Penguin Books, 1975).

United Nations, *Year Book on Human Rights* (biennial) (Geneva).

Vallet, F. (ed.), *Introduction to the Study of Human Rights*, (Europa, 1970).

Zimmern, A., *The League of Nations and the Rule of Law* (Macmillan, 1935).

Index